Diagram Design
A Constructive Theory

Springer
Berlin
Heidelberg
New York
Barcelona
Hong Kong
London
Milan
Paris
Singapore
Tokyo

Thomas Kamps

Diagram Design

A Constructive Theory

With 84 Figures, 8 of them in Colour

 Springer

Thomas Kamps

Heidelberger Landstr. 224A
D-64297 Darmstadt, Germany

ISBN 3-540-65439-9 Springer-Verlag Berlin Heidelberg New York

Library of Congress Cataloging-in-Publication Data applied for

Die Deutsche Bibliothek - CIP-Einheitsaufnahme
Kamps, Thomas: Diagramm design: a constructive theory/Thomas Kamps.-
Berlin; Heidelberg; New York; Barcelona; Hong Kong; London; Milan; Paris;
Singapore; Tokyo: Springer, 1999
ISBN 3-540-65439-9

© Springer-Verlag Berlin Heidelberg 1999
Printed in Germany

Cover design: Künkel + Lopka, Heidelberg
Typesetting: Computer to film from author's data
Printed on acid-free paper   SPIN 10703650   33/3142PS   5 4 3 2 1 0

Preface

To Farah and Chiara

Diagrams are known as grapical visualisations of facts. Some of them, e.g., bar charts, pie-charts or network diagrams represent well established, conventional diagram types that are given names. Indefinitely many unconventional types exist – derivatives of those mentioned before, intermediary types, or just novel types of visualisations created by information designers. They may be in 2-D or in 3-D space, using colours or grey-scale, representing temporal, geographical, or other aspects. Whatever the aspects they differ in, all of them have one thing in common: to a large extent their construction obeys formal rules. The main purpose of this book is to capture these rules, analyse them and provide a formal theory for diagram design that serves as a basis for automatic design approaches.

Automatic diagram design is becoming more and more important, especially where on-demand generation of graphics is inevitable. A major field of application certainly is the enormously growing field of knowledge management. Knowledge, besides capital and labour, has in recent years become a more and more important factor of productivity. Knowledge occurs in many business contexts, e.g., as domain knowledge, as expert knowledge concerning the modelling of work-flows, as technological expertise that companies need to preserve, but also in the form of customer databases. In any case, the particular knowledge needs to be accessed to become operational. This is where diagram generation may play a major supporting role, since an important type of knowledge represenation are facts, mathematically expressed by means of relations.

In this book the application scenario is concerned with an electronic encyclopaedia of art consisting of a domain knowledge base representing object-relations (a semantic index). The objects connected by the relations are art-specific entities such as 'artists', 'works of art', 'artistic professions', abstract concepts such as 'modern art', or 'architecture', but also objects acting as containers for text and image materials. The semantic relations connecting these entities are given in the form of events, but also as instances of thesaurus relations. In this way, all knowledge particles are mutually interconnected and structured in a large semantic network. Suppose a query tool, being able to retrieve information from the knowledge base by extracting subsets of this network, would be used for interactive data exploration. In this case, generated diagrams might be the output of the query. This, in turn, could be the starting point for the succeeding query – in this way establishing a diagram generation-based graphical exploration process. A bottleneck in such a model would certainly be related to the fact that the output structures could be very heterogeneous. This is why a rather flexible generation process, that takes the different data characteristics into account, would be a great help.

The art-centered scenario in this book represents, of course, only one impressive example application for the combination of knowledge and diagram visualisation. Other application contexts might be related to data mining problems where large amounts of relation tuples need to be classified and drilled down so that, e.g., marketing experts gain more insight into customer behaviour. In a similar way, graphical analysis of web-site related logfile data might be a fruitful field of application. Beyond that, a high-level diagram system could become a design assistant in a desktop-publishing system. With such a system a user could automatically produce a set of alternative designs within a reasonable amount of time.

Chapter 1 will give a short introduction to the problem and chapter 2 will discuss related works and theories. Chapter 3 will define the terminology for the data structure, followed by an example-driven motivation of the theory and algorithms in chapter 4. Chapter 5 will discuss data characteristics relevant for the designs, whereas chapter 6 will outline how such data characteristics may be translated into visual encodings given complex structures of facts. Chapter 7 will account for the realisations of the graphical encodings using procedural layout techniques and for the system EAVE (Extended Automatic Visualisation System) that prototypically implements the diagram design theory. Chapter 8 will provide a summary and conclusions.

Thanks to all those people who helped me in producing this book. First of all, I want to thank my wife for all the patience and support without which this work had not been possible. Then, I owe a great deal to Dr. E.J. Neuhold and Dr. J.D. Foley who made many valuable criticsms and suggestions throughout the entire preparation of this book. I would also like to thank Dr. R. Steinmetz who supported me in moving forward during the final phase of preparation. A great many thanks, to all colleagues of my former GMD-IPSI department PaVE and to the department COMET, especially to K. Reichenberger, Dr. J. Bateman and C. Hüser who proofread many versions of the manuscript and discussed thousands of relevant issues concerning diagram generation and related topics.

K. Reichenberger and I hope to turn as many theoretical results as possible pragmatically into technology within the framework of our knowledge-based visualisation focussed company Intelligent Views Software and Consulting GmbH (http://www.i-views.de).

Summer 1999

Thomas M. Kamps

Contents

List of Figures

Chapter 1

Introduction

This book is concerned with the automatic generation of diagrams. Diagrams are a familiar, widespread means for the communication of relational data. They occur in scientific papers, business reports, newspapers, magazines, technical manuals and many other types of publications. Their task is to communicate complex, abstract matters in an intuitive, graphical way.

Traditionally, diagrams are manually produced by graphic designers, cartographers, and other layout experts. Since the design of a complex diagram may in certain cases take up to several hours, automatisation of the design process will help reducing the production time and costs, and is thus highly desirable from a business point of view.

Commercially available diagram visualisation systems – we only mention Microsoft Excel's design assistant [eta95] as a representative – are not sufficient for three reasons: first, they are not flexible enough to deal with a broad range of relational data, second, they offer only predefined diagram types so that variety in design depending on the data type is impossible, and third, most of the design process is still a task the user has to perform by selecting the appropriate diagram type for the data he needs to visualise.

To fill the gap, we introduce the diagram visualisation system EAVE (Extended Automatic Visualisation Engine) that takes arbitrary relational data as input and generates designs primarily depending on data characteristics and graphical knowledge, but also, by taking user preferences into account. Since EAVE's design process is constructive, a broad range of diagrams can be produced fully automatically in this way. The paradigm pertaining to our approach is, however, not as in many scientific visualisation approaches to discover "new designs" (see [MBC93] and [USM95] for visualisation of vector fields and [MRC91] as well as [Hem95] for visualisation of abstract data) or to simulate the real world (see [YLRM95]), but rather to automatise the generation of "traditional" types of diagrams as they are commonly used in publications as those mentioned above.

In the next section, we will also discuss the publication process in which the diagram visualisation system EAVE is used. Beginning the discussion with a historical review of publishing which is followed by an outline of a three-step electronic publication process, we will continue the outline describing the publication environment as the software architecture in which EAVE is embedded. At the end of the introduction, we will discuss the problem the visualisation system is designed to solve in the context of being applied as a presentation component of an electronic publishing product.

1.1   Historical Review of Publishing

Gutenberg's invention of book printing opened up new opportunities for the dissemination of ideas in the form of printed products. With his improvement of the printing technology, resulting in lower manufacturing costs, mass production of print products became possible. This, in turn, was responsible for the establishment of a new industrial branch – the publishing industries. Throughout the last five hundred years publishing has been the only form of mass communication available to mankind. As a consequence, it has been the strongest vehicle for the development and circulation of new ideas, and on a scale large enough to influence the course of civilization. Only in this century has the introduction of computer-based communication technologies led to a revolution of publishing – from conventional print publishing via desktop publishing towards hypermedia publishing. The rapid advance in information and communication technologies in recent years has had a major impact on this development. The late 1960s and early 1970s witnessed the widespread replacement of mechanical methods of typesetting by computerized phototypesetting. At the same time, word processors were beginning to replace typewriters for office use, and this has led to their increasing use by authors and editors in preparing text for publication. However, these two related developments did not come together fully until the development of "desktop publishing", the first form of electronic publishing, in the early to mid 1980s (cf. [WN91]). For many publishing activities the role of the specialist typesetter has all but disappeared, as it has become increasingly cost-effective for graphic designers, previously employed on preparing instructions for typesetters, to perform composition and layout tasks directly.

Today, the increasing sophistication of low-cost workstations, as well as the development of international broadband-communication infrastructures make it possible to distribute a mixture of modalities such as text, graphics, still images, video, sound etc. over the internet. This challenges the cooperation of information retrieval systems, text generation systems, sound generation systems, and visualisation systems to make interactive information access, even from remote sites, an on-demand publishing task.

To illustrate this, let us consider an art history student in the United States interested in the German art school Bauhaus. He may start a remote login on the Dictionary of Art database ([RMF94]) that is established at the Integrated Publication and Information Systems Institute of GMD in Darmstadt and ask for certain Bauhaus members who left Germany after the Nazis came into power in 1933. As a result, the query retrieves a collection of facts that form the input to a diagram generation process as well as to a text generation process. The output of both processes is synthesised into a presentation containing text, graphics, and image.

Figure 1.1 illustrates a possible outcome of the query retrieving automatically generated artist biography texts, a generated time-chart , and a set of still images that are composed into an overall page layout. In the remainder, we will describe a publishing environment that makes such an information access scenario possible.

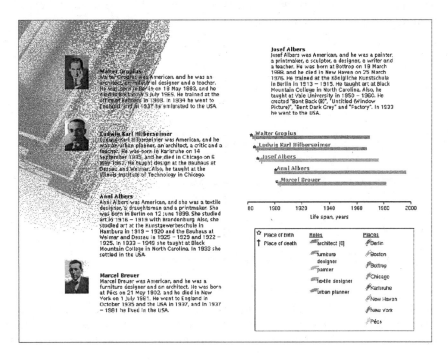

Figure 1.1: *Query result synthesised into a presentation.*

1.2   The Publication Process

Traditional print and also desktop publications are hierarchically organised, linear documents that may contain additional structure in the form of cross references and bibliographic information. For electronic publications [Haa96] considered an electronic publishing process on the basis of non-linear hyperdocuments[1]. She described the objective of the publication process as the preparation of publications in view of compatible data formats readable by application programs, e.g., hypertext authoring tools. Her model of the process distinguished three consecutive phases (see Figure 1.2): a *Content Acquisition Phase* in which hyperdocuments are created, an *Editing and Value-Adding Phase* in which documents are revised until they are ready for publication, and a *Production and Distribution Phase* in which selected subsets of the hyperdocuments stored in the publisher's data base are composed into a publication that may be distributed on different hardware platforms such as CD-Rom, CD-I, DVD, and Internet, but also as print products in linearised form. In our approach, we will follow Haake's model, but need to make some extensions concerning the publisher's database. This will be the topic of the next section.

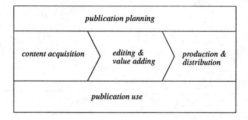

Figure 1.2: *Haake's Publication model*

1.3   The Publication Environment

As indicated above, [Haa96] considered a two-level architecture consisting of a publisher's database on the bottom-level and application programs on the top-level. The publisher's database comprises a document pool storing the set of all hyperdocuments and a database management system controlling the application programs'

---

[1] The concept *hyperdocument* is derived from the concept *hypertext* that is defined as a directed graph structuring a database in such a way that its vertices, called the *nodes*, may contain arbitrary content, and its edges, called the *links*, connect the nodes [Con87]. For a hyperdocument, in contrast, [Haa96] requires a well defined, author-intended structure as well as closedness properties for the graph.

data access. In contrast, the application programs are publishing tools supporting the three phases of the publishing process. She concretely listed the hypertext authoring tool SEPIA ([SHT89]) for content acquisition, the terminology editor ([MR93] for editing and value adding, and the Automatic Visualisation Engine
AVE ([RKG95]) – the forerunner of EAVE – for production and distribution.

For the extension of the publisher's database we adopt the ideas developed in
the department Publication and Visualisation Environment (PaVE) of IPSI, which
proposed the use of meta-knowledge to provide additional access structures to the
data. The meta-knowledge consists both of facts extracted from text material stored
in the document pool and of domain-dependent terminology. The use of meta-
knowledge has proven useful, particularly when dealing with large-scale document
pools, because it makes searching more effective by allowing application of fulltext retrieval techniques such as [TC91] [Sal89] in combination with retrieval techniques operating on the meta-knowledge. Formally representing both, extracted
facts and terminological facts, as relation tuples established between abstract data
objects we may interpret the meta-knowledge to be organised as a network of relations, called the *Object Network*, that resides on top of the document pool. As
a requirement for the above mentioned meta-knowledge-driven retrieval mechanism, the network objects need to be directly connected to the documents in the
document pool (cf. [RM94], [AR96]). Figure 1.3 illustrates this situation

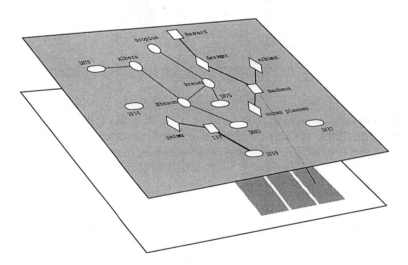

Figure 1.3: *The two data levels of the publisher's databases.*

Besides the improved retrieval possibilities we may identify another advantage of adding an additional layer of abstract meta-knowledge to the publisher's

database. The circumstance that the facts are represented as tuples of formal relations allows them to be the input of the diagram visualisation and the text generation tools needed for the composition of synthetic multimodal documents, as shown in Figure 1.1. Presuming also a page layout system composing documents of different modalities into a coherent multi-modal design we have now identified the generation tools necessary for the presentation environment we consider. More concretely, using EAVE together with the text generation system KOMET ([TB94]) and the page layout system APALO ([RRKB96]), that were both developed at GMD-IPSI, we propose the presentation architecture for on-line publishing products displayed in Figure 1.4.

Figure 1.4: *Adopted presentation architecture.*

The presentation architecture shows that, unlike both the KOMET and the EAVE system, the APALO system accepts either generated textual or graphical input, or prefabricated texts and images stored in the document pool.

1.4   The Problem

In the context of the presentation environment as we have sketched it above we will now describe the diagram visualisation problem to be tackled in this book. As we have already indicated before, the diagram visualisation algorithm is considered to be used as a means to graphically convey relational information that is collected by a query. As the query extracts portions of the Object Network, the most general data constellation we may expect is a subnet containing different relations defined on domains of arbitrary types. They may be set-valued, discrete or real-valued. They may even be relations themselves. The task is now to specify an algorithm that can deal with such a variety of differently typed data, that is, it must be able to generate effective graphical designs whatever the relational input is. Since the algorithm functions as a component of an on-line publishing product the designs must be adequate in quality to be used as the presentation results. This means, e.g., that the number of graphical elements must be moderate in size to keep the diagram readable. Readability depends on the application of graphical resources, but also on the limited capabilities of the human perceptual system. [KR95] and [KHMS96] have argued that this is already a problem the query has to deal with. They propose a restriction of the retrieved number of data elements to a size manageable by the visualisation process. This interesting topic lies, however, outside the range of this work. The second important issue concerning the quality of an online publication is that the designs, as part of the interaction behaviour, must be generated within interaction time requiring careful and effective modelling of the employed algorithms with respect to time complexity aspects.

1.5   A Solution

In this book we present an approach to automatic diagram design comprising three process phases: a *data classification phase*, a *graphical resource allocation phase*, and a *layout phase*.

The data analysis phase takes an object network of moderate size as input. The latter is decomposed into its constituents that may be arbitrary nested n-ary data relations. To classify a data relation we distinguish its schema from an instance conforming to the schema. This is important, because data relations, particularly binary data relations, may be typed on the schema level using relational properties as formal semantics. Since an instance of a binary relation schema may comprise more specific formal semantics than those defined on the schema level, it is a goal of data classification to analyse a given data relation instance to detect its most specific properties. These will be graphically communicated in the diagram.

For the more general nested n-ary relations there exist no such properties by which they could be typed. However, they may be described by means of their binary components, particularly, set-valued mappings, unique mappings and bijective mappings established between the domains on which the relations are defined. A data analysis process will detect such instance-based components and represents them using a dependency lattice. Binary components that are not interpreted as mappings, that is, directed graphs defined on one domain such as order relations, trees etc., cannot be represented by means of dependency lattices. A nested n-ary relation instance will thus be described by means of a tree structure containing dependency lattices and directed graphs as its nodes. A nested n-ary relation that is classified in this way represents the input to the resource allocation process.

The goal of the resource allocation process is to encode the data relations using graphical relations. Graphical binary relations may be qualified by the same properties as binary data relations. To graphically encode a binary data relation in an expressive way it will be assigned a graphical binary relation matching its relational properties. Since generally there exists more than one graphical relation that meets this requirement we must find the most effective among those graphical relations that are expressive. This selection takes quantitative, perceptual as well as graphical aspects into account.

The encoding of nested n-ary data relations is modelled as a composition of the encodings of its binary components. To this purpose, we have designed a hierarchical resource allocation algorithm that processes the nested relational data input top-down and assigns each binary component a graphical resource according to the encoding principle outlined above.

The layout phase is responsible for the realisation of the design decisions. It must work down the nested relation and trigger the procedural layout techniques by which the graphical relations are implemented.

1.6   Overview

This book is organised in the following way: in chapter 2 we will outline the state of the art concerning automatic diagram design which is limited to approaches producing designs in the 'traditional' sense. In chapter 3, we will discuss a definition of the input to the visualisation algorithm. After that follows in chapter 4 an introduction to our approach in which the main concepts are illustrated using examples. In chapter 5, the discussion will continue with a formal classification of relations leading to the introduction of a hierarchic classification algorithm for Object Networks. In chapter 6, we will first specify the graphical vocabulary and the mapping of binary *data relations* into binary *graphical relations*. Then we will outline how this process can be generalised for arbitrary (possibly nested) n-ary relations leading to the presentation of a resource allocation algorithm for such data. At the end of this chapter, we will discuss how the graphical encoding problem for Object Networks can be solved. In chapter 7, we will show how the encoding structure computed during the resource allocation process may be processed and concretely realised by applying procedural layout techniques. After that we will sketch an implementation in VisualWorks/Smalltalk ([Par92]). Finally, chapter 8 contains a summary and conclusions.

At this point, we should remark that the main body of this book will, due to restrictions from the publisher, not include coloured diagram illustrations. In this case colour will be 'substituted' by grey-scale values. Wherever this occurrs in the text, however, it will be referred to appendix D that lists the corresponding coloured illustrations.

Chapter 2

Related Work in Automatic Diagram Design

The paradigm pertaining to most automatic diagram presentation systems presumes an application program retrieving database facts (relation tuples) that have to be graphically communicated. The goal of such presentation systems is to eliminate the need for end-users and application programmers to specify, design and arrange a display each time output is required from the application program. A prerequisite is therefore to separate the presentation from the rest of an application.

Research on automatic diagram design can be classified according to the design decisions an automatic visualisation system has to make. In this context design decisions concern the selection of graphical resources to visually encode the relation tuples. Historically, there is a distinction in the state of the art between *decision-based approaches*, considering the selection process itself to be in the focus of research, and *procedural layout techniques*, graphically realising design decisions. The advantage of decision-based approaches is their potential to generate a variety of designs. In contrast, procedural techniques compute exactly one visualisation type such as network diagrams or topographic maps. However, decision-based approaches clearly depend on procedural layout techniques once a decision is made in favour of a particular graphical resource. For instance, if the system decides to visualise tuples of a given relation using 'arrows' then a network drawing algorithm must realise this decision. Apart from decision-based approaches and procedural layout techniques we also distinguish *hybrid approaches*. Hybrid approaches are procedural layout techniques allowing for a limited decision process.

We further classify decision-based approaches into *template-based approaches* and *constructive approaches*. Templates describe the structural and semantic properties of potential presentation types. Typically, a set of predefined templates is compared with the input information in order to find a match. Once a match is found, procedural attachments in the chosen template can be used to generate an information display. Gnanamgari's BHARAT system [Gna81] is representative of this class of decision-based approaches. Depending on data characteristics, it can decide for pie-charts, bar-charts, or line charts. The major problem with such approaches is, of course, their limitation to fixed designs. In order to allow for flexible design strategies constructive approaches are inevitable. They require on the one side a characterisation of the data and on the other side a set of graphical languages into which the data are mapped. However, unlike template-based approaches, they consist of composition rules allowing the flexible synthesis of designs in a constructive process. This superiority in flexibility over template-based approaches is also responsible for the fact that constructive design approaches have prevailed in the course of time.

In the remainder of this chapter, we will focus on a chronological presentation of the state of the art concerning constructive approaches, and omit a discussion of procedural layout techniques, because the EAVE approach we will introduce later is essentially a constuctive one. At this point, we will, however, refer to chapter 7 where we will show how particular layout techniques fit into EAVE. Finally, a discussion that serves as a basis to derive requirements for a visualisation system is presented.

2.1   Constructive Decision-Based Design Approaches

2.1.1   Bertin's Approach

We begin the discussion of constructive approaches with an appreciation of Jacques Bertin, a graphic designer, who aimed in his book 'The Semiology of Graphics' [Ber83] at proposing guidelines for good manually created diagram designs. Remarkable is his analytical approach which, however, was not meant to be implemented in a computer program. Nevertheless, his work strongly influenced all constructive approaches to automatic diagram design until today and this justifies a discussion of his ideas at this point.

Comprehending a diagram to Bertin meant more than just processing elementary information given by the relation tuples. Instead, he considered understanding to be based on classification processes. To support comprehension of a given set of relational data he introduced a graphical data analysis method called "normal construction". The rationale behind this method is to perform data analysis graphically in a constructive process comprising three steps. The first step of this process is the transcription of the data matrix into a graphical construction. Examples of graphical constructions he took into account were (visual) matrix constructions, chart constructions, network constructions and topographic constructions, as the most important types. This differentiation reveals Bertin's functional notion of diagram design in the sense that data characteristics to a large extent determine the layout. To graphically encode them Bertin used a vocabulary comprising 'points', 'lines', and 'areas' as the objects and 'x-dimension', 'y-dimension', 'colour', 'shape', 'size', 'value', 'texture' and 'orientation' as their attributes. The second step consists of a simplification of the given construct. In the case of the visual matrix, which is the most general construction, because every binary relation can be represented in visual matrix form and every other construction may be derived from it, the simplification happens by performing permutations of the rows and the columns of this matrix and by combining either similar columns or rows in order to discover the desired groups. The simplification process is illustrated in Figure 2.1. The third step is concerned with the interpretation of the resulting graphic.

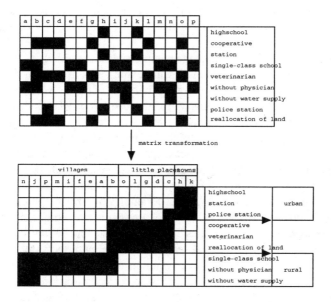

Figure 2.1: *The upper matrix provides the 'raw' data. Applying row and column transformations results in the lower matrix. This representation exposes relationships established between groups of row and column elements. For instance, villages correspond to the 'rural' properties.*

A problem of normal construction is that it only works sensibly for mappings, because, in this case, the range set can be used to classify the domain set if the mapping is interpreted as a classification function. However, such a classification is generally not possible, since not all binary relations are mappings (see chapter 5). A more general problem is concerned with the automatisation of Bertin's non-automatic method, because it requires the mapping of the rows to semantic categories such as 'urban' or 'rural' but also the definition of an effective band-diagonalisation algorithm for the rearrangement of the matrix. A problem concerned with the graphical presentation of classified data is the absence of a formal specification that could be used to develop a visualisation algorithm for diagram design.

2.1.2 Mackinlay's Approach

Mackinlay's [Mac86] goal was to develop an automatic visualisation algorithm that could decide for the most effective presentation, given an arbitrary set of relational data. The cornerstone of his research was to introduce a formalism allowing diagrams to be expressed as sentences of graphical languages that have the same precise syntax and semantics as propositional formalisms. As such, a graphical language can be understood as a formalisation of Bertin's concept of a graphical construction.

The syntax of a graphical language comprises visual symbols as the alphabet and syntactic rules (formulae) defining valid expressions of the language. These definitions include a specification of connectivity and domain sets of the relation to be encoded. To specify the domains Mackinlay distinguished quantitative, nominal and ordinal sets. Moreover, he assumed that every graphical object could be described as a set of primitive objects (pixels) together with their associated colours and positions. This led him to construct graphical languages from such primitives. For example, he defined a horizontal axis language by a formula that relates pixel positions on a horizontal line. Each instantiation of this formula is thus a valid sentence of the horizontal axis language. Examples of other graphical languages he specified in this way are vertical axis, colour, shape (rectangle, disc), bar-chart, pie-chart, network etc. The semantics of these languages are defined by specifying the relationship between a graphical sentence and the set of facts (relation tuples) that are encoded given the semantic conventions of the language.

To make sure that a set of facts is expressed correctly Mackinlay used the formal definition of graphical languages to prove positive and negative expressiveness theorems. A graphical language is expressive for a set of facts if the language contains a sentence that encodes all the facts and only the facts in the given set. A horizontal axis language, for instance, is expressive for a function with nominal domain and quantitative range, but it is not expressive for a mapping.

Since a given relation can generally not be expected to be expressed by only one graphical language, the question of how to select the most effective among those that are expressive needed to be answered. Mackinlay's answer was to base effectiveness criteria on a number of different factors. A design can be judged effective if it can be interpreted accurately or quickly, if it has visual impact, or if it can be rendered in a cost-effective manner. Thus, unlike expressiveness, which only depends on the syntax and the semantics of the graphical language, effectiveness to him depended essentially on the capabilities of the observer. However, a major problem that occurred to him was the absence of an emprically verified theory of human perceptual capabilities. So, he conjectured his own theory based on the results of Cleveland and McGill [CM84], who found that people accomplish perceptual tasks, such as searching or comparing (in the flight information example above: searching for departure times or comparing them) associated with the interpretation of graphical presentations, with different degrees of accuracy. Mackinlay extended their ranking of perceptual tasks, which was restricted to only quantitative data sets, to cover also ordinal and nominal data. However, he never evaluated his task ranking empirically.

Above, we argued that the design process should be constructive in order to ensure a flexible visualisation process. To this purpose, Mackinlay presented an algebraic approach comprising primitive graphical languages and a set of composition rules that allow for the constructive generation of different designs. The composition principle is to merge those parts of two graphical sentences that encode the same information.

To my knowledge, Mackinlay was the first who aimed at developing an automatic algorithm for diagram design that takes any relational information as input and decides how to allocate graphical resources in order to convey the input information effectively. He implemented his theory for diagram design in A Presentation Tool (APT).

Mackinlay's research was strongly influenced by Jacques Bertin's work, and not just, because of the fact that he aimed at formalising Bertin's graphical techniques. He also adopted Bertin's philosophy of functional design which means that the data and their characteristics essentially determine the aesthetics of the computed diagrams. However, he also recognised that functional design is only one side of the coin. The other side needs to capture the human perceptual abilities. The unity of functional design and perceptual design expressed through expressiveness and effectiveness criteria together with his constructive approach is perhaps responsible for the success and significance of Mackinlay's approach that has influenced many other researchers who came after him, including myself.

2.1.3   The Approach of Roth et.al.

[RM90] followed up on Mackinlay's approach. However, they felt the need for a stronger characterisation of the input information in order to obtain a richer variety of characteristics that could be exploited for the graphical presentation. Recall that Mackinlay's data description was limited to domain set characterisations distinguishing nominal, quantitative, and ordered sets. Roth and Mattis introduced the following differentiation of data characteristics: coordinates vs. amounts, domain of membership, relational structure and algebraic dependencies.

Elements of ordered sets are coordinates if each element specifies a point or location temporally, spatially or otherwise. In contrast, amounts are not embedded in particular frames of reference. The domain of membership provides semantics of specific domain sets, such as time, space, currency, temperature etc. that can be used to visualise according to conventions. Relational structure rather specifies relation characteristics. In this way, relational coverage corresponds to the classical mathematical concept of a surjective mapping (see appendix A), whereas cardinality expresses the number of elements of a set to which a relation can map from one element of another set. Uniqueness refers to the concept of a unique mapping and arity specifies the number of dimensions on which the relation is defined. Finally, algebraic dependencies specify the relationship between values of the domain set of a relation, or between values of the domain sets of different relations in terms of equations and inequalities.

Roth and Mattis built the visualisation system SAGE upon this additional data knowledge. It is also remarkable that they defined a presentation system to be intelligent if it comprised not only an automatic visualisation component, but also one that generates text. However, the first implementation of SAGE did not provide any textual output. Based on the technology outlined above [GRKM84] developed a visualisation environment comprising the interactive graphics construction tool SageBrush and the graphics retrieval tool SageBook beside SAGE.

2.1.4   Casner's Approach

[Cas91] followed a task-analytic approach to automatic diagram design, implemented in BOZ, because he was convinced that graphics are only successful when they are developed explicitly to support tasks. Hence, he considered their usefulness to be task-dependent. Two consequences of his thinking were: first, different presentations of the same information best support different tasks, and second, the interesting aspects of a presentation are the efficient perceptual procedures (searching, comparing) that users can perform using the presentation to quickly arrive at the desired result. Moreover, Casner believed that task knowledge is sufficient to decide for the best design among those that are expressive. Therefore, he saw no need to adhere to Mackinlay's concept of effectiveness.

He described tasks as logical procedures that are composed of sequences of logical operators, each representing a program whose return value is a relation. To illustrate this, we refer to his airline reservation application. Tasks in this example may be to find the cheapest flight from one destination to another, or to find the fastest connection from one destination to another. The second task involves, for instance, the logical operator *computeLayover* that pairwise maps arrival times and departure times to layovers. The return value of this operator is then a set of triples comprising arrival time, departure time, and layover.

To graphically realise a task, a logical procedure is substituted by a perceptual procedure by replacing each logical operator in the logical procedure by its respective perceptual operator. Thus, *computeLayover* may be replaced by the perceptual operator *comparison*. The underlying assumption is that users can perform perceptual inferences more efficiently than those demanding logical inferences. An example may be that checking flight layovers by comparing time bars in a time chart is more efficiently performed than calculating flight layovers mentally from a number of time-stamps representing departure and arrival times. A justification for this is perhaps that time-charts support compare operations on the time-bars efficiently, because their relative location as well as their length can be graphically, and thus directly, inferred through a perceptual compare operation. Unlike this comparatively easy perceptual inference a logical inference would require a mental comparison of dates which again would require complex mental computations to obtain the same result.

Logical and perceptual operators are classified according to a set of task equivalence classes such as 'search', 'lookup', 'difference', 'greater than' etc. Since logical operators represent relations this classification is a task-oriented categorisation of the input data. According to this classification *computeLayover* represents a computation task, whereas *determineDeparture* represents a lookup task.

A necessary condition for the replacement of a logical operator is the following: a logical operator can be substituted by a perceptual operator if and only if both operators belong to the same class. Orthogonal to this task classification, logical operators and perceptual operators are assigned to graphical languages. This guarantees operator expressiveness in the sense of Mackinlay. A sufficient condition for replacement is finally given by a combination of an estimation of the relative performance efficiency of a perceptual operator with the potential combinations of the primitive graphical languages assigned to it.

2.1.5   The Approach of Mittal et al.

[MRM$^+$96] realised that novel graphical presentations are often difficult to understand completely until explained. This problem particularly occurs when several relations are to be displayed at the same time. Also, Mackinlay realised this difficulty before and circumvented the problem by constraining APT to generate conventional designs (bar-charts, pie-charts, node-link diagrams etc.) only.

Mittal et.al. took a new approach to tackle this problem by adopting the idea of Roth and Mattis to synthesise text and graphics into a multimodal presentation. Their assumption was that natural language generation would be able to produce explanatory captions to facilitate comprehension for the designs. In this way, nonconventional designs could also be integrated into a graphical vocabulary. To my knowledge, Mittal and Roth et al. were the first to realise a multimodal presentation engine in which the graphics component was an automatic diagram design tool — the SAGE system described before.

In addition to adding a text generation component that complements the plain visualisation-based presentation system, Mittal et.al. also saw a need to base the presentation process on a task model. In accordance with Casner they found a high performance of problem-solving tasks to be one of the main goals for automatic presentation systems. Likewise, they considered user-defined layout preferences important. These insights resulted in a modification of SAGE's data input which is now extended by specifications of tasks and user preferences.

2.1.6 Marks' Approach

According to the classification of diagram visualisation approaches presented in the introduction of this chapter, the approach of [Mar91] may be classified as a hybrid ranging between constructive approaches and network diagram design. His model is limited to the visualisation of network diagrams, but within this class it describes how a decision process based on a formal specification of the syntax, semantics and pragmatics of network diagrams could come up with a variety of networks.

The syntax includes an explicit representation of the perceptual organisation of a network diagram. It can be expressed in terms of a graphical alphabet containing the usual symbols (shape, area, line, text string etc.) and the perceived groupings, orderings and magnitude relationships established among the elements of the alphabet.

The semantics of a network diagram are specified in the obvious way by mapping the nodes as well as the edges of the network model to graphical elements which constitute the network diagram. Nodes can be mapped to different types of shapes and areas, whereas edges can only be graphically realised using lines. This establishes a trivial expressive mapping from the network model into the network diagram. However, Marks' approach also includes the definition of non-trivial expressive mapping formulae that individually assign graphical symbols to particular elements of the model. This guarantees a variation of design for network diagrams. In addition, his model allows the grouping of subsets of the network model to form semantic units. Expressiveness for such composite objects is guaranteed by their representation as enclosure objects constraining all graphical symbols representing vertices of the composite to be positioned within the boundaries of the enclosure object. Particular types of such composites are 'hub-shapes' and T-shapes'. Both are subnetworks of the given input network and are discovered, similar to Bertin and Casner, using data analysis methods. In this case, however, the method is a pattern matching technique.

Marks allowed design decisions not only to be affected by the semantics, but also by pragmatic concerns, called design directives. These are reader-defined tasks similar to those defined by Casner. However, Marks introduced only such pragmatic concerns that directly influenced the relationship of syntax and semantics.

2.1.7 The Approach of Reichenberger et.al.

Unlike all other approaches [RKG95] describe the visualisation process by means of three consecutive subprocesses: a *data classification process* identifying the most specific properties of the given data, an *encoding process* in which the data are graphically encoded, and a *layout process* in which the drawn decisions are graphically realised using procedural layout techniques. Together they are implemented in the Automatic Visualisation Engine (AVE).

In their approach [RKG95] distinguish a number of binary relation types that are organised in form of a Relation Type Tree whose hierarchic structure represents the specificity of the types by means of the relational properties defining them. Thus, e.g., the StrictOrderRelationType is more specific than the acyclic relation type, because its properties 'antisymmetric' and 'transitive' imply acyclicity, but the converse, that every acyclic graph is at the same time a strict order, is not true. In the same way a 'tree order' relation is more specific than a 'strict order' relation, because it has the additional property 'tree'. [1]

In their model [RKG95] consider the Relation Type Tree to be a persistent meta knowledge structure that can be used to type data relations on the schema level. The data classification process exploits this circumstance by decomposing the input, which is given as a network of binary relations, into its binary relation components. For each component the most specific type is determined by applying a so called 'type refinement algorithm' that checks (in linear time) for a given data relation if its schematically assigned type is more specific for this instance. This is desired, because, similar to Bertin, [RKG95] felt the need to communicate the most specific information about the data in the design including such statements only implicitly encoded.

Apart from instance-based data classification purposes the Relation Type Tree persistently classifies so called graphical relations by defining them at the types. A graphical relation or combination of graphical relations may only be defined at a given type if it visually communicates all of its relational properties. For instance, the graphical relation 'lineWithOneArrow' is antisymmetric and may thus be defined at the AntisymmetricRelationType. Consequently, a data relation of this type may be communicated using 'lineWithOneArrow', whereas a symmetric data relation or a mapping may not use it. The example demonstrates that in their approach

---

[1] For a formal definition of the relational properties above see appendix A

expressiveness is given whenever a graphical relation is chosen that matches the data relation's type.

noindent Effectiveness is based on two criteria: the first is a qualitative one, presuming that the more specific relation types organise the data more strongly than the more general types. For instance, linear order relations organise the data more strongly than strict order relations, or unique mappings organise the data more strongly than set-valued functions. Thus effectiveness is bound to the type and the visualisation algorithm should always use the resources defined at the most specific type. This is, however, not always possible, particularly when more than one data relation needs to be visualised at the same time (this will be discussed in more depth in chapter 4). In this case the data relations compete for the best graphical resources. Then, a quantitative aspect of effectiveness relating the share of a given data relation, measured in the number of tuples, to the overall network of relations comes into play. Both, the quantitative and the qualitative, type-based aspect, are computed into a rank for a data relation and the ranked relations are input into a resource allocation algorithm optimising the graphical encoding, that is, the assignment of graphical relations to all involved data relations. [RKG95] did not take task modelling into account. Instead, they based their model only on data characterisation that became, however, in comparison with all approaches discussed before much broader and more systematic.

To realise the design decisions made in the encoding process AVE applies procedural layout techniques. One of them, described in [KKR95], is applied to draw networks, another one, described in [Wil95], to position included rectangles. Still others are employed for colouring and for the realisation of other graphical means of expression.

2.2   Summary and Discussion

In this chapter, we have discussed the state of the art in decision-based automatic approaches. Decision-based approaches mainly focus on the selection process concerning the choice of graphical language that a visualisation system has in order to produce effective presentations for a given relational input. These approaches were further classified into template-based and constructive approaches. Template-based approaches use predefined presentation types into which the data are mapped, whereas constructive approaches are based on a composition algebra to ensure a flexible design process.

Although Bertin was not engaged in automatic diagram design, his analytical explanation of the matter was essential for all constructive approaches after him. He understood diagram design as a constructive analysis process in which the data are graphically transcribed using different types of visual constructions. Following Bertin's notion of functional design, Mackinlay was the first to introduce an automatic design process in which the involved relations were effectively mapped into composable graphical languages. His theory of expressiveness and effectiveness of graphical languages and the constructive design model he introduced were fundamental for all following diagram visualisation models. [RM90] saw a need to extend Mackinlay's notion of data characterisation which was limited to the specification of domain sets. Besides additional domain set specifications they proposed algebraic dependencies and relational properties as further characteristics. [Cas91] modified this theory by introducing tasks into the visualisation process that replaced Mackinlay's concept of effectiveness. In addition, he proposed data analysis methods to discover patterns of connectivity not explicitly encoded in the data. [MRM+96] introduced the first multimodal approach in which the graphics component is an automatic diagram visualisation algorithm. Moreover, they took up Casner's idea of a task-oriented design process and introduced user-defined presentation styles.

The data classification mechanism Reichenberger et al. proposed goes far beyond Mackinlay's characterisation. They systematically classify binary relations resulting in a set of relation types including qualitative, quantitative, and nominal types. Moreover, in their approach the relation types are not just unrelated, but instead organised in a Relation Type Tree which is used as a persistent data structure that serves for typing and instance-based type refinement of the data. At the same time, the relation types store the graphical resources possible to communicate the data. In this way a simple expressiveness mechanism is obtained.

An advantage of constructive approaches over template-based approaches is the constructive design process that flexibly arranges varieties of diagrams depending on data characteristics, effectiveness criteria, tasks and user-defined presentation styles. Although much progress has been made in the development of constructive visualisation systems, there remain some problems to be fixed. One important dilemma of current decision-based approaches is a still insufficient characterisation of relations. Even the extension of Mackinlay's original data description by [RKG95] is not sufficient, because the relation types are only organised in a tree and not in a more general hierarchy that would allow for multiple inheritance which is more appropriate in the general case. Moreover, the descriptive power of the classification mechanisms introduced is limited to the specification of binary relations and a systematic classification of relations with arity > 2 is still lacking.

From the discussion in this chapter we may derive the following requirements that an automatic diagram design system must meet. We must provide

- a systematic classification of binary relations and n-ary relations (for $n > 2$),

- a data analysis component discovering implicitly encoded data characteristics,

- a systematic classification of graphical resources, and

- a specification of user preferences influencing the design

upon which we may construct a fast resource allocation algorithm that generates effective diagrams while at the same time allowing for a broad variety in design.

Chapter 3

Data Structure

In this chapter, we will define basic concepts concerning both the input data and the graphics to realise them in the form of diagrams. The input is considered an object-network that is composed of nested n-ary data relations whose domains are sets of objects. Since relations themselves become objects in the proposed approach they may be nested. The graphics will be expressed by means of graphical relations.

Next, we will introduce the formal machinery that is required to define these concepts. We begin with the introduction of standard data types as the basic value sets upon which the object world is defined. Then, we will introduce algebraic construction rules that allow for the composition of complex data types. After that follows the central definition specifying what is meant by an object. This is followed by an introduction to object classes as containers of objects with similar properties and behaviour. Thereafter, we will present the important concepts 'Data Object Class' and 'Relation Object Class' whose instances constitute the essential components of object networks. The latter will be introduced subsequently. Then we will define the graphical concepts 'Graphical Object Class' and 'Graphical Relation Class'. Finally, we will provide an example-based, graphical illustration of the discussed concepts.

Definition 3.1 (standard data type) *A standard data type consists of an unstructured set of values, called the domain, and a set of type-specific operations that return a unique value.*

- *Integer*
  domain: the set of integers
  operations: +,-,*,/,mod,div, etc.: $Integer \times Integer \mapsto Integer$.

- *Real*
  domain: the set of real numbers
  operations: +,-,*,/ etc.: $Real \times Real \mapsto Real$.

- *Boolean*
  domain: $\{true, false\}$
  operations: $\vee, \wedge$, *etc:* $Boolean \times Boolean \mapsto Boolean$,
  $\neg$: $Boolean \mapsto Boolean$.

- *String*
  domain: the set of finite strings
  operations: $\leq$: $String \times String \mapsto Boolean$, *concatenation:* $String \times$
  $String \mapsto String$, *etc.*

- *OID*
  domain: the set of object ids
  operations: =: $OID \times OID \mapsto Boolean$.

- $\emptyset$
  domain: the empty set $\emptyset$
  *operations: the set of operations defined for all other types. Any operation
  applied to the empty type will result in the empty type.*

Using a set of algebraic rules, as proposed in the next definition, standard types
may be composed into so called complex data types.

Definition 3.2 (type, type constructors) *A data type (type) is either a standard
type T or a constructed (complex) type T^c. Let $T_1 \ldots T_m$ be data types and $m \in$
$\mathbb{N}$ an arbitrary number. Then, we define the following type constructors:*

- $\wp(T)$ *denotes the data type composed of subsets of T. The elements of $\wp(T)$
  are defined by the power set of T. We will presume the usual set operations
  such as $\in, \cup, \cap, =, \neq$, etc. to be applicable to $\wp(T)$.*

- $T_\times = T_1 \times \cdots \times T_m$ *denotes the product data type. Its elements are n-tuples
  $\mathbf{t} = (t_1, \ldots, t_m)$ and $\mathbf{t} \in T_\times :\Longleftrightarrow t_1 \in T_1 \wedge \ldots \wedge t_m \in T_m$. We use the
  symbol T^m to denote m-fold application of the product of T with itself. For
  an m-tuple $\mathbf{t}$ and an arbitrary number i for which $1 \leq i \leq m$ we define $\pi_i(\mathbf{t})$
  to be the projection into $\mathbf{t}$'s ith component.*

Definition 3.3 (specificity, type hierarchy) *Let $\mathcal{T}$ denote the set of types and let
$T_1 := (D_1, Op_1) \in \mathcal{T}$, $T_2 := (D_2, Op_2) \in \mathcal{T}$ be types with D_1 and D_2 as their
domains and Op_1 as well as Op_2 as their operation sets. Then, T_1 is said to be a
subtype of T_2 iff D_2 includes D_1 and Op_1 includes Op_2, more formally*

$$T_1 <_T T_2 \Leftrightarrow D_1 \subset D_2 \wedge Op_2 \subset Op_1.$$

We call the relation $<_T$ that imposes a strict order on $\mathcal{T}$ the Type Hierarchy.

Based on the definitions of types we may now proceed to define the central concept of an object. An object will be characterised by a unique object identifier oid $\in$ OID and by a state. The state of an object is defined to be a set of object attributes each comprising a possibly complex type as its value. Formally, we may express these characterisations as follows:

Definition 3.4 (domain, object, attributes, operations) *Let OBJECT be a global, infinite set of elements and $\mathcal{O}$ a set of disjoint infinite subsets of OBJECT, then we call any $O \in \mathcal{O}$ a domain and any element $o \in O$ an object. We assign each object a unique object identifier, a set of attributes and a set of methods (operations). If the finite integers n, m denote the number of attributes and the number of methods respectively, we may express these assignments formally as:*

$$oid(o) : OBJECT \mapsto OID \tag{3.1}$$

$$attribute_i(o) : OBJECT \mapsto \mathcal{T} \quad for\ 1 \leq i \leq n \tag{3.2}$$

$$method_s(o) : OBJECT \mapsto OBJECT \quad for\ 1 \leq s \leq m \tag{3.3}$$

Omitting object identifications in the following outline (to keep the formal description simpler) we will next introduce an object class as a specific object that determines the properties and the behaviour of its instance objects by means of attributes and operations.

Definition 3.5 (object class, instance, class domain) *An object class is defined by the triple (A,M,C) in which A specifies a set of attributes, M a set of methods applicable to the objects of this class, and C represents a finite set of objects, called the instance of (A,M,C) whose elements $c \in C$ are generated from (A,M,C) by applying the object creation function new : $C \mapsto$ OBJECT that is defined on the set of all classes $\mathcal{C}$. The class domain $O_{(A,M,C)} \in \mathcal{O}$ consists then of the set of all possible objects that can be created by appying the function new and for the instance we obtain $C \subset O_{(A,M,C)}$.*

In addition to the object identification we require each object class to specify the attribute 'className' that assigns each class its unique name. We will write the class name using brackets and capital letters . To denote the instance we just omit the brackets. Thus, the string [ExampleClass] denotes the class 'ExampleClass' whereas the string ExampleClass refers to its instance. For the identification of the domain of an object class we will use the function dom: $\mathcal{C} \mapsto \mathcal{O}$ from now on. Next we specify the data input to the visualisation algorithm. To this purpose we introduce the concept of a data object class.

Definition 3.6 (data object class) *A data object class $[D] \in C$ is an object class that defines only a bijective name attribute $name : [D] \mapsto \mathcal{T}$.*

In the outline below we will use the term *data element* as a synonyme for data object and call the domain of a data object class also by the name *data domain*. In our object-oriented approach data relations will be schematically modelled by means of relation object classes. For the definition of relation object classes we will require the object identification attribute oid to be bijective, that is, oid^{-1} exists and is a unique mapping as well.

Definition 3.7 (data relation class, data relation instance, data relation tuple)
A data relation class $[R]$ is an object class that defines besides its bijective name attribute $name : [R] \mapsto String$ an additional finite number $n \in \mathbf{N}$ of attributes specifying the domain object classes on which it operates. Let $[\mathcal{DOC}]$ denote the set of data object classes ($\mathcal{DOC}$ denotes the set of data object class instances)and $[\mathcal{DRC}]$ denote the set of data relation classes ($\mathcal{DRC}$ denotes the set of data relation class instances), then we define the domain attribute formally as: $domain_i : [R] \mapsto \{o \in OID \mid oid^{-1}(o) \in \mathcal{DOC} \cup \mathcal{DRC}\}$ for $1 \leq i \leq n$. The set of objects generated from $[R]$, that is, $\{r = (d_1, \ldots, d_n) \in R \mid d_i := domain_i(R)\}$ is called the data relation instance R. Each element $r \in R$ is called a data relation tuple (data tuple).

Note, that the condition expressed in the domain attribute is important since it ensures that the object identifier really points to an object that is an instance of either a data object class or a relation object class. Moreover, because the domain attribute accepts tuples as its values the definition implies the modelling of *nested relational domains*. In the remainder the notation $R_1 < R_2$ will indicate that relation R_1 is nested in relation R_2.

In the specific case where a relation object class specifies exactly two domain attributes we will call its instance a *binary data relation* and write $\mathcal{DRC}_2$ to indicate the set of binary data relation classes. For mappings as a particular type of binary relations (cf. appendix A) we will speak of the *domain* and the *range* attribute instead of calling them domain attributes in general. In our model the instances of domain object classes are seen to establish *unary data relations*.

We may now go on defining an object network as a set of data relation instances.

Definition 3.8 (object network) *Let for some constant $k \in \mathbf{N} [R_1] \ldots [R_k] \in \mathcal{DRC}$ be a set of data relation classes. Then we call the set of relation instance sets $\{R_1, \ldots R_k\}$ conforming to these classes an object network.*

Next we need to introduce the concepts graphical object class and graphical relation class. Objects conforming to these classes will be used to visually transcribe data objects and data relations respectively.

Definition 3.9 (graphical object class) *A graphical object class* $[G] \in C$ *is an object class that defines, besides name:* $[G] \mapsto String$, *a finite set of graphical attributes* $graphAtt_i : [G] \mapsto T$, *for* $1 \le i \le n$ *whose values determine the visual appearance of the object.*

In the outline below we will use the term *graphical element* as a synonyme for graphical object. Moreover, we will call the domain of a graphical object class also by the name *graphical domain*. Graphical domains are the sets on which *graphical relations* are defined. In our object-oriented approach graphical relations will be modelled by means of graphical relation classes.

Definition 3.10 (graphical relation class) *A graphical relation class* $[GR] \in C$ *is an object class that defines, besides name:* $[GR] \mapsto String$, *a finite set of attributes specifying the graphical object classes on which the graphical relation is defined. Let [$\mathcal{GOC}$] denote the set of graphical object classes, then* $graphDomain_i :$ $[GR] \mapsto \{o \in OID \mid oid^{-1}(o) \in \mathcal{GOC}\}$ *for* $1 \le i \le n$. *The set of objects generated from [GR], that is* $\{gr = (g_1 \ldots, g_n) \mid g_i := graphDomain_i(GR)\}$ *is called the graphical relation instance GR. Each element* $gr \in GR$ *is called a graphical relation tuple (graphical tuple).*

In the remainder we will refer to the set of graphical relation classes by the term $\mathcal{GRC}$. In the specific case where a graphical relation class defines exactly two graphical domains we call it a *binary graphical relation class* and refer to the set of binary graphical relation classes by the term $\mathcal{GRC}_2$. In analogy to a data object class an instance of a graphical object class establishes a *unary graphical relation* The number n of domains of an n-ary data or graphical relation is called its *arity*.

To illustrate the definitions above we will provide three data examples and a graphics example next. For the sake of simplicity we will renounce of presenting the oid attributes in the examples as well. In the first data example a binary terminological relation relates concepts to their broader concepts, in the second data example measurement tuples, as they may be the output of scientific experiments, are modelled, and in the last data example we model facts about univerisity faculty members in the form of nested relation schemata. The graphics example illustrates how a schema for the graphical relation 'line' may be defined.
Data Examples

Example 3.1 (BroaderConcept (NarrowerConcept) schema) *Let [BroaderConceptOf]* $\in [\mathcal{DRC}_2]$, *[Concept]* $\in [\mathcal{DOC}]$, *and*

A_1 *(broaderConceptOf): [BroaderConceptOf]* $\mapsto$ *[Concept]*,
A_2 *(narrowerConceptOf): [BroaderConceptOf]* $\mapsto$ *[Concept]*),

If $bt_i \in BroaderConceptOf$ and $t_j \in Concept$, for $1 \leq i \leq m$, and $1 \leq j \leq 2m$ denote objects, then the class instance BroaderConceptOf is presented in Figure 3.1.

BroaderConceptOf =

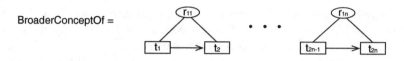

Figure 3.1: *Broader concept tuples.*

Note that from a non-object oriented, pure formal point of view the arrows represent the actual relation tuples. The bt_i are only needed as linking objects.

Example 3.2 (Measurement schema) *Let $[Measurement] \in [\mathcal{DRC}]$, [TimeInstance], [Material], [Density], [Temperature] $\in [\mathcal{DOC}]$, and*

A_1 *(time): [Measurement] $\mapsto$ [TimeInstance],*
A_2 *(material): [Measurement] $\mapsto$ [Material],*
A_3 *(density): [Measurement] $\mapsto$ [Density],*
A_4 *(meltingPoint): [Measurement] $\mapsto$ [Temperature],*
A_5 *(boilingPoint): [Measurement] $\mapsto$ [Temperature],*

If $m_i \in Measurement$, $t_i \in TimeInstance$, $ma_i \in Material$, $d_i \in Density$, and $tp_i, tp_j \in Temperature$, for $1 \leq i, j \leq m$, denote objects then the relation instance Measurement is schematically presented in Figure 3.2.

Measurement =

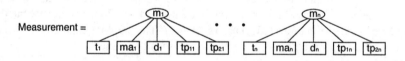

Figure 3.2: *Measurement tuples.*

Example 3.3 (FacultyAt schema) *Let $[FacultyAt] \in [\mathcal{DRC}]$, [DurationPeriod] $\in [\mathcal{DRC}_2]$, [Person], [School] $\in [\mathcal{DOC}]$, and*

A_1 *(teacher): [FacultyAt] $\mapsto$ [Person],*

A_2 *(Duration): [FacultyAt]* $\mapsto$ *[DurationPeriod],*
A_3 *(school): [FacultyAt]* $\mapsto$ *[School].*

Let furthermore [Date] $\in \mathcal{DOC}$ *and*

A_1 *(startTime): [DurationPeriod]* $\mapsto$ *[Date],*
A_2 *(endTime): [DurationPeriod]* $\mapsto$ *[Date],*

If $f_i \in FacultyAt$, $p_i \in Person$, $dp_i \in DurationPeriod$, $s_i \in School$, *and* $d_i, d_j \in Date$, *for* $1 \le i, j \le m$ *denote objects, then FacultyAt is given in Figure 3.3.*

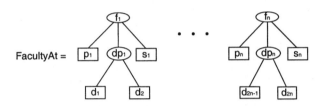

Figure 3.3: *Nested tuples.*

Graphics Example

Example 3.4 (line schema) *Let [Line] be* $\in \mathcal{GRC}_2$, *[Rectangle] , [Circle], [Diamond], [Triangle] be*$\in \mathcal{GOC}$ *and*

A_1 *(firstEnd): [Line]* $\mapsto$ $[Rectangle] \cup [Circle] \cup [Diamond] \cup [Triangle]$

A_2 *(secondEnd): [Line]* $\mapsto$ $[Rectangle] \cup [Circle] \cup [Diamond] \cup [Triangle]$

For a deeper understanding of object-oriented databases we refer the interested reader also to the discussions of the different object-oriented models introduced by [ABD+89], [Bee89], [Heu92], and [KAN93]. A formal definition and classification of all graphical relations used in this approach is presented in chapter 6.

Chapter 4

Introduction To the Approach

As the general problem we consider the visualisation of an object network as it may be extracted by a query. In the previous chapter we have explained that an object network is generally composed of a set of data relations. As indicated before, a fundamental feature of the approach we will describe is to conceive both the data and the graphics (visually displaying them) to be representable by means of relations and their characteristics.

Data relations are visually transcribed by selecting adequate graphical relations and mapping data elements and data tuples into graphical elements and graphical tuples respectively. Such a mapping is expressive if both the data relation and the graphical relation share the same relational characteristics. In general, however, there exists a variety of distinct graphical relations to expressively represent one data relation. To ensure an effective design the most effective graphical relation needs to be selected out of this variety. As discussed in chapter 2, this selection depends on user tasks as well as on quantitative, perceptual, and graphical aspects.

For the schematic specification of n-ary data relations we will also make use of the less formal and more intuitive notation below in which the name of the relation and the name of the data domain are set in upper case. In parentheses we indicate the relation types associated with this notation. [1]. In this way, the symbols $\longrightarrow$, $\longmapsto$ or $\longleftrightarrow$ represent set-valued functions, unique mappings and bijective mappings in the following text.

$RelationName(D_1, \ldots, D_n)$ (relations in general)

$RelationName(D_1, D_1)$ (directed graphs defined on one domain),

$RelationName : D_1 \longrightarrow D_2$ (set-valued function),

---

[1] A formal introduction of binary relation properties and types is given in appendix A

$RelationName : D_1 \mapsto D_2$ (unique mappings),

$RelationName : D_1 \leftrightarrow D_2$ (bijective mappings).

Graphical relations are written in the same way, except that relation names are set in lower case and italics, whereas the name of graphical domains are set in upper case and italics. Within formulae both data and graphical relations are set in italics so that only the lower case / upper case setting and the semantics, expressed by the name, will distinguish the latter from the first.

This chapter is organised as follows: The first section discusses the problems of expressiveness and data interdependencies using six example diagrams. This is followed by an outline of inexpressive visualisations, and then we explain the criteria of effectiveness mentioned above. Then we will discuss conflicts occurring while allocating graphical resources, and finally we will provide a summary of the discussion.

4.1   How to Establish Expressiveness

In this chapter, we will introduce graphical techniques that may be used to expressively visualise a given network. To this purpose, examples A), B), and C) discuss graphical realisations of differently typed binary relations, for which the typing is achieved by assignment of relational properties such as 'transitive', 'antisymmetric', 'irreflexive', 'tree', or by assignment of aggregations of such properties to the particular relations. Example D) shows how an n-ary relation (n > 2) may be visualised. After that, example E) demonstrates the use of classification techniques to structure an n-ary relation and then how such a structured relation may be graphically conveyed. Finally, example F) discusses the most general visualisation case in which a network comprising a set of relations of different arity and structure need to be graphically encoded.

The domains on which the data relations are defined throughout this section are predominantly sets of differently typed art concepts such as sets of artists, art works, art styles etc. Since art concepts are technically represented by means of data objects that are in a one-to-one correspondence with their names (the value defined at their value attribute, see last chapter) we will graphically convey this identity either by encoding (dataElement,name)-tuples using simple text strings as the graphical means, or by using the graphical binary relation *textAttachment* that composes name strings and abstract graphical elements such as rectangles into a visual unit. Alternative visualisations are presented in Figure 4.1.

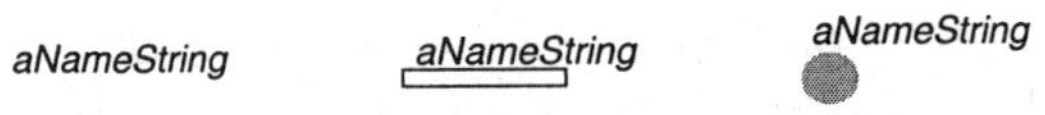

aNameString   aNameString   aNameString

Figure 4.1: *Alternative visualisations of (dataElement,name)-tuples.*

Example A)

The information underlying the diagram in Figure 4.2 is represented by the binary data relation NarrowerDiscipline(Discipline,Discipline) linking art disciplines. The following sets of relation tuples are given:

NarrowerDiscipline: {(product design,applied arts), (architecture, applied arts), (fashion design,product design), (furniture design,product design), (building design,architecture), (interior design,building design), (furniture design,interior design), (urban planning,architecture)}

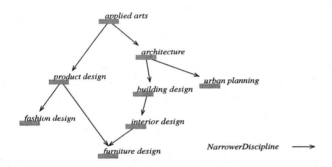

Figure 4.2: *Diagram A) represents art disciplines and their relationships.*

As NarrowerDiscipline is a strict order relation, and thus a specific type of a directed graph, we may communicate its connectivity using the graphical binary relation *arrow(attachment, attachment)* that pairwise connects the (Rectangle,Text) attachments. To achieve expressiveness, additional constraints must be imposed on *arrow* in order to properly communicate the relational properties. First, irreflexivity requires that none of the arrows may point back to the graphical element 'attachment' from which it emanates; second, antisymmetry requires that no pair of elements may be graphically connected more than once, and third, the transitivity of the relation generates 'relative position' constraints for the elements in such a way that any element representing a concept is placed below any other element representing one of the concept's broader concepts. However, the 'relative position' constraints, expressed by the graphical relation *below(attachment,attachment)*, do not fully specifiy the position of each attachment. To achieve this, a procedural graph drawing technique needs to be applied which computes the final positions according to a set of aesthetic rules while respecting the imposed constraints. Finally, NarrowerDiscipline needs to be explained in the legend, since the arrows alone would not indicate the meaning of the relation tuples. This graphical measurement may be interpreted as a visual consequence of factoring out information that all tuples share - in this case the fact that all tuples are of the kind "NarrowerDiscipline".

Example B)

In this example the data are similar to those in example A). They comprise the binary relations NarrowerStyle(ArtStyle,ArtStyle) connecting art styles. The following relation tuples are given:

NarrowerStyle: {*(Impressionism, Modernism), (Cubism, Modernism), (Futurism, Modernism), (Expressionism, Modernism), (Pointillism, Impressionism), (Fauve, Expressionism),(Die Brücke, Expressionism), (Blauer Reiter, Expressionism)*}.

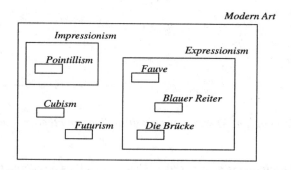

Figure 4.3: *Diagram B) represents art styles and their differentiation.*

In contrast to example A), NarrowerStyle forms a tree-order relation (with respect to the definition in appendix A) which is more specific than a strict order. We may visualise it using the more specific graphical binary relation *inclusion (attachment, attachment)* operating on *(Rectangle,Text) attachments*. Inclusion realises the NarrowerStyle tuples by nesting the rectangles of the involved concepts. The nesting process works in such a way that an attachment representing a more specific style is placed within the boundaries of the rectangle that is part of the attachment representing the more general style. A recursive construction according to this antisymmetric principle is by definition transitive. Irreflexivity is ensured by ruling out that two nested rectangles are congruent. Finally, the tree property requires that none of the rectangles representing siblings in the tree intersect. However, similar to example A), the recursive construction of inclusions generates only 'relative position' constraints for the attachments requiring their final positions to be computed again by a procedural graph drawing technique that is seeking to achieve a set of aesthetic goals while respecting the imposed constraints.

Example C)

The data underlying the visualisation in Figure 4.4 are quite different from those in the two examples before. There, they described specific types of directed graphs, whereas here they are given as sets of tuples (timeInterval, numberOfRelevant Articles) relating time intervals to the number of relevant articles (concerning the subject 'painting') in a database (cf. [Mic96]). The tuples are *(1200-1300,7), (1300-1400,8), (1400-1500,32), (1500-1600,25), (1600-1700, 17), (1700-1800, 25), (1800-1900,77), (1900-1996,16)*. These tuples may formally be described by the unique mapping $distribution : DateInterval \mapsto NumberOfRelevantArticles$. Both the domain and the range of the function are linear orders defined on quantitative sets. The elements of the domain are intervals of equal length, and thus, we may encode them by mapping them to the *width* of a set of rectangles. The range may in the same way be mapped to the *height* of the rectangles. Since the width of the rectangles is equal they may be set to to "zero" and this leads to the visualisation of vertical lines. It must, however, be ensured that the lines appear at the right position on the x-axis. To this purpose, the linear order of intervals needs to be realised by assigning *fixed x-positions* to the rectangles. The resulting diagram is presented in Figure 4.4

At this point, we should remark that also points could be used to represent the tuples, instead of the vertical lines. However, an increasing number of tuples corresponding to an increasing granularity of the time intervals may lead to the representation of a curve, instead of the discrete vertical lines. This is caused by the fact that in this case pure quantity would approximate the discrete points into a 'continuous' set of points so that the distinction between the accumulation of points and the curve is blurred.

Example D)

The information to be graphically encoded for the design presented in Figure 4.5 is the ternary relation EmigrateTo(Artist,Country,Date) for which the following tu-

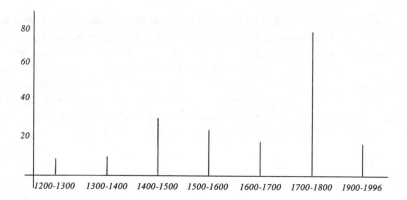

Figure 4.4: *Diagram C) represents a temporal distribution of the number of relevant articles concerning the subject painting.*

ples are given:

EmigrateTo: {*(Walter Gropius ,USA, 1931), (Anni Albers, France, 1933), (Marcel Breuer, UK, 1933), (Olav Stoemme, Norway, 1938), (Ernst May, Kenya, 1935}*

These data are different from the data in the examples before with respect to the arity of the relation (which is three here) and with respect to redundancies encoded in the data. The graphs given in example A) and B) naturally comprise redundancies of the form "domain element 'applied arts' occurs in the tuples (product design, applied arts) and (architecture, applied arts)". Such redundancies characterise, at least to some degree, the connectivity of graphs in general. Redundancies also occur in the data of example C). The fact that the distribution is not injective allows assignments of the same range values to different domain elements. However, in the data of this example we find no redundancies at all, because no data objects occur twice. Thus, the given instance of EmigrateTo establishes a one-to-one-to-one relation among its domain sets.

   The visualisation process is not much different from the process in the other examples, although in the graph examples before we had to be more careful in order to prevent redundant graphical encoding. We visualise the triples by selecting adequate graphical elements (point, rectangle, circle, ellipse, line etc.) that may expressively encode each of the triple's values. We may even use the elements' attributes (width, height, position, colour etc.) to represent those values. The expressiveness criterion that the graphical mapping must meet is that the characterisation of a domain set must match the characterisation of the chosen graphical element's attribute value set. Concretely, in the diagram below we have chosen a circle to represent an artist. To distinguish the artists with respect to where they emigrated we set the colour attributes of the circles to distinct values. This is appropriate if we visualise a set of different qualities. Given the circles as the visual representation of the artists, their position attributes were used to graphically encode the temporal data domain. The continuity of time, indicated by a timescale, connects the data in a more subtle way than the graphs, because time implies a linear order relation (also a graph) established on quantities whose edges do not need to be drawn explicitly. To represent the third dimension, text strings were employed as the graphical means of expression. Eventually, circles and text strings were attached to compose visual units. The graphical relation representing the triples is formally given by the expression *attachment(Circle,Text)* in combination with *colour(Circle,ColourValue)* and *fixedXPosition(Circle,PositionValue)*. Spatial grouping techniques need to be applied to compute the y-coordinates of the attachments' positions. Finally, the legend needs to describe the assignment of colour values.

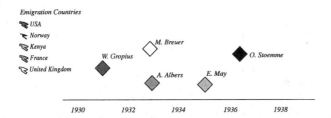

Figure 4.5: *Diagram D) represents artists emigrating to different countries (see appendix D for a coloured illustration).*

Example E)
The data underlying this example are triples conforming to the relation FacultyAt (Artist, School, WorkPeriod). In contrast to the MigrateTo relation discussed in the example before, FacultyAt contains a nested relation - the mapping WorkPeriod(Date, Date). Thus, FacultyAt may be considered to be more structured than MigrateTo. Therefore, we have to actually speak of a ternary relation of which one domain is itself a relation. Using this example we will show how the structuring may even be increased by eliminating redundancies encoded in the data and how this will affect their graphical realisation. The following FacultyAt tuples are visually encoded in the design displayed in Figure 4.6.

FacultyAt {(Ludwig Mies van der Rohe, Illinois Institute of Technology, 1938-1958), (Anni Albers, Black Mountain College, 1933-1949), (Marcel Breuer, Harvard Uni-

versity, 1937-1946), (Walter Peterhans, Illinois Institute of Technology, 1938-1960),
(Josef Albers, Black Mountain College, 1933-1949), (Laszlo Moholy-Nagy, New
Bauhaus, 1937-1938), (Xanti Schawinsky, Black Mountain College, 1936-1938),
(Walter Gropius, Harvard University, 1937-1951), (K.L Hilberseimer, Illinois In-
stitute of Technology, 1939-1967)}

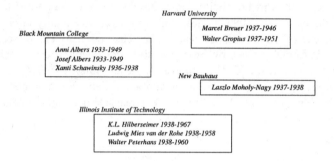

Figure 4.6: *Diagram E) represents former Bauhaus members teaching at American art schools.*

A classification of all involved relation tuples with respect to the different schools
results in a grouping of the tuples in four categories. The grouping may be expressed by rewriting FacultyAt as the classification function

$$FacultyAt^* : \{(Artist, WorkPeriod)\} \mapsto Schools$$

that uniquely maps binary tuples connecting artists and working periods to schools.
The concrete tuples conforming to this function are:

FacultyAt:

{(LudwigMies van der Rohe, 1938-1958),
(Walter Peterhans, 1938-1960),
(K.L. Hilberseimer, 1938-1967)} ↦ *Illinois Institute of Technology*

{(Anni Albers, 1933-1949),
(Josef Albers, 1933-1949),
(Xanti Schawinsky, 1936-1938)} ↦ *Black Mountain College*

$\{(Marcel\ Breuer,\ 1937\text{-}1946),$
$(Walter\ Gropius,\ 1937\text{-}1951)\} \mapsto Harvard\ University$

$\{(Laszlo\ Moholy\text{-}Nagy,\ 1937\text{-}1938)\} \mapsto New\ Bauhaus$

Since it is certainly a goal to graphically represent the information completely, it is important to mention that this classification factored out redundant information without losing information. However, in the given case we may even refine our knowledge about the data. Investigating the domain of FacultyAt we find a unique mapping established between artists and schools; also the time intervals may be understood as a mapping from the set of time instances into itself. Now, FacultyAt may be further rewritten and as a result we obtain the structured relation

$$FacultyAt^{**} : Artist \mapsto WorkPeriod \mapsto School, \quad where$$

$$WorkPeriod : (Date, Date).$$

The first line indicates that FacultyAt can be interpreted by means of two consecutive unique mappings, one from artists to work periods and the other from work periods to schools.

The rewritten relation FacultyAt** incorporates also predefined *nested dependencies* describing the internal structure of the work periods as a directed graph defined on the domain Date as well as instance-based *functional dependencies* interrelating the domains Artist, WorkPeriod and School. Apart from nested dependencies and functional dependencies we consider also *set-valued function dependencies* in our approach

Using the facultyAt example classification we will next show how such a structurally enriched description of the data, containing less redundancies than before, can be exploited for the graphical encoding. Concretely, the work periods are composed of two text strings representing the dates and the graphical relation *hyphen (Text,Text)* connecting them. In this way 'hyphen' expressively encodes the tuples of the work period relation. The artists are also encoded as text strings and the composed work period strings are uniquely assigned to them using the graphical relation *concatenation* operating on text strings. Finally, the encoded subtuples are grouped with respect to the schools and this grouping is reinforced by placing the concatenated text strings within the frame rectangles. Also, the school names are represented using text elements that are placed on top of the rectangles. The visual analog to the rewritten data relation is now given by the graphical function:

$$FrameRectangle : concatenation \mapsto Rectangle,$$

$$concatenation : Text \mapsto hyphen,$$

$$hyphen : (Text, Text)$$

To increase readability, the text lines in each rectangle are sorted alphabetically. As in example C), a spatial grouping algorithm seeking to achieve an aesthetically pleasing arrangement of the attachments, is needed to compute their positions within the display area. A legend is not necessary for the resulting diagram, since the information that is factored out (the names of the groups) is still present in the diagram.

Example F)
In this example we will show how the visualisation process may work if a set of relations of different arity and structure need to be graphically realised at the same time. The input information consists of the tree-order EvolvedFrom, the mappings PerformedBy and DurationPeriod, and finally by the one-to-one correspondence DurationPeriod. These relations are defined as follows.

$$EvolvedFrom(Profession, Profession)$$

$$PerformedBy : Profession \longrightarrow Person$$

$$Duration : Profession :\leftrightarrow DurationPeriod$$

$$DurationPeriod : Date \longrightarrow Date$$

The list of facts conforming to these relations are presented below:

EvolvedFrom: {*(graphic design, sign painting), (display design, sign painting), (advertising copyediting, sign painting), (typography, graphic design), (advertising arts, graphic design)*}

PerformedBy: {*(sign painting,herbert bayer), (sign painting,jan tschichold), (advertising arts, herbert bayer), (typography, jan tschichold), (graphic design, john heartfield), (advertising copyediting, herbert bayer), (typography, herbert bayer), (display design, john heartfield), (advertising arts, john heartfield), (graphic design, jan tschichold), (graphic design, herbert bayer)*}

Duration: {*(sign painting, DurationPeriod(1835,1910)), (graphic design, DurationPeriod(1835,1910)), (advertising arts, DurationPeriod(1860,1930)), (display design, DurationPeriod(1835,open)), (advertising copyediting, DurationPeriod (1835,open)), (typography, DurationPeriod (1835,open))*}

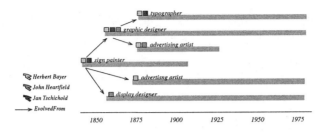

Figure 4.7: *Diagram F) describes how and when different professions in advertising emerged (see appendix D for a coloured illustration).*

The bijective mapping Duration nests DurationPeriod in its range. Thus, a nested visualisation strategy may be employed here as well. Apart from the nesting of Duration and DurationPeriod there exist no other nestings on the given input relations. However, the network containing all input relations is not disconnected, because Duration, EvolvedFrom and PerformedBy share the professions as a commmon domain set. Also, such weaker types of domain dependencies which we call *shared domain dependencies,* have to be discovered in order to avoid redundant graphical encoding. Another important aspect of the data concerns the correlation of EvolvedFrom and DurationPeriod which may be expressed by the following implication: Whenever a profession evolved from another this profession emerged later than the other. Next, we will discuss how the data together with their characteristics may be graphically encoded.

The circumstance that the three weakly dependent data relations share the professions as a common domain is responsible for first encoding the professions as *(Rectangle,Text) -attachments* in the diagram above. However, we must ensure that this design decision does not hinder the visualisation of the remaining not yet graphically represented domains. Therefore, we have to check how all three relations may be graphically realised on the pre-condition that this decision was made. To obtain the diagram above we first graphically encoded the range of Duration using the rectangles' quantitative attributes *extent.* The assignment of fixed rectangle extents induces *absolute position constraints* with respect to a time scale. These constraints are consistent with *'rightOf' relative position constraints* that have to be imposed if EvolvedFrom is visualised using arrows. The rectangles' heights do not encode any information, and therefore, they are all set to the same value. Moreover, the fact that the ratio of *height* and *width* is comparatively small for each rectangle creates the visual impression of a bar, instead of a rectangle. The PerformedBy relation is graphically encoded by attaching sets of little icons, representing the artists performing a profession, to the (Rectangle,Text) attachments. To distinguish the different artists the icons may be coloured. We could, of course, select different shapes, instead of colouring the icons to obtain the distinction. The

graphical relations underlying the diagram in Figure 4.7 are formally expressed as
follows:

$$anAttachment : Rectangle \leftrightarrow Text$$

$$extent : Rectangle \mapsto (Real, Real)$$

$$icon : AnAttachment \mapsto Rectangle$$

$$colour : Icon \mapsto ColourValue$$

$$arrow(AnAttachment, AnAttachment), \quad constrainedby$$

$$rightOf(AnAttachment, AnAttachment)$$

$$anotherAttachment : Rectangle \mapsto anAttachment$$

As the reader may easily verify, all of the data relation's characteristics are graphically represented. The presented network diagram is irreflexive, antisymmetric,
transitive and a tree. In contrast to example A) and B), a procedural graph drawing technique only needs to compute the y-coordinates of the attachments, since
the x-coordinates are fixed by the absolute position constraints. The PerformedBy
relation and the EvolvedFrom relation need to be explained in the legend.

4.1.1   Inexpressive Visualisations

The following example illustrates how important it is to insist on an expressive
graphical realisation of data characteristics. A symmetric graphical display of the
same information as in example A) would be nicely symmetric, and perhaps easy
to remember, but it would also convey wrong information, since the symmetry of
the displayed graph is not a property of the data.

4.2   How to Establish Effectiveness

During the discussion so far we always selected exactly one graphical relation to
represent a given data relation. Generally, however, there exist several choices
of graphical means that may be utilised to communicate a data relation expressively. For instance, in example B) the graphical relation inclusion, defined on
(Rectangle,Text)-attachments, could have been replaced by the relation *arrow (attachment,attachment)* in combination with 'below' relative position constraints as

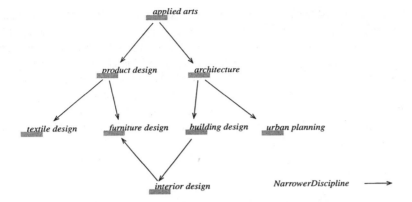

Figure 4.8: *Diagram G) represents a wrong symmetric display. The arc from interior design to building design violates the transitivity of the data relation.*

in example A). A possible visual outcome of this kind is displayed in Figure 4.9.

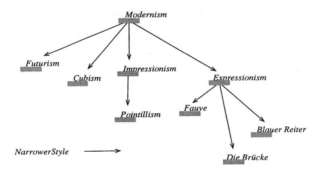

Figure 4.9: *Diagram H) represents an alternative display for the data in example B).*

Also, the data given in example D) could have been visualised in an alternative way, for instance, as in Figure 4.10. Unlike Figure 4.6, which stressed the 'grouping' aspects of the data, the time-bar visualisation clearly underlines their temporal aspects. In this diagram, the graphical mapping $extent : Rectangle \mapsto (Real, Real)$ serves, as in Figure 4.7, to represent the unique mapping between artists and working periods. The top level of the rewritten FacultyAt** function is visually encoded twice to increase readability: first, *spatialGrouping(attachment,*

attachment) is used to ensure that attachments associated with the same school are positioned close to one another. However, in the given case the realisation of this graphical relation effects only on the computation of the y-coordinates, since the x-coordinates are fixed. Second, the fact that FacultyAt** is a function, mapping into a qualitative range, allows the use of the graphical relation $colour : Rectangle \mapsto Colour$ to assign each rectangle the colour of the school the artist belongs to and thus to reinforce the distinction between the different blocks of schools. To reinforce readability within the groups, the attachments are visually sorted top-down by the begins of the working periods.

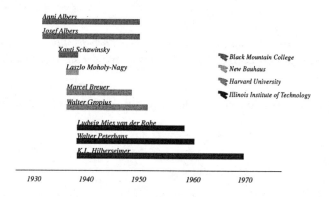

Figure 4.10: *Diagram I) represents an alternative design for the data underlying diagram E).*

In the remainder of this section we will discuss different aspects that influence the selection of effective graphical means of expression.

4.2.1   Task and Data Aspects of Effectiveness

Both examples make plain that we may find different expressive visualisations for a given data relation. An important issue arising now is concerned with the selection of graphical means of expression if multiple relations are involved. An obvious answer to this question is to presume a task-model as [Cas91] proposed it. Such a model would explain the emphasis of the grouping aspects in Figure 4.6 as a result of an explicit user wish. It implies that the grouping of artists into schools of artists in case of the FacultyAt** relation is ranked more important than any other level of the same relation. In other words, user-defined tasks induce an importance ranking on the involved data relations that should have a strong impact on the selection of graphical resources.

However, what happens if such demands are missing, for instance, because the task is not sufficiently well specified by the user? Is there a chance that an effective visualisation may still be generated? In other words, is the visualisation system able to manage, at least to some extent, without relying on a task model? We claim this to be possible. The way to ensure it, is to establish objective criteria upon which a ranking of data relations can still be based. As [RKG95] have proposed, a simple measure is, e.g., to compute the share of each relation among all relations to determine the allocation of graphical resources in this way. This computation can be done counting the tuples of a relation and dividing this number by the total number of tuples involved in all relations. For the three weakly interdependent relations in example F) we obtain the following ranking:

$$EvolvedFrom : \frac{7}{90}, PerformedBy : \frac{11}{90},$$

$$Duration : \frac{6}{90}, DurationPeriod : \frac{66}{90}$$

This ranking, in which DurationPeriod gets the highest score, clearly underlines the power of linear order relations in organising the data. The high score is due to the fact that all time instances are pairwise comparable which makes a total of $\binom{12}{2}$ = 66 tuples. The second highest ranking is assigned to the PerformedBy relation that counts 11 tuples, the third highest to EvolvedFrom that contains 7 tuples and the lowest rank is assigned to the Duration relation which has only 6 tuples.

4.2.2 Perceptual Aspects of Effectiveness

So far, we have described the data aspects of effectiveness that concern a model of user tasks but also objective criteria on which an importance ranking of the given relations may be founded. The second important aspect of graphical resource selection is concerned with the human perceptual capabilities, as was stressed by [Mac86] and [Cas91]. In example E), for instance, we applied two alternative graphical resources, text strings and bars (Figure 4.6 and Figure 4.10), that are both expressive for linear orders defined on continuous domains. However, in chapter 2 we conceived the hypothesis that a time-bar visualisation is more effective than the text strings, because the user may apply efficient perceptual operations to compare the bars, instead of performing awkward logical compare operations that are required in the case of textual representations. This suggests to rank the bars higher than the text strings with respect to their effectiveness. More generally, graphical resources that are assigned the same relation type should be ranked, because such a ranking allows the selection of the best graphical relation among those that are expressive for a data relation. Such rankings, however, must be determined empirically in a similar way as [Mac86] has done to rank graphical means of encoding quantitative data.

4.2.3   Graphical Aspects of Effectiveness

Complementary to choosing alternative graphical relations assigned to the same relation type it is also conceivable to choose graphical relations that are expressive for relation types of higher generality (see figure 4.11). In this case, we may identify an objective criterion that allows a ranking of the alternatives based on the visual specificity of the used graphical relation. Visual specificity may be quantified by counting the number of visual elements (visual symbols) required to layout a given data relation. This implies counting, besides explicit visual symbols such as rectangles, text strings, arrows etc., also 'implicit symbols' such as constraint tuples establishing relative positions between explicit symbols. The difference in graphical salience of both types of symbols should be captured by assigning different ratings to explicit and implicit symbols. Figure 4.11 illustrates a set of ranked visualisations for a linear order and a unique mapping. There, explicit symbols are assigned the value 1 and implicit symbols the value $\frac{1}{2}$. The graphical relations employed for the first relation (a linear order) are, from left to right: *unconstrained arrow*, *arrow* constrained by the relative position relation below, *inclusion*, only relative position relation *belowOf*. The fact that the vertical sequence of symbols on the right gets the lowest score tells us that this graphical realisation is the one with the lowest visual complexity for the given data structure. Perhaps, this is responsible for the circumstance that such visual arrangements appear to be the most natural way to graphically convey such data. However, to find evidence for this conjecture, which would to some extent explain why certain graphical conventions developed, must also be subject to empirical studies that are, however, out of the scope of this book. For the second relation (a unique mapping) the visual means are: arrow, attachment, and merge, a graphical relation that composes two explicit symbols into one. Note that none of the graphical relations used may be applied to a data relation of a more general relation type as the one indicated in the figure. The relative position relation *belowOf*, for example, is not expressive, i.e. wrong, when applied to a DAG as the sole graphical means.

What we have not considered so far is how the number of graphical elements impacts on the visualisation. For instance, in the linear order example above the pure arrow representation would become very complex, because the number of transitive edges is drastically increasing. As a consequence, the readability of the diagram will suffer. On the other side, the other visualisations still remain readable, because, at least to some extent, it is possible to identify the graphical elements, since no additional explicit elements are introduced. Readability is even amplified

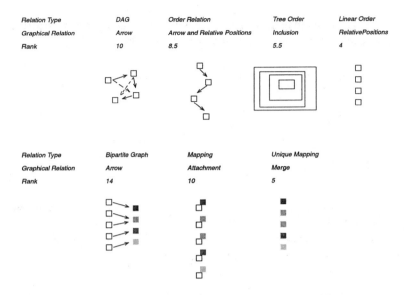

Relation Type	DAG	Order Relation	Tree Order	Linear Order
Graphical Relation	Arrow	Arrow and Relative Positions	Inclusion	RelativePositions
Rank	10	8.5	5.5	4

Relation Type	Bipartite Graph	Mapping	Unique Mapping
Graphical Relation	Arrow	Attachment	Merge
Rank	14	10	5

Figure 4.11: *Rankings of graphical relations of different types.*

when alignments and equal distances between graphical elements are paired with relative position constraints.

4.3 Conflicts in Graphical Resource Allocation

The discussion in the last section showed that a given data structure may be visualised using different graphical relations corresponding to different values of effectiveness. An additional, seemingly natural visualisation principle would be to always allocate the most effective graphical relation for any data relation, that is, the one with maximum specificity, highest perceptual and lowest graphical ranking. However, this principle may not always be followed, especially if there is more than one data relation involved in the visualisation process. In this case, allocation problems may occur, because the graphical resources are not arbitrarily often applicable, and not arbitrarily combinable in one design. For instance, if arrow is more than once applied in combination with a relative position relation this may quickly lead to inconsistent designs, which is exactly the case in design a) of Figure 4.12, where both data relations are presumed to represent strict order relations that are encoded using arrows and 'below' constraints. Since $R_1(2, 4)$ and $R_2(4, 2)$ both hold, a conflict occurs, because R_1 wants to position node '2' below node '4' and R_2 wants to position them the other way around. Such a choice of graphical

relation assignments may thus lead to a real expressiveness problem, because the
two graphical resources are not compatible for these data.

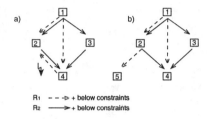

Figure 4.12: *Diagram a) shows a resource allocation conflict: R_1 is expressively
represented by arrow and below, whereas the encoding of R_2 is wrong, because
the transitivity is graphically not expressed. Diagram b) , in constrast, is conflict
free.*

Network diagram b) is free from conflicts although it is based on the same design decisions applied to the same type of data. The difference results from the
fact that the connectivity of R_2 is different from that of R_1. Diagram b) illustrates
that graphical relations are not per se incompatible. Instead, resource allocation
conflicts rather need to be detected on the tuple level. This problem represents a
typical constraint solving task which is particularly difficult when the tuple set is
large. However, there are many ways to resolve the conflict occurring in example
a). One design decision could be to position nodes 2 and 4 on the same horizontal
level to treat R_1 and R_2 equally badly. Another one could be to select different
graphical reations for the realisation.

The example shows that resource allocation may be understood as an optimisation process that must avoid conflicting assignments of graphical relations, because
they may lead to expressiveness errors causing serious readability problems.

4.4   Summary and Discussion

In this chapter, we have motivated our data regularities-driven approach to automatic diagram design. The discussion of the example visualisations A), B), and C)
has shown how aggregations of relational properties, describing data characteristics in the form of binary relation types (strict order relation, set-valued function,
function etc.), may be utilised to construct expressive designs. In example D) and
E) we have demonstrated how even n-ary relations could be characterised in this
way by breaking them up in a set of binary relations, particularly into unique mappings (functional dependencies) and set-valued mappings (set-valued mapping de-

pendencies). We have, however, also identified nested dependencies as a specific kind of domain dependency of n-ary relations. In example F) we have, in addition, identified 'shared domain dependencies' as a property of object networks. All these characteristics represent structural properties of the data.

Common to all examples was the exploitation of these structural data characteristics for the relation's graphical encoding, because this, first, helpes reducing redundancies in the data and thus the complexity of the graphical design, and second, it suggests particular structure-dependent visualisation strategies.

The fundamental method to achieve expressiveness was in all examples based on the assumption that *data relations* may be visually encoded using *graphical relations* matching the data relation's characteristics.

After giving an example for inexpressive visualisations we have addressed effectiveness problems in which the selection of the 'best' design among those that were expressive was the focus of interest. Outlining this problem we have distinguished data and task-dependent aspects, but also perceptual and graphical aspects of effectiveness. Finally, we have adressed resource allocation conflicts which may result from the circumstance that different data relations compete for the same graphical resources.

As a result of the discussion of the state of the art and of the previous chapter, we will propose a visualisation approach comprising three consecutive processes: a *data classification process*, a *graphical resource allocation process*, and a *layout process*. The theoretic assumptions underlying these processes, as well as their algorithmic implementations, will be the subject of chapters 5, 6, and 7 which constitute the core of this work.

In chapter 5 we will outline our model of data characterisation beginning with a discussion of binary relation classification. This includes the construction of a relation type lattice modelling the correct logical implications between the binary relation types we consider. In this context, we will show how data relations may be schematically qualified using relation types that add *formal semantics* to the data. We will also show how a type refinement algorithm may exploit the type lattice for the computation of the most specific type of a given binary relation instance. After that we will discuss the classification of n-ary relations. Important topics in this context are the systematic detection and representation of functional and set-valued functional domain dependencies using so called 'dependency lattices'. We will further address nested dependencies and demonstrate how in particular cases such dependencies can also be found on the instance level. At the end of chapter 5 we will discuss the classification of networks which includes the detection of shared domain dependencies as well as a data ranking, as an aspect of effectiveness, that is determined by quantitative factors, but also by external factors such as tasks, presentation styles etc.

Eventually, the discussion will result in a uniform classification routine for networks that hierarchically integrates the algorithmic components presented below:

- a type refinement algorithm for binary relation instances,

- a classification algorithm for the detection of functional (unique) and set-valued function (set-valued) dependencies,

- a classification algorithm for the detection of shared domain dependencies in networks, and

- a ranking function modelling quantitative and external factors of the design

In chapter 6 we will discuss the graphical resource allocation for the refined relational input, starting with a formalisation and a classification of 'graphical relations'. We will then illustrate our notion of expressiveness as an assignment of appropriate combinations of graphical binary relations to relation types. The order in which the graphical resources are assigned can be seen as an implementation of the perceptual aspects of effectiveness discussed above. After that we discuss structure-driven resource allocation strategies for n-ary relations. Using examples we will first derive an encoding strategy for functional dependencies that will be generalised to work for:

- set-valued functional dependencies,

- mixed functional and set-valued functional dependencies, and

- nested dependencies.

During this discussion we will develop qualitative, type-dependent effectiveness criteria relating to the specificity of the types, and thus realising the graphical aspects of effectiveness outlined above. We will further introduce additional graphical criteria determining the use of graphical relations with respect to frequency, and other aspects, by which they may be applied in a design. For the allocation of graphical resources we will formulate a uniform and general algorithm able to encode arbitrary n-ary relations. Concerning the encoding of networks we will, however, only provide a problem-oriented discussion in which possible solutions are indicated.

The layout process, emphasising the concrete realisation of the encoding decisions made during the resource allocation process, will be discussed in chapter 7. There, we will begin with an introduction of the algorithm that processes the given encoding structure and then we will discuss the role and complexity of procedural layout techniques that concretely realise graphical decisions.

Chapter 5

Relation Classification

In the introduction to the approach in chapter 4, we have outlined how relational data characteristics may be exploited to realise expressive graphical designs. As we consider the input data to be organised in object networks composed of object relations, we understand data characterisation to be based on a classification of relations and their relational characteristics.

For binary relations we will propose relation types that are defined by assignments of binary relation properties (cf. A). Data relations may then be qualified by these types on the schema level. The relation types will be organised in a Relation Type Lattice modelling the logical dependencies between the types. We will show how this type lattice may be interactively constructed and then automatically implemented as a Type Object Lattice so that updates of the classification structure may be achieved conveniently. Convenient updates of the classification structure are important, because the graphical knowledge that is assigned to the relation types as well as the classification structure itself may be subject to changes due to the requirements of the given application. For instance, certain relation types may be required and others may not be required for a given application. The most important purpose of the Type Lattice is that it may be exploited for instance-based type refinement. This means that a relation which is assigned a certain type, say a 'Strict Order', on the schema level may turn out to be a 'Tree Order' on the instance level. For example, if in the NarrowerDiscipline data of example A) in chapter 4 the tuple (furniture design, interior design) was missing, we would — according to the definitions in appendix A — obtain a tree-order relation, instead of only a strict order. This can only be found out by analysis of the given relation instance. As a consequence, we could visualise these data using the more specific graphical relation inclusion. The difference is illustrated in Figure 5.1.

We will exploit such knowledge to graphically encode the relation using the more specific resources defined at the 'Tree Order' type (see chapter 6).

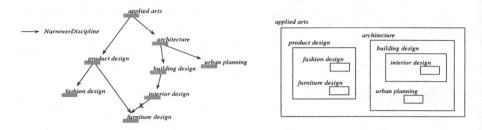

Figure 5.1: *On the left we have displayed the line diagram of the given relation instance as it was displayed in Figure 4.2. The potentially missing tuple is marked by an 'X'. On the right we have presented the more specific inclusion diagram that is only expressive if the marked edge is missing.*

In section 5.2 we will discuss the treatment of n-ary relations for $n > 2$. In this case, there is no rich variety of conventionalised relational properties that we can exploit to establish a classification structure similar to the Relation Type Lattice mentioned above. Nevertheless, we will show how functional and set-valued functional dependencies between the domains of a given relation may be described by means of Mixed Dependency Lattices. A mixed dependency lattice can thus be seen as a means to represent an n-ary relation in terms of its functional and set-valued functional binary components.

We will distinguish 'horizontal' functional dependencies, well known from the theory of relational databases (see [Cod88]), as well as 'vertical' dependencies that describe the nesting structure of data relations. We will further provide an n-ary relation classification algorithm that detects functional and set-valued functional dependencies for a given relation instance and represents them in a dependency lattice. As the latter describes the relation instance by means of a structure imposed on its binary relation components, we may exploit this circumstance to compose the visualisation along this structure using the resources defined at the corresponding binary relation types (this will be addressed in chapter 6). It will also be shown how in specific cases vertical dependencies may be derived from this lattice. Moreover, the binary relation classification algorithm will be embedded in the n-ary relation classification algorithm, since the latter may be seen as performing a binary decomposition of n-ary relations in case of $n > 2$. We will thus establish a hierarchic classification framework which mirrors the fact that n-ary relations are the more general and binary relations are the more specific data structure.

In section 5.3 we will discuss object networks as the top of the data structure hierarchy, because each network may include a set of relations of arbitrary arity. The approach is here to apply a divide and conquer algorithm that decomposes the network into its semantic units — the relational subcomponents — which we know how to visualise and then to compose them together in the end. We must, however,take into consideration that domains may be shared by different relations, since this may lead to conflicts in the graphical resource allocation process. Therefore, we will also propose how to compute the Network Dependency Lattice that represents shared domain dependencies for the relations of a given object net. However, in contrast to the Relation Type Lattice, neither the Network Dependency Lattice nor the Mixed Dependency Lattice will constitute persistent data structures. They must be computed anew whenever new data instances are given as input and disappear when the visualisation is done.

5.1 Binary Relation Classification

In chapter 3 we have described the input to the visualisation algorithm as a network of relations defined on data domains. As mentioned above, we will, in this section, take up the idea outlined in chapter 4 to classify binary relations using formal relational properties. In order to do this, we will make use of Formal Concept Analysis (FCA) [GW96], a mathematical theory for structural data analysis and will show how this theory may be applied to classify binary relations. The result of the classification will be a complete lattice structure whose nodes, implemented as type concept objects, may be used to type relation schemata. Thus, we will develop a means to add formal semantics to the data on the class level that, as we will see in chapter 6, may be exploited for visualisation purposes.

There is a broad variety of relational properties that could be used to qualify binary relations. In fact, there are arbitrarily many, since their existence is only a matter of definition, although some of them have been established as well-known conventions. However, we will subsequently only consider such properties that promise to be useful in the context of diagram visualisation. In the approach to be discussed, we follow a pragmatic directive which says that a property is useful as long as there is a graphical realisation for it. Since we cannot anticipate all possible properties and all their visualisations we will only present a set that is large enough to cover a broad variety of visualisation types. It is important, though, that the applied classification method is powerful enough to easily extend the relation classification, if necessary.

Figure 5.2 below, shows a matrix assigning relation types (rows) to their defining properties (columns). We will call such a matrix a *relation type context* or simply a *type context*. The 'Function' type in row 3, for example, is assigned the properties 'bipartite', 'oriented', and 'unique', whereas the 'Injective Function' type in row 5 has the additional property ' injective ' [1].

Obviously, there are logical interrelations between the types, caused by the fact that sets of types share relational properties. To represent such interrelationships,

---

[1] These assignments are consistent with the definitions in appendix A.

	bipartite	oriented	unique	surjective	injective
Bipartite Relation	X				
Set-Valued Function	X	X			
Function	X	X	X		
Surjective Function	X	X	X	X	
Injective Function	X	X	X		X
Bijective Function	X	X	X	X	X

Figure 5.2: *Type matrix defining relation types by assigning relational properties.*

concept lattices are an appropriate mathematical structure. The lattice diagram corresponding to the type context displayed above is presented in Figure 5.3. There the relation types are printed in bold type face and the properties in normal type face. To find the properties assigned to a relation type, we must follow all arcs in the upward direction, starting at the node representing the given relation type. Note that the properties we collect in this way match the row entries at the relation type in the context. In the next subsection we will outline how such a lattice structure may be systematically constructed.

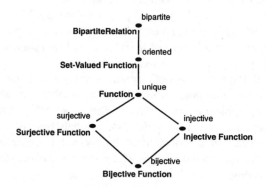

Figure 5.3: *Lattice modelling bipartite relations.*

5.1.1 Relation Types

To formally introduce the Relation Type Lattice we must first present as much of the theory of FCA as is necessary for explanation. Then we will show how the Relation Type Context may generally be constructed in such a way that it represents all the relational properties we want to model. This is followed by a description of the Relation Type Lattice. After that we will discuss the implementation of the lattice in an object-oriented way. Then we will explain how relation schemata may be typed, and finally we will introduce a type refinement algorithm for relation instances.

Introduction to Formal Concept Analysis

Formal Concept Analysis is an applied mathematical discipline based on a formal notion of concepts and concept hierarchies and allowing the exploitation of mathematical reasoning for conceptual data analysis and processing. FCA was developed by [Wil82] at the Department of Mathematics of the Technische Hochschule (Darmstadt) in the early 1980s. We refer the interested reader to the textbook [GW96].

FCA starts from the basic notion of a formal context representing the data. An example of such a context is the one in Figure 5.2 that defines relation types. The formal definition of a context follows.

Definition 5.1 (context) *A formal context is defined as a triple (G,M,I), where G and M are sets and I is a binary relation between G and M. The elements of G and M are called objects and attributes, respectively, and I(g,m) is read "object g has attribute m" for $g \in G$ and $m \in M$.*

For a context (G,M,I), two important derivation operators (Galois-Connections) are defined as follows.

$$\alpha: \quad A \mapsto A' := \{m \in M | I(g,m) \forall g \in A\}, for A \subseteq G, \qquad (5.1)$$

$$\beta: \quad B \mapsto B' := \{g \in G | I(g,m) \forall m \in B\}, for B \subseteq M. \qquad (5.2)$$

Using these operators we are in a position to define a formal concept in accordance with the traditional theory of concepts [Wagner73] consisting of an intension and an extension.

Definition 5.2 (formal concept, extent, intent, object intent) *A formal concept of a context is defined as a pair (A,B) with $A \subseteq G$, $B \subseteq M$, A' = B, and B' = A. A and B are called the extent and the intent of the concept, respectively. The set $\{m \in M \mid I(g,m)\}$ is called the object intent of g.*

Note that (A",A') is, for arbitrary $A \subseteq G$, a concept according to this definition. To illustrate formal concepts let us consider the context displayed in Figure 5.2 again for the following example. Let $G_1 := \{$ BipartiteRelation, Set-ValuedFunction$\}$, then $G_1' = \{$bipartite$\}$ and $G_1'' = \{$ bipartite $\}' = \{$ BipartiteRelation, Set-ValuedFunction, Function, SurjectiveFunction, InjectiveFunction, BijectiveFunction$\}$; thus (G_1'', G_1') forms a formal concept. It is represented by the topmost node in the lattice diagram in Figure 5.3. It has all objects in its extent but only the property ' bipartite' in its intent. We may now establish a hierarchy relation ' $\leq$', called ' subconcept-superconcept' , on the concepts in the following way:

$$(A_1, B_1) \leq (A_2, B_2) :\Longleftrightarrow A_1 \subseteq A_2 (\Longleftrightarrow B_1 \supseteq B_2) \tag{5.3}$$

To illustrate this definition let $G_2 = \{$ Function $\}$. Then $G_2' = \{$ bipartite, oriented, unique $\}$ and $G_2'' = \{$Function, Injective Function, Surjective Function, Bijective Function $\}$. The concept (G_2'', G_2') is represented as the node labeled by the strings ' Function' and ' unique' in the type lattice diagram and clearly $(G_2'', G_2') \leq (G_1'', G_1')$.

The following theorem states that for each concept lattice there exists a smallest common superconcept and a greatest common subconcept. A proof of the theorem can be found in [GW96].

Theorem 5.1 (concept lattice) *The set of all concepts of (G,M,I) together with the relation ' $\leq$' forms a complete lattice (see [GW96]) which we call the the concept lattice of (G,M,I) denoted by $B(G, M, I)$. For any set of concepts $(A_t, B_t)_{t \in T}$ there exists always a smallest common superconcept, given by*

$$((\bigcup_{t \in T} A_t)'', \bigcap_{t \in T} B_t), \tag{5.4}$$

called the supremum (sup) of $(A_t, B_t)_t \in T$ in B(G,M,I) and a greatest common subconcept

$$((\bigcap_{t \in T} A_t, (\bigcup_{t \in T} B_t)'') \tag{5.5}$$

called the infimum (inf) of $(A_t, B_t)_t \in T$ in B(G,M,I).

More importantly, the theorem indicates a solution for an algorithmic construction of the concept lattice which is based on a further implication saying that every concept extent is an intersection of attribute extents and, vice versa, every concept intent is an intersection of object intents. This may be exploited to model a naive algorithm for the computation of all concepts of a context: a list of concept extents that is empty in the beginning needs to be generated (the extents are sufficient, since α may be applied to compute the corresponding intent). The initial step is to add the concept extent G to the list. The ith step is then to check for every attribute $m \in M$ and for every $A \subseteq G$ that is added to the list whether $A \cap m'$ is in the list. If it is not it needs to be added.

Since the algorithm described above needs too many list look-ups it becomes awkward for larger contexts. Therefore, [Gan87] introduced a more efficient algorithm, called "Next Closure", to compute the lattice based on a lexicographic ordering of the concepts. An important impact of the fact that such an algorithm exists is that the concept lattice may be automatically updated whenever the (predefined) context has changed.

Constructing the Relation Type Context

In this subsection we will discuss how the Relation Type Context may be interactively constructed in such a way that the context implications induced by the properties' definitions are correct. The correct modelling of relation type interdependencies is important for the relation type refinement algorithm, introduced later in this chapter, which effectively exploits the property logic to detect instance-based data regularities.

Informally, implications between attributes of a context are statements of the form: 'Every object that has the attributes a, b and c (premise) has also the attributes x, y and z (conclusion). To formally explain what we mean by context implications we will introduce this concept next.

Definition 5.3 (Context Implications) *A subset $T \subseteq M$ respects an implication $A \Longrightarrow B$ if $A \not\subseteq T$ or $B \subseteq T$. T respects a set $\mathcal{L}$ of implications if T respects each implication in $\mathcal{L}$. $A \Longrightarrow B$ is true for a set $\{T_1, T_2, \ldots\}$ of subsets if each T_i respects $A \Longrightarrow B$. $A \Longrightarrow B$ is true in a context (G,M,I) if it is true in the system of object intents. In this case we call $A \Longrightarrow B$ an implication of the context.*

To illustrate this definition we consider again the context introduced in Figure 5.2. There we may easily verify that ' unique' $\Longrightarrow$ 'oriented' is an implication of the context, because whenever a relation type has the property 'unique' it has at the same time the property 'oriented' .

In the opening example in Figure 5.3 the relation types were specified by assigning to them their defining properties. However, if the property logic needs to be preserved in the type context such a construction may lead to inconsistencies in the system of context implications. This is illustrated by the example presented in Figure 5.4 which at first glance seems to be correct, since the property assignments are correctly made. However, a more careful investigation of the lattice shows that the properties 'transitive' and 'irreflexive' both imply the properties 'acyclic' and 'antisymmetric' which is certainly not consistent with respect to the definitions in appendix A, since, e.g., 'transitive and irreflexive imply acyclic' cannot be derived from these definitions.

To circumvent this problem we need to find out the implications that hold between the properties. To this purpose, we will apply a program called 'Interactive Attribute Exploration' [Bur91] that serves to explore attribute implications in an interactive fashion. The result will be a context describing the property logic correctly so that the derived concept lattice properly reflects the implications between the properties. The exploration program is based on a simple principle: The first step is to provide an initial set G^* of objects that have to be correctly qualified using a given set M of attributes. In our application the initial context will contain binary relation instances as its objects and relational properties as its attributes. Then, the program systematically computes suggestions for implications based on

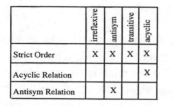
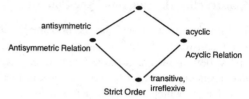

Figure 5.4: *Example showing incorrect property implications.*

this context. The user is then requested either to verify the implication by proving the statement or to falsify it by providing a counter example that needs to be added to the context. In this way the context is enlarged by adding counterexamples until all possible suggestions are processed. In our case we choose the initial set

$$G^* := \{g_1, \ldots, g_{15}\}$$

of objects (see Figure 5.5 for the definitions of the g_i) and the set

M := {symmetric, symmetric tree, equivalence relation, antisymmetric, antisymmetric tree, strict order, complete lattice order, tree order, discrete linear order, real-valued linear order, acyclic, bipartite, oriented, unique, surjective, injective, bijective}

of relational properties some of which already represent complex aggregations of primitive properties (see appendix A for their definitions).
After applying the implication exploration program G^* is extended by the counter examples

$$G^{**} = \{g_{16}, g_{17}, g_{18}\}$$

to form the final object set G, so that the Relation Type Context may be defined by the triple $C_T(G, M, I)$. It is presented in Figure 5.6. This context consists of 24 concepts (they are listed in appendix B) and a minimum number of 24 non-redundant attribute implications. From this so called "implication base" the whole universe of possible implications, which is, of course, much larger, may be derived (see [Bur91] and [Zic91]). The implication base of $C_T(G, M, I)$ is presented below.

- real-valued linear order $\Longrightarrow$ complete lattice order $\wedge$ tree order,

- equivalence relation $\Longrightarrow$ symmetric,

- symmetric tree $\Longrightarrow$ symmetric $\wedge$ acyclic,

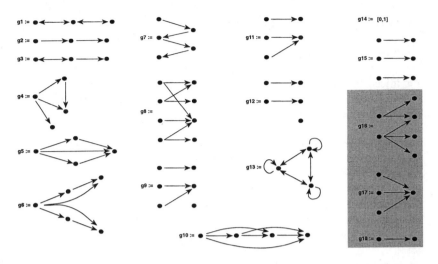

Figure 5.5: *The set G of objects. The explored objects are indicated by the grey background.*

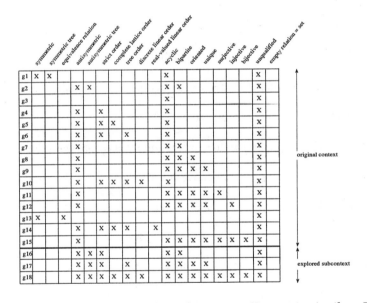

	symmetric	symmetric tree	equivalence relation	antisymmetric	antisymmetric tree	strict order	complete lattice order	tree order	discrete linear order	real-valued linear order	acyclic	bipartite	oriented	unique	surjective	injective	bijective	unqualified	empty relation = set
g1	X	X									X							X	
g2				X	X						X	X						X	
g3											X							X	
g4				X		X					X							X	
g5				X		X	X				X							X	
g6				X		X		X			X							X	
g7				X							X	X						X	
g8				X							X	X	X					X	
g9				X							X	X	X	X				X	
g10				X		X	X	X	X		X							X	
g11				X							X	X	X	X	X			X	
g12				X							X	X	X	X		X		X	
g13	X		X															X	
g14				X		X	X	X		X								X	
g15				X							X	X	X	X	X	X	X	X	
g16				X	X	X					X	X						X	
g17				X	X	X			X		X	X	X	X				X	
g18					X	X	X	X	X	X	X	X	X	X	X	X	X	X	

original context

explored subcontext

Figure 5.6: *Final context after applying the program 'Interactive Attribute Exploration'.*

- antisymmetric tree $\implies$ bipartite,

- bijective $\implies$ surjective $\wedge$ injective,

- injective $\implies$ unique,

- surjective $\implies$ unique,

- unique $\implies$ oriented,

- oriented $\implies$ bipartite,

- bipartite $\implies$ antisymmetric $\wedge$ acyclic,

- discrete linear order $\implies$ complete lattice order $\wedge$ tree order,

- complete lattice order $\implies$ lattice order,

- tree order $\implies$ strict order,

- complete lattice order $\implies$ strict order,

- strict order $\implies$ antisymmetric $\wedge$ acyclic,

- oriented $\wedge$ antisymmetric tree $\implies$ strict order,

- surjective $\wedge$ injective $\implies$ bijective,

- strict order $\wedge$ bipartite $\implies$ tree order $\wedge$ oriented $\wedge$ antisymmetric tree,

- strict order $\wedge$ unique $\implies$ surjective function,

- strict order $\wedge$ injective $\implies$ complete lattice order,

- complete lattice order $\wedge$ bipartite $\implies$ discrete linear order $\wedge$ injective,

- discrete linear order $\wedge$ real-valued linear order $\implies$ symmetric,

- symmetric $\wedge$ acyclic $\implies$ symmetric tree,

- acyclic $\wedge$ equivalence relation $\implies$ antisymmetric,

- symmetric $\wedge$ antisymmetric $\implies$ bipartite $\wedge$ equivalence relation $\wedge$ real-valued linear order,

The Relation Type Lattice

As already mentioned in the last section, the type context and thus the Relation Type Lattice $B_T(G, M, I)$ consists of 24 concepts. A line diagram representing the Type Lattice is presented in Figure 5.7. Its nodes represent the concepts visually. For instance, we may identify the concept $B := (\{g_4, g_5, g_6, g_{10}, g_{14}, g_{16}, g_{17}, g_{18}\}, \{antisymmetric, strictorder, acyclic, unqualified\})$ as the one marked in the line diagram. For our purposes, however, the example relation instances g_i, that is, the elements of the concept extents, are of no significance anymore, since they have only served to develop the property logic consistently. This is the reason why we have not displayed them in the diagram. The properties and their logic, though, are general and thus serve for the classification of other relation instances as well. This is guaranteed by the generality and the correct use of the attribute exploration program. Using this method we have achieved a complete and consistent representation of implications that are induced by the property definitions (in appendix A). The example relations could therefore be replaced by other examples and another implication base could be computed, but the universe of implications induced by the two bases would definitely be the same.

In the remainder we will thus identify the relation types by the properties assigned to the lattice nodes, particularly by those directly assigned to them. For instance, the marked concept B in the diagram will represent the 'Strict Order' relation type and from B's concept intent we know that a strict order relation is at the same time acyclic, antisymmetric etc. This means that we may distinguish among 24 different relation types induced by the property logic, given the relational property set M we took into consideration.

The Type Lattice reflects the pragmatic principle we followed according to which only those relational properties that may be visually represented are considered. This means that not all defining relational properties (with respect to the definitions in appendix A) should be explicitly modelled in the type lattice. For instance, we do not consider the property 'transitive' to be visualisable as such, because we know of no sensible case where transitivity alone could be visualised. Therefore, this property is not explicitly represented as an attribute. For the same reason we have not represented the property 'irreflexive' or the combination of the two properties. Nevertheless, we have outlined in chapter 4 that the two properties can be visualised in the context of a strict order relation. However, if it should turn out that one of these properties, or any other property or combination of properties become 'visual types' it is comparatively easy to extend the given Type Lattice by just extending its corresponding Type Context.

The actual use of the distinction into different relation types lies in their potential to qualify the data relations by adding relation type information, i.e. formal semantics, to them (this is the topic of subsection 5.1.1). Moreover, as we have demonstrated in chapter 4, explicit knowledge of the relation type of a given input

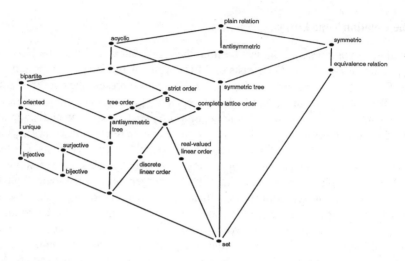

Figure 5.7: *Lattice modelling relation types.*

relation allows the application of type-specific visualisation strategies. The relation types thus represent persistent graphical knowledge. As we will explain later on, we will implement the types as 'type objects' at which the graphical resources are bound. These type objects, connected by a 'subtype' attribute storing the given type's subtypes, will represent the implementation of the Type Lattice. Instead of storing this lattice persistently it will rather be computed each time when the visualisation algorithm is set up (this will be discussed in greater detail in the next section). The relation types may then be used to type relation schemata on the class level. In addition, we may exploit the lattice structure to analyse a given binary relation instance for its relation type, since a relation instance may show a more specific type than the one that is assigned to its relation schema on the class level. Since the Relation Type Lattice represents exactly and effectively the logical implications between the relation types, an efficient algorithm may be designed to compute the instance-based type refinement. Before we go on outlining this algorithm we first need to relate the Relation Type Lattice to the world of object-oriented modelling. This will be the next topic.

Generating the Relation Type Lattice

In this subsection we will describe how the Relation Type Lattice may be implemented using an object-oriented design. As a result of applying the algorithm "Next Closure", we presume we are given the set of type concepts $\{t | t \in B_T(G, M, I)\}$. Although these concepts make up the Relation Type Lattice we do not know much about the lattice connectivity, since this information is only implicitly encoded in the extents and intents of the concepts. To make this connectivity information explicitly available we need to compute it algorithmically. How this can be achieved will be discussed below.

Before we come to the explanation of the algorithm that constructs the Type Lattice from the set of type concepts we need to give some explanation of the object-oriented implementation of the basic data structure including context objects, context attributes, contexts, and concepts as the building blocks of the Type Lattice.

Let $[BinaryMatrix] \in C$ be the object class whose instantiations represent $\mid G \mid \times \mid M \mid$ binary matrices and let $[G], [M] \in C$ be arbitrary object classes. Then we define a context $C_T(G, M, I)$ in the following way:

Definition 5.4 (TwoValuedContext) *A context $C_T(G, M, I)$ will be represented as an instantiation of the class $[TwoValuedContext] \in C$ that owns the attributes contextObjects : $[TwoValuedContext] \mapsto [G]$, contextAttributes : $[Two ValuedContext] \mapsto [M]$, and $I : [TwoValuedContext] \mapsto [BinaryMatrix]$.*

Both, the program "Interactive Attribute Exploration" and the program "NextClosure" need to be defined as procedures operating on instances of [TwoValuedContext] [2]. To create a new type lattice they must be performed one after the other in the above order. The resulting type concepts are represented as objects conforming to the class $[TypeConcept]$ that is defined next. Let $[G], [M] \in C$ represent classes of context objects and context attributes respectively:

Definition 5.5 (TypeConcept) *A type concept will be represented as an instantiation of the class $[TypeConcept] \in C$ that defines the attributes name : $[TypeConcept] \mapsto String$, extent : $[TypeConcept] \mapsto [G]$, intent : $[TypeConcept] \mapsto [M]$, and subtypes : $[TypeConcept] \mapsto [TypeConcept]$.*

In addition to contexts and type concepts, we need a data structure for the representation of the Type Lattice. To this purpose, we define:

Definition 5.6 (TypeLattice) *The TypeLattice $B_T(G, M, I)$ will be represented as an object conforming to the class $[TypeLattice] \in C$ that defines the attribute typeConcepts : $[TypeLattice] \mapsto [TypeConcept]$ which stores the set of type concepts of the lattice. For arbitrary types $T_1, T_2 \subseteq TypeConcept$ the TypeLattice also implements the functions smallest common supertype ($sup(T_1, T_2)$) and greatest common subtype ($inf(T_1, T_2)$) according to the definitions given in formula 5.4 and formula 5.5.*

An important issue concerning the implementation of the type lattice relates to the fact that its elements not only serve as a means for adding formal semantics to

---

[2] We will not discuss the two programs in detail here. The interested reader is referred to [Bur91] and [Gan87] where they are explained in depth.

the data relations but also to bind type-specific graphical knowledge (cf. chapter 6). As a consequence, it is necessary to preserve this information. To this pupose we generate a corresponding data type for each type concept at which the graphical resources may be persistently stored. The resulting Relation Type Lattice is then a subset of the Type Hierarchy defined in definition 3 in chapter 3. Whenever the visualisation system is started anew it must, however, guarantee that the type concepts find the corresponding data types again. This can be realised by assigning both the type concepts and the data types the same name in the first run so that a name string matching can be performed in subsequent runs. To the set of relation types we will refer by the term Types in the remainder.

For the construction of the lattice the following operations must be performed: Given the set of type concepts as constructed by "NextClosure", the Type Lattice is generated by recursively calling the procedure *createTypeLattice* that invokes the procedure *nextSubtypes*. The latter computes for a given type $t \in TypeLattice$ its immediate subtypes.

Next, we will explain the procedure *nextSubtypes*. Thereafter follows an outline of *createTypeLattice*.

Let $C_T(G, M, I)$ be the type context and $t \in TypeConcept$ be an arbitrary relation type concept. We further presume the derivation operators α and β, introduced in subsection 5.1.1, to be implemented as context operations at the class [TwoValuedContext]. Then, we formulate the following algorithm:

Algorithm 5.1 (Next Subtypes)

Input: *a relation type $t \in TypeConcept$ for which $A := extent(t)$ and*
            $B := intent(t)$ and the set M of attributes.

Output: *all immediate subtypes of t with respect to the type lattice.*

function nextSubtypes(t,M)
        local variables: S, m, S_m, subTypes, B.

        $S := \emptyset$. *subTypes* $:= \emptyset$.
        $S := S \cup (S_m := M)$.
        forall $m \in M \setminus B$ *do:[*
                $S_m := \alpha(\beta(B \cup \{m\}))$.
                for all $S_n \in S$ *do:* [
                        if $S_m \subset S_n$
                                then $S := S \cup S_m \setminus S_n$.
                                else $S := S \cup S_m.$]]
        forall $S_n \in S$ *do: [subTypes* $:= subTypes \cup (S_n, \alpha(S_n)).$]
        return(subTypes).

Explanation 5.1 *Let $t^* := (A^*, B^*) < t := (A, B)$. Then we know from definition 5.2 that $B \subseteq B^*$. This justifies the construction of the set $B \cup \{m\}$ for $m \in M \setminus B$ (the outer for-loop) that contains B. Since $B \cup \{m\}$ is not a concept intent we must apply the derivation operator $(B \cup \{m\})''$ twice to obtain its closure under β, that is, the smallest concept intent that contains $B \cup \{m\}$. Since $B \subset B \cup \{m\} \subseteq (B \cup \{m\})''$ we know now we have found a subconcept t^* of t with intent $(B \cup \{m\})''$. We do not know, however, if this is an immediate subconcept or not. To detect the immediate subintents we need (the inner for-loop) to exclude those subintents S_i from the set of all constructed subintents S that include other subintents S_j. The collection of pairwise non-inclusive subintents created in this way then contains the concept intents we are looking for. To eventually obtain the immediate subconcepts, we need to apply the derivation operator β to all elements of S to find the corresponding subextents. The collection of (subextent, subintent) pairs in the set subtypes is then the wanted set of immediate subconcepts. Finally, the subconcepts (subtypes) are returned.* ◇*

Starting at the top-type of the type lattice we may consecutively compute the subconcepts down to the bottom-type by applying the procedure *createTypeLattice*.

Algorithm 5.2 (Create Type Lattice) *Let subtypes be the attribute defined at the class [TypeConcept] storing the immediate subtypes of a given type. Then we may formulate the procedure createTypeLattice as follows:*

Input: the relation type $t := sup(TypeConcepts)$.

Output: a TypeLattice representing $B_T(G, M, I)$ by means of connected type concept objects.

```
procedure createTypeLattice(t)
        local variables: tp.
        subtypes(t) := nextSubtypes(t).
        if subtypes(t) = inf(TypeConcepts).
        then [terminate]
        else [  forall tp ∈ subtypes(t) do: [
                    createTypeLattice(tp)]]
```

Explanation 5.2 *The algorithm starts with the topmost type of the TypeLattice. For an arbitrary type $t \in TypeLattice$ it computes the immediate subtypes. If inf(TypeLattice) is reached the algorithm terminates and the Relation Type Lattice is instantiated.*◇

Now, that we have established the Type Lattice we may use the more convenient operation *subTypes* retrieving the value of a type concept's subtype attribute, instead of using the computationally more expensive operation *nextSubTypes* defined on the TypeContext that was necssary to construct the TypeLattice from the set of type concepts. Dually, we obtain the operations *nextSuperTypes* and *superTypes* respectively. Moreover, once the type lattice has been constructed it is also convenient to precompute the set of suprema (least upper bounds) and infima (greatest lower bounds) and store them in a list from which they can be looked up whenever they are needed, instead of computing them anew according to formula 5.5.

Typing Binary Data Relations

This subsection is dedicated to the description of the typing of binary relations using the relation types introduced above. Recall that we have distinguished in chapter 3 between the schematic description of relations and the relation instances that may be instantiated from the schema. To introduce binary relation types in the object-oriented design we need to extend relation schemata by adding a new 'relationType' attribute that uniquely assigns a unique relation type to each binary relation.

$$relationType : [\mathcal{DRC}_2] \mapsto Types$$

At this point, we must not forget however, that the domains may be interpreted as relations (unary relations in case the domain is a plain set, cf. chapter 3). In case a domain represents an unstructured set it is assigned the SetType. We are therefore allowed to characterise them using the same relation types. To illustrate this consider example 3.1 in chapter 3 again. There we have defined the relation schema for the 'BroaderConceptOf' relation. To specify its relation type we need to add the attribute

relationType: [BroaderConceptOf] $\mapsto$ StrictOrderType

and at the class [Concept] we need to add the attribute

relationType: [Concept] $\rightarrow$ SetType

In example 3.3 we need to add the following type definitions to the FacultyAt relation schema:

relationType: [Person] $\mapsto$ SetType,

relationType: [DurationPeriod] $\mapsto$ BijectiveFunctionType, and relationType: [School] ↦ SetType.

Note that the FacultyAt relation itself cannot be typed at this point, since it is not a binary relation. We will postpone the treatment of the more general n-ary relations to the next section. We may, however, further qualify the domain Date appearing in the DurationPeriod schema by defining

relationType: [Date] ↦ [RealValuedLinearOrderType],

so that we know that DurationPeriod is a bijective function from a set of reals into itself. Such a typing of relations allows for arbitrary combinations of domain types. This is particularly interesting in the case of functional relations where the distinction of domain and range according to the following combinations alone

$$\{SetType, DiscreteLinearOrderType, RealValuedLinearOrderType\} \times$$

$$\{SetType, DiscreteLinearOrderType, RealValuedLinearOrderType\}$$

leads to a broad variety of function types each corresponding to a specific design, as discussed in chapter 4.

In this subsection we have demonstrated how binary relations may be schematically typed using the relation types constituting the type lattice. In the next subsection we will show how instance-based type refinement may be performed in order to find the most specific type of a given binary data relation.

Type Refinement Algorithm for Binary Relations

Before we proceed to outline the type refinement algorithm, we need to define the subprocedure *checkProps* that returns the value true if a relation instance R has the properties defining type t. Let $\mathcal{P}$ denote the relational properties we consider (e.g., those defined in appendix A) and let

$$relationalProperties : Types \mapsto \wp(\mathcal{P})$$

be the attribute specified at a given relation type $T \in Types$, that stores the relational properties defining this type. Note that for the context $C_T(G, M, I)$ the attribute set M is generally included in the set $\mathcal{P}$, because not all defining properties of a relation type are modelled in the Type Lattice $B_T(G, M, I)$, but only those that we considered visually significant. We may now formulate the property testing algorithm as follows:

Algorithm 5.3 (Relational Property Testing) *Let $p \in \mathcal{P}$ be a relational property, $R \in [\mathcal{DRC}_2]$ be a binary relation instance and isPropertyOf(p,R) be the function returning true if p is a property of R. Then we define the function checkProps in the following way:*

Input: *a binary relation instance R conforming to* $[R] \in [\mathcal{DRC}_2]$ *and*
            a type concept $t \in TypeLattice$

Output: *the return value is 'true' if all of t' s defining properties are true for R.*

function checkProps(R,t)
            local variables: DefProps, check, p.

            DefProps := ∅.
            check := true.
            DefProps := relationalProperties(t)
            for all $p \in DefProps$ *do: [*
                    if isPropertyOf(p,R) = false
                            then check := false.]
            return(check)

Explanation 5.3 *The function iterates over the relational properties defining a given relation type* $t \in TypeLattice$ *that are defined as testing functions at the corresponding type concept t. If all tests return 'true' the function returns 'true', otherwise 'false' .*

We may now go on to present the type refinement algorithm for binary relation instances. Assuming we compute $\inf(\{t_i, t_j\})$ for arbitrary $t_i, t_j \in TypeLattice$ according to formula 5.5 we formulate the algorithm in the following way:

Algorithm 5.4 (Type Refinement)

Input: *a binary relation instance R conforming to* $[R] \in [\mathcal{DRC}_2]$ *together*
            with its predefined relation type $t \in TypeLattice$

Output: *the most specific type of R with respect to the type lattice.*

procedure typeRefinement(R,t)
            local variables: validTypes, Types, i.
            validTypes := new(Set).
            Types := subtypes(t).
            i := 1 to $|Types|$ *do: [*
                    if checkProps(R, t_i *) = true then validTypes := validTypes* $\cup \{t_i\}$ *].*
            if validTypes isEmpty then return(t)
                    else typeRefinement(R,inf(validTypes))

Explanation 5.4 *In the do-loop the program checks for all subtypes of t whether their defining properties are valid for the given relation instance R. If this is the case, it adds the subtype to the set validTypes. Otherwise, it is ignored. If valid-Types is empty we have already found the most specific type. It is t itself. If valid-Types is not empty the procedure is recursively applied until validTypes is empty. This will be the case for some type $t \in TypeLattice$, since the lattice is finite and the procedure converges strongly monotonically.*

That the most specific type is unique can be seen from the following argument: If the types $t_1, \ldots, t_n$ are true for the given relation instance then their conjunction, that is, inf($\{t_1, \ldots, t_n\}$) is true and inf is uniquely determined according to theorem 5.1. This is the reason why we may apply the infimum operator to jump from a given set of true subtypes directly to their infimum, instead of consecutively working down the immediate subclasses of a given type to reach the infimum. ◇

To illustrate the algorithm we will present an example next.

Example 5.1 (Type Refinement) *Let NarrowerDiscipline be an instance of the binary relation [NarrowerDiscipline] $\in [\mathcal{DRC}_2]$ with the following tuples:*

NarrowerDiscipline:= { (visual arts, arts), (performing arts, arts), (painting, visual arts), (painting, arts), (sculpture, visual arts), (sculpture, arts), (theatre, performing arts),(theatre, arts), (opera, performing arts), (opera, arts), (music, performing arts), (music, arts)}.

The corresponding line diagram is presented in Figure 5.8. The operation *relation-Type(NarrowerDiscipline)* returns the relation type 'StrictOrder', since this is the default type we have assigned to the relation on the schema level (cf. example A) in chapter 4). Relation instance and type are then input to the procedure. The operation *subTypes(StrictOrder)* returns the set Types := $\{TreeOrder, CompleteLat-ticeOrder\}$. The procedure *checkProps(T_i)* returns false for 'CompleteLattice-Order' and true for 'TreeOrder', since the transitive kernel (the set of tuples without the transitive tuples, cf. Appendix A.) of the relation instance is clearly a tree. Thus the type 'TreeOrder' will be returned as the refined type of the relation instance.

5.1.2 Summary of Binary Relation Classification

In this section, we have introduced an applied mathematical technique by which binary relations can be effectively classified. The advantages of organising the emerging relation types in a concept lattice are manifold. First, updates of the classification structure are comparatively easy to perform, since they only require a

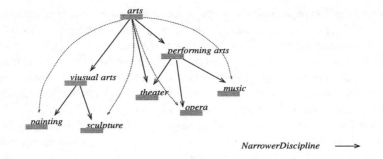

Figure 5.8: *Type refinement example. Transitive edges are displayed using dotted arrows.*

change of the given type context. Changing the context is supported by the program 'Interactive Attribute Exploration' which assures a logically consistent type modelling. Given the list of type concepts as computed by the program "NextClosure" the Type Lattice itself can be automatically constructed by applying the procedure *createTypeLattice*. For its implementation we have proposed an object-oriented design in which the types are represented as type concept object s whose connectivity is established by the values stored in their subTypes attribute. The Type Lattice is stored in a database and retrieved in a set up operation whenever the visualisation algorithm is started. The idea behind this model is that the lattice represents persistent knowledge by which the data relations, and as we will see later, also the 'graphical relations' may receive formal semantics forming the basis of expressive graphical mappings in the sense of [Mac86]. Moreover, since the type lattice correctly reflects the system of logical implications between the relational properties that constitute the relation types we may exploit the lattice structure for refinement of relation instance types. This is important, because it reveals valuable information about the given input data which is not encoded on the class level but may be exploited to graphically represent the most specific properties, or regularities, of the data.

In the next section we will discuss classification in the case where we are given relations of arity > 2. We will also show how the the binary relation classification introduced in this section may be embedded in the more general case.

5.2 Classification of n-ary Relations

For relations of arity > 2 there exist no relational properties which we could exploit for classification in the way we have for binary relations in the last section, but this does not mean that n-ary relations are completely unstructured. As we have seen in chapter 3, they may be nested, which implies that each relation tuple forms a tree, instead of plain sequences of values. We may interpret the nesting structure to establish a grouping of domains into semantic units. In chapter 4 we have referred to such a grouping of domains by the term nested dependencies. The following March relation schema illustrates this again:

March(Troop,((Location,Date),(Location,Date)))

This relation schema, whose visualisation has been discussed by [Tuf83] and by [RM90], represents 5-tuples whose acyclic graph structure result from a double nesting of domains. The inner parentheses indicate that Location and Date instances form units. In this case we interpret the first (location,date)-tuple to encode where and when a troop started its march and the second where and when its march stopped. The next outer parentheses represent the sequence of the march, and the outer most parentheses relate the subject to its march. Clearly, we could not have the grouping information at our disposal if the March relation schema was defined as follows:

March(Troop,Location,Date,Location,Date)

In this case we would not know how to relate the involved domains. Grouping of different domains of a relation may also be understood as a form of domain dependencies (we call them nested dependencies) by which some of the domains are more strongly tied together than others. Another form of domain dependencies (which we also have addressed in chapter 4 already) are so called functional dependencies that are well known from the theory of relational databases. In case of such dependencies, however, domains may not be tied together by meaning, but by means of syntactic data analysis techniques.

As we will see later, explicit knowledge of such dependencies will have a strong impact on the visualisation process. Therefore, such information needs to be found out on the instance level if it is not already encoded in the relation schema. For nested dependencies, this is unfortunately in the general case a non-trivial, computationally expensive task, since it needs to be found out which subsets of a relation' s domain correlate. However, there exist heuristic approaches, particularly in the field of knowledge discovery and data mining, that show how such groupings can be found from the instances of unstructured relations. The applied techniques range from statistical methods to detect quantitative and qualitative laws, e.g., [ZB91] and [CW91] over knowledge-based approaches such as [CCH91]to domain-specific discovery methods such as [ABL91] and formal logic-based techniques, e.g. [SSS91] and [Zic91] .

From the discussion so far, it is clear that the input to the visualisation algorithm may range between completely unstructured relation tuples, as was, e.g., the case for the measurement tuples in chapter 3, and well structured tuples as was the case in the march example above. In analogy to the last section we need to provide data classification techniques which we can apply to analyse arbitrary n-ary relation instances for implicitly encoded, that is, instance-based data regularities. To this purpose, we will apply Formal Concept Analysis (FCA) again, since it provides us with a structural representation of the functional dependencies in the form of a 'dependency lattice' which we may exploit to conveniently design visualisation strategies. We will also show that the same techniques may in certain cases be used to detect even nested dependencies. Moreover, application of FCA has the additional advantage that a reuse of the machinery introduced to classify binary relations is ensured to keep the classification algorithm simple. Before we go on to outline these problems we will introduce a relation table in Figure 5.9 that represents the "example database" from which most of the data, used in the remainder of this chapter and in chapter 6, will be extracted.

5.2.1   Functional Dependencies

Presuming we are given an arbitrary n-ary relation schema $[R] \in [\mathcal{DRC}]$ with semantically independent domains, then we may qualify the binary relations established between pairs of domains using the binary UnqualifiedRelationType in the general case. The question is then if there exists a type refinement for the instances of these relations and how these relations are structurally organised. In this section, we focus on the detection of mappings which means we consider the SetValuedMappingType to be the most general type established between two relation domains. To tackle these problems using FCA we must first represent n-ary relation instances in an adequate form. To this purpose, we introduce multivalued contexts as a generalisation of 2-valued contexts introduced in the last section.

Definition 5.7 (Multivalued Context) *A multivalued context (G,M,W,I) consists of the sets G, M, W and of a ternary relation $I \subseteq G \times M \times W$ such that*

$$\forall_{g \in G}, \forall_{m \in M}, \forall_{w,v \in W} : (g, m, w) \wedge (g, m, v) \Rightarrow w = v \qquad (5.6)$$

As in the case of 2-valued contexts, the elements of G are called the objects and the elements of M the attributes. The elements of W are called the attribute values. We read I(g,m,w) as follows: 'attribute m of object g is assigned the value w' .

According to the definition above the generalisation of 2-valued contexts is established by introducing the non-trivial value set W generally comprising more than

	Person	Profession	School	WorkPeriod	LifeSpan
g1	A.Albers	Designer	Bauhaus	1924-1933	1899-s.a.
g2	A.Albers	Designer	BMC	1933-1949	1899-s.a.
g3	J.Albers	Urban Planner	BMC	1933-1949	1888-1976
g4	Bartning	Architect	Bauhaus	1923-1928	1883-1959
g5	Breuer	Architect	Bauhaus	1928-1932	1897-1972
g6	Breuer	Architect	Harvard	1937-1946	1897-1972
g7	Breuer	Urban Planner	Harvard	1937-1946	1897-1972
g8	Feininger	Urban Planner	Bauhaus	1927-1931	1906-s.a.
g9	Gropius	Architect	Bauhaus	1925-1933	1883-1969
g10	Gropius	Architect	Harvard	1937-1951	1883-1969
g11	Hilberseimer	Architect	Bauhaus	1925-1929	1885-1967
g12	Hilberseimer	Architect	IIT	1938-1967	1885-1967
g13	Johnson	Architect	Harvard	1949-1965	1895-1973
g14	Johnson	Urban Planner	Harvard	1933-1949	1895-1973
g15	Kandinsky	Painter	Bauhaus	1925-1933	1866-1944
g16	Klein	Urban Planner	IIT	1944-1952	1928-1962
g17	Le Corbusier	Architect	Bauhaus	1923-1927	1887-1865
g18	Maki	Architect	Harvard	1939-1948	1908-s.a.
g19	Manning	Urban Planner	IIT	1955-1964	1921-s.a.
g20	Mies v. d. R.	Architect	Harvard	1938-1958	1886-1869
g21	Moholy-Nagy	Urban Planner	New Bauhaus	1937-1938	1855-1946
g22	Gupcic	Sculptor	Harvard	1933-1949	1905-1967
g23	Soltan	Urban Planner	Harvard	1944-1953	1913-s.a.
g24	Fuller	Architect	Harvard	1942-1949	1895-1983
g25	Goldsmith	Urban Planner	IIT	1939-1947	1918-s.a.
g26	Schawinsky	Urban Planner	BMC	1936-1938	1895-1961
g27	Peterhans	Urban Planner	IIT	1938-1960	1899-1975

Figure 5.9: *Example database containing facts about the domain of art. The abbreviation 's.a.' indicates that the artist is still alive.*

two values. To identify the value $w \in W$ of attribute $m \in M$ for an object $g \in G$ we will also adopt the notation m(g) = w, instead of $(g, m, w) \in I$ in the remainder. This function-driven notation indicates perhaps more directly that context entries are well defined (c.f. formula 5.6), since m(g) = w and m(g) = v iff w = v.
Relation tables such as the one presented in Figure 5.9, are examples of multivalued contexts. The value set of the attribute Person comprises the set of entries in the first column and and $Person(g_2) = Albers$ indicates that the entry of 'Person' at g_2 is 'Albers'.

Apart from the fact that a context should be well defined we will also require the data to be complete in the sense that no context entries are missing. A multivalued context meeting this requirement is then called a *complete context*. Clearly, the facultyAt context introduced above meets this requirement.

Next, we will discuss how functional dependencies may be described in multivalued contexts. In order to do this, we need to provide a formal definition of functional dependencies.

Definition 5.8 (Functional Dependency) *Let $X \subseteq M$ and $Y \subseteq M$ be sets of attributes of a complete multivalued context (G,M,W,I), then we say Y depends functionally on X if for any pair of objects $g, h \in G$ the following implication is true*

$$(\forall_{m \in X} m(g) = m(h)) \Rightarrow (\forall_{n \in Y} n(g) = n(h)) \tag{5.7}$$

To paraphrase this definition, a functional relationship between two attribute sets X and Y is given, whenever the fact that two arbitrary objects have the same values with respect to the attributes in X implies that they have the same values with respect to the attributes in Y. The term functional may be explained as follows: Y depends functionally on X if and only if there exists a function $f : W^X \mapsto W^Y$ [3] for which

$$f(m(g)|m \in X) = (n(g)|n \in Y) \quad for \ all \ g \in G \tag{5.8}$$

is true. Important is that functional dependencies may be expressed as implications in 2-valued contexts. This can be done using the dependency context

$$K_N(\wp_2(G), M, I_N) \tag{5.9}$$

which is defined by the rule

$$I_N(\{g, h\}, m) :\Leftrightarrow m(g) = m(h), \tag{5.10}$$

given that $\wp_2(G) := \{\{g, h\}|g, h \in G, g \neq h\}$. The context object set of the dependency context thus consists of all pairwise combinations of objects of the original context, whereas the context attribute set remains the same. In analogy to the dependency context we call $B_N(\wp_2(G), M, I_N)$ the dependency lattice. The following proposition recapitulates the relationship between functional dependencies in multivalued contexts and implications in 2-valued contexts.

Proposition 5.1 *The attribute set Y depends functionally on X in (G,M,W,I) iff the implication $X \Rightarrow Y$ is true in the context K_N.*

Proof 5.1 *The proof of the proposition is trivial, since*

$$(\forall_{m \in X} m(g) = m(h)) \Rightarrow (\forall_{n \in Y} n(g) = n(h))$$

$$\Leftrightarrow$$

$$(\forall_{m \in X} I_N(\{g, h\}, m) \Rightarrow (\forall_{n \in Y} I_N(\{g, h\}, n)$$

---

[3] The notation indicates the cartesian product of value sets with respect to the attributes in X and Y

The statement made by the proposition is important, since it ensures that we may use the algorithms designed for the 2-valued case for the detection of functional dependencies.

Before we proceed to the next subsection where nested dependencies will be discussed, we will provide two examples that illustrate the transformation of multivalued contexts into 2-valued contexts. The first example is based on the extraction of relation tuples (from our example database presented in Figure 5.9) representing FacultyAt facts.

	Person	School	WorkPeriod
$g1$	Gropius	Harvard	1937-1951
$g2$	Breuer	Harvard	1937-1946
$g3$	A.Albers	BMC	1933-1949
$g4$	J.Albers	BMC	1933-1949
$g5$	Moholy Nagy	New Bauhaus	1937-1938
$g6$	Hilberseimer	IIT	1938-1967

BMC: Black Mountain College
IIT: Illinois Institute of Technology

Figure 5.10: *Multivalued context representing FacultyAt facts.*

According to formula 5.9 and formula 5.10 respectively the dependency context of the multivalued FacultyAt context introduced above is generated by taking all pairwise combinations of original objects as the dependency context objects, leaving the attributes as they are and writing the value 'x' at an arbitrary entry ($\{g, h\}$,m) of the dependency context if g and h have the same attribute value in the FacultyAt context. This condition is in the given example only true for (g_1, g_2) in combination with the attribute 'School' and for (g_3, g_4) in combination with the attributes 'School' and 'WorkPeriod'. Therefore, we obtain a rather sparse dependency context that is presented in Figure 5.11

	g1g2	g1g3	g1g4	g1g5	g1g6	g2g3	g2g4	g2g5	g2g6	g3g4	g3g5	g3g6	g4g5	g4g6	g5g6
Person															
School	x									x					
Period										x					

Figure 5.11: *Dependency context corresponding to the multivalued FacultyAt context presented in Figure 5.10. To consume less space it is displayed up-side down.*

The given dependency context may be reduced by removing all blank columns and rows, since they have no effect on the information the context provides. For the construction of the dependency lattice, however, we have to keep row eleminations in mind, since the corresponding attributes (in this example 'Person') are assigned to the lattice infimum, because they qualify none of the objects. As a consequence, they occur at the lowest node in the diagram. The reduced context and its assigned lattice are displayed in Figure 5.12.

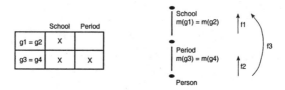

Figure 5.12: *The Reduction of the dependency context 5.11 and the corresponding dependency lattice.*

The FacultyAt example shows a rather clear dependency structure. The lower line, read in the upward direction, indicates the function f_1 that maps from the set of persons into the set of time periods, and the upper line indicates the function f_2 uniquely mapping periods into schools. Note that the transitivity of the concept lattice implies also a mapping f_3 from the persons into the schools. Moreover, the lattice additionally shows the following *redundancy information*. 1) the objects g_1 and g_2 have the same value at the attribute 'School' whereas 2) g_3 and g_4 even share the values of 'WorkPeriod' and 'School'. Since there are as many persons as there are tuples in this FacultyAt context we may conclude that in the first case Gropius and Breuer were in different times at the same school, whereas in the second case A. Albers and J. Albers were at the same time at the same schools.

To explain why we need to find out such redundancy information we have to anticipate the visualisation principles introduced in chapter 6 to some extent at this point. Suppose we visualise this functional dependency structure bottom-up which means, we first encode the persons using rectangles, then we assign the rectangles positions and extents to represent the temporal information, and finally, we use colours to represent the schools. In this case we additionally know that the rectangles representing 'A. Albers' and 'J. Albers' must be horizontally aligned and they must obtain the same colour (because of 1)), whereas the rectangles representing 'Gropius' and 'Breuer' are only assigned the same colour (because of 2)). In other words, besides the functional information that tells us how data domains are graphically encoded we obtain helpful constraints expressing how the graphical elements relate to one another (e.g., elements have the same colour or have the same position).

A clear linearly ordered dependency structure as above can be effectively visualised. However, we cannot always expect such a simple dependency lattice. In the next example we investigate the extracted PerformedProfession facts in Figure 5.13:

	Person	Profession	School	WorkPeriod
g1	Gropius	Architect	Bauhaus	1937-1951
g2	Breuer	Architect	Bauhaus	1937-1946
g3	A.Albers	Designer	BMC	1933-1949
g4	J.Albers	Urban Planner	BMC	1933-1949
g5	Moholy-Nagy	Urban Planner	New Bauhaus	1937-1938
g6	Hilberseimer	Architect	IIT	1938-1967

Figure 5.13: *Multivalued context representing PerformedProfession facts.*

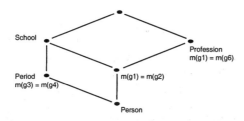

Figure 5.14: *Dependency lattice corresponding to the multivalued context in Figure 5.13.*

The structure of the lattice (see Figure 5.14) is in this case more complex. We may draw the following conclusions: There are functional relationships from the set of persons into the set of professions, the set of periods and the set of schools. A further functional relationship exists from the set of periods into the set of schools. From the fact that the professions and the periods as well as the professions and the schools are incomparable we may conclude that the connectivity between both professions and periods as well as professions and schools is only a set-valued mapping, and thus, not unique. In chapter 6 we will thus refer to such dependencies by the term *set-valued functional dependencies*, and in case both types of dependencies occur at the same time, as in Figure 5.14, we call that a *mixed dependency*. The redundancy of the first and the second tuple '$m(g_1) = m(g_2)$' with respect to the schools and professions indicates that Gropius and Breuer were at the same school and had the same professions, whereas the redundancy of the first and the sixth tuple '$m(g_1) = m(g_6)$' with respect to the professions shows that Gropius and Hilberseimer had the same profession. Finally, the redundancy of the third and the fourth tuple '$m(g_3) = m(g_4)$' with respect to the periods means that A.Albers and J.Albers were in the same school at the same time. In the same way as above we may use these redundancies for the generation of constraints that relate the used graphical elements and their attributes. Therefore, such facts are valuable information we may exploit for the visualisation process.

In summary, we may say that a dependency lattice expresses an n-ary relation by means of its binary components and their mutual interdependencies as well as by the redundancies of tuples with respect to particular domains. As we will see in chapter 6 and chapter 7 respectively, the structure of the lattice and the relationtype-specific information of its binary components will be used to allocate the proper graphical resources to the domains, whereas the redundancy information is exploited to guide the final layout process.

5.2.2   Nested Dependencies

Nesting of relations may be understood as a form of domain dependency that is orthogonal to functional dependencies. We may, however, also say that nested dependencies represent functional dependencies between the domains. The difference is that "classical" functional dependencies, as described in the last subsection, organise the domains horizontally, whereas nested relations organise them vertically.

Horizontal organisation essentially refers to the presence of functional dependencies on the same level of nesting while disregarding that a domain may itself be a relation. Thus, in the classification process described so far, we did not distinguish between domain classes that are relation classes themselves and those that are not.

Vertical organisation , in constrast, means, we can describe the relation in terms of nested relations. To illustrate this, we will rewrite the opening example of this section in this way:

$$March :\subseteq Troop \times Move$$

$$Move :\subseteq LocDate \times LocDate$$

$$LocDate :\subseteq Location \times Date$$

As we already know from the last section, binary relations may have different relation types. For instance, if March is specified as a unique mapping in the following way $March : Move \mapsto Troop$, then we know that the relation Move represents a directed graph and LocDate a set-valued mapping relation in the general case. According to our philosophy, this implies the need to perform type refinement for a given instance of the March relation schema. Using type refinement we may, e.g., find out whether the given schema describes the move of one troop, and if this is so, that the directed graph describing the moves represents a sequence of moves, because a troop can only make one move at the same time. An intuitive illustration of the March schema is the nesting tree presented in Figure 5.15.

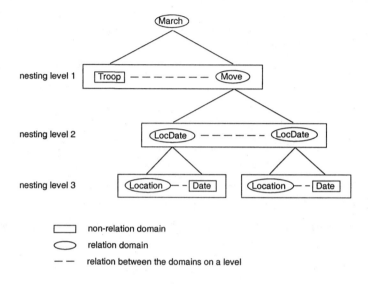

Figure 5.15: *Nesting tree of March relation.*

A more abstract description of the problem by which the domain dependencies become apparent may be formulated in the following way: suppose we are given a linear sequence of nested relations $[R_n] < \ldots < [R_1] \in [\mathcal{DRC}]$ and a set of non-relational (plain) domains $[D_1], \ldots, [D_s] \in [\mathcal{DOC}]$ that constitute the range sets of the non-relational domain attributes of some $[R_i]$ for $i \in \{1, \ldots, n\}$, then the sequence of functions defined by:

$$f_i : [D_1] \times \ldots \times [D_{s_i}] \times [R_{i-1}] \mapsto [R_i] \tag{5.11}$$

recursively expresses the vertical dependency of the domains $[R_1], \ldots, [R_n]$. We will interpret the arguments of the vertical functions to represent the *nesting levels* of the relation. As the formalism indicates, they may generally be relations of arity > 2 themselves and as such they must be subject to n-ary relation classification themselves to find out their most specific properties. Moreover, the vertical dependencies occur in this case only in a linear form, since we were given a sequence of nested relations. We will only consider such cases in this book.

So far, we have assumed the nestings to be defined on the schema level. As we have outlined before, the detection of vertical dependencies on the instance level is a quite difficult task since the grouping of domain sets is essentially determined by the semantics of the data. However, in certain cases we may use the results of horizontal dependency analysis to find vertical dependencies as well. The key concept we need for this are *bijective dependencies*, that is, a stronger form of functional dependencies in which two domains of a relation are in a one-to-one correspondence with one another. In this case we can group the two domains together to form a nested binary subrelation of the original relation. To illustrate this we consider another extraction of facts creating the PerformedProfession relation instance presented in Figure 5.16:

	Person	Profession	School	WorkPeriod
g1	Architect	Gropius	Bauhaus	1925-1933
g2	Sculptor	Gupcic	Harvard	1933-1949
g3	Painter	Kandinsky	Bauhaus	1925-1933
g4	Architect	Gropius	Harvard	1933-1949

Figure 5.16: *Multivalued context also representing PerformedProfession facts.*

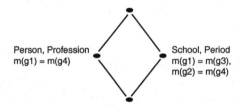

Person, Profession
m(g1) = m(g4)

School, Period
m(g1) = m(g3),
m(g2) = m(g4)

Figure 5.17: *Dependency lattice corresponding to the multivalued context presented in Figure 5.16.*

From the diagram of the dependency lattice corresponding to these facts (presented in Figure 5.17) we learn that both the domains Profession and Artist as well as the domains School and Date are in a one-to-one correspondence which justifies the rewriting of the schema describing the given relation instance as

PerformedArtisticProfessions((Profession, Artist), (School, Date))

However, such a nesting of domains is only sensible if we have initially ensured that the domains are semantically independent. Otherwise, we might obtain sense-less groupings of domains. To illustrate such a case consider the following March facts in which $FromLocation, ToLocation \subseteq Location$ and $FromDate, To-Date \subseteq Date$.

	Troop	Location1	FromDate	Location2	ToDate
g1	Napoleon	Paris	1800	Luxembourg	1801
g2	Napoleon	Luxembourg	1801	Köln	1802
g3	Napoleon	Köln	1802	Berlin	1804
g4	Napoleon	Berlin	1804	Warschau	1805

Figure 5.18: *Multivalued context representing March facts.*

Figure 5.19: *Dependency lattice representing corresponding to the context above.*

Computing the functional dependencies leads to the dependency lattice displayed in Figure 5.19. We see that the FromLocations correspond to the ToDates in the same way as they correspond to the FromDates. A relation (FromLocation,ToDate) would, however,be a semantically false grouping information. This example un-derlines, however, how important a rich semantic data model is, since, as we will see, such knowledge represents valuable information for the fact visualisation pro-cess.

In summary we may say that nested relations reflect groupings of domains into semantic units. To detect such groupings on the instance level is comparatively difficult, since it requires to find correspondences between the involved domains. However, if we can detect instance-based bijective relations between domains we recognise these to form such correspondences.

5.2.3   Classification Algorithm for n-ary Relations

To analyse a possibly nested n-ary relation structure the classification algorithm recursively processes the given input relation's nesting hierarchy top-down and performs type refinement for nested binary subrelations using the type refinement algorithm introduced in the last section. For nested subrelations with arity greater than 2 it computes its corresponding dependency lattice. Functional dependencies in the dependency lattice are subject to type refinement as well.

To implement this algorithm, called *functionalDependencies*, we first need to explain the subprocedures *multivaluedContext, dependencyContext, dependencyLattice, nestedDomains*, and *refineAllFunctions*.

The operation *multivaluedContext* computes a multivalued context for a given relation instance from which *dependencyContext* computes its corresponding dependency context. The algorithm *dependencyLattice* computes a dependency lattice from a dependency context and *nestedDomains* returns the set of nested subrelations of a relation instance. Eventually, *refineAllFunctions* computes a type refinement for all functional dependencies established between relation domains represented in the dependency lattice.

Before we start with the outline of the classification algorithm's main components using pseudo-code we will provide some explanations, especially for those auxiliary routines ocurring within the code that may be understood intuitively and therefore not explained in detail.

Let $cM_{context}$ be the notation to denote the contextMatrix attribute of a given context in the following pseudo-code, let Array(n,m) be an $n \times m$ array instance of the class [Array], and let furthermore $domObj_j(r_i)$ be the operation defined for each data relation class $[R] \in [\mathcal{DRC}]$ returning the data object at the j-th component of the i-th tuple of a given relation instance R.

We may now start with the outline of the function that computes multivalued contexts from arbitrary n-ary relation instances. Multivalued contexts are, in analogy to 2-valued contexts, represented as objects conforming to the class $[Multi\text{-}valuedContext] \in \mathcal{C}$ that is defined analogously. The difference between multivalued contexts and 2-valued contexts is only that the contextMatrix stores an $| G | \times | M |$ matrix whose entries may be arbitrary values, instead of binary values.

Algorithm 5.5 (Multivalued Context)

Input: *an n-ary relation instance R conforming to* $[R] \in [\mathcal{DRC}]$

Output: *an mvc conforming to* $[MultivaluedContext] \in \mathcal{C}$

      function multivaluedContext(R)

local variables: arity, mvc, cM_{mvc}, i,j.

$$arity := arity(R).$$
$$mvc := new([MultivaluedContext]).$$
$$cM_{mvc} := new([Array(|R|, arity)]).$$
$$for\ i = 1\ to\ |R|\ do:\ [$$
$$\qquad for\ j = 1\ to\ arity\ do:\ [$$
$$\qquad\qquad cM_{mvc}(i, j) := domOb_j(r_i)]]$$
$$return(mvc)$$

Explanation 5.5 *The function iterates over the set of tuples in R and over the set of domains and assigns each entry of the* $|R| \times arity(R)$ *context mvc the corresponding domain value.*

The function dependencyContext, to be specified next, transforms a given multivalued context into a 2-valued dependency context by applying formula 5.9.

Algorithm 5.6 (Dependency Context)

Input: an mvc conforming to $[MultivaluedContext] \in C$

Output: a tvc conforming to $[TwovaluedContext] \in C$

function dependencyContext(mvc)
local variables: arity, tvc, cM_{tvc}, i, j, k.

$$arity := arity(R).$$
$$tvc := new(TwovaluedContext)$$
$$cM_{tvc} := new([Array(|R|, |R|, arity)]).$$
$$for\ i = 1\ to\ |R|\ do:\ [$$
$$\qquad for\ j = 1\ to\ |R|\ do:\ [$$
$$\qquad\qquad for\ k = 1\ to\ arity\ do:\ [$$
$$\qquad\qquad if\ i \neq j\ and\ (cM_{mvc}(i, k) = cM_{mvc}(j, k))$$
$$\qquad\qquad\qquad then\ cM_{tvc}(i, j, k) := 'x'$$
$$\qquad\qquad\qquad else\ cM_{tvc}(i, j, k) := '\ '\ ]]]$$
$$return(tvc)$$

Explanation 5.6 *For each pair of non-identical context objects the value 'x' is set in the contextMatrix belonging to the dependency context tvc if the two objects have the same attribute value in the multivalued context mvc and ' ' otherwise.* ◇

The function *dependencyLattice* works in analogy to the function *createTypeLattice* described in section 5.1 except that the nodes of a dependency lattice represent the domain object instances of a given a relation instance and not the relation types. Therefore, we renounce of a detailed description of *dependencyLattice* at this point, since it would only repeat what has been said already. Before we go on outlining *nestedDomains* we will, however, define the class [DependencyLattice] whose instantiations represent dependency lattices.

Definition 5.9 (DependencyLattice) *A dependency lattice DL is an instantiation of the class* $[DependencyLattice] \in \mathcal{C}$ *that defines the attributes* $latticeNodes :$ $[DependencyLattice] \mapsto [\mathcal{DOC}] \cup [\mathcal{DRC}]$

Next we will discuss the function *nestedDomains* that returns those domains of a relation instance that are themselves relation instances.

Algorithm 5.7 (Nested Domains) *Let* $domain_i(R)$ *be the operation defined at all data relation classes* $[R] \in [\mathcal{DRC}]$ *returning the i-th domain on which the relation is defined.*

Input: *an n-ary relation instance R of* $[R] \in [\mathcal{DRC}]$

Output: *the set relSet of immediately nested (relational) domains*

> *function nestedDomains(R)*
>   *local variables: relSet, i, n, D,*
>
>   *relSet :=* $\emptyset$.
>   *for i = 1 to n do:[*
> $D := domain_i(R)$.
>   *if* $[D] \in [\mathcal{DRC}]$
>   *then relSet := relSet* $\cup \{D\}$.
>   *return(relSet)*

Obviously, the function above adds all relation domains to the set relSet which is returned.

Before we may introduce the classification algorithm for n-ary relations we need to specify *refineAllFunctions* that is called by this algorithm. As we have already pointed out above, *refineAllFunctions* refines all functional dependencies found in the dependency lattice. Thus, ad-hoc functions have to be generated for all those pairs of domains that are in such relationships with one another. To this purpose, *refineAllFunctions* calls the subroutine *createFun* that generates an adhoc-function (unique mapping) from a multivalued context $mvc \in MultiValuedContext$, a domain instance D conforming to $[D] \in [\mathcal{DOC}]$ and another domain instance D^* conforming to $[D^*] \in [\mathcal{DOC}]$. If $Dis\,a\,subTypeof\,D^*$ in the dependency lattice then D represents the domain of the function and D^* represents its range. The function *subDomains* that returns the immediate subdomains of a given domain is defined in analogy to subTypes in section 5.1 which returns the immediate subtypes of a given relation type

Algorithm 5.8 (Refinement of a Dependency Lattice)

Input: *a dependency lattice dl, a concept B, and a multivalued context mvc.*

Output: *a refinement of the functional dependencies between the domains.*

function refineAllFunctions(dl,B ,mvc)
        local variables: nextDomains, D, fun.

        if B = nil
            then B := sup(dl).
            else [
                nextDomains := subDomains(B).
                if nextDomains = ∅
                    then return
                    else [
                        forall D ∈ nextDomains do: [
                            fun := createFun(D,B,mvc).
                            typeRefinement(fun).
                            refineAllFunctions(dl,D,mvc)]]]

Explanation 5.7 *Initially the parameter B representing concepts of dl is set nil and thus the function initialises B by sup(dl). It then computes its subconcepts, stores them into the variable nextCon and checks whether this set is empty. Note that this is in a complete lattice only the case for inf(dl). If this is the case, the function terminates and returns the set types that contains all refined functional dependencies computed so far. Otherwise, it iterates over the subconcepts of B and calls createFun that generates adhoc function instances from mvc with D as its domain and B as its range. These function instances are further analysed by the binary classification algorithm typeRefinement to find their most specific description with respect to the binary Relation Type Lattice. All refined dependencies are then added to the set types. The function is recursively called with the lattice dl, the current subconcept D, and the multivalued context mvc as its parameters. ◇*

Now we may go on formulating the dependency detection algorithm for n-ary relations. It distinguishes between binary relation schemata and schemata of higher

arity. In the first case it applies the binary classification algorithm *typeRefinement*
and in the second it pairwise computes the functional dependencies for all involved
domains and represents them by means of a dependency lattice. Each functional
dependency is, of course, subject to further refinement by applying the binary relation classification algorithm once again.

Algorithm 5.9 (Classification of Nested n-ary Relations)

Input:　　an n-ary relation instance R conforming to $[R] \in [\mathcal{DRC}]$
　　　　　　and a set dependencySet of dependency contexts.

Output:　the most specific set of dependency lattices characterising R.

function functionalDependencies(setOfRelationInstances,dependencySet)
　　　local variables: dSet, R, i, mvc, tvc, dl.

　　　　　dSet := dependencySet.
　　　　　nextSubrelations := ∅ .
　　　　　for i = 1 to | setOfRelationInstances | do:[
　　　　　　if [R_i] \in [\mathcal{DRC_2}]
　　　　　　　then [typeRefinement(R_i)]
　　　　　　　else [
　　　　　　　　mvc := multivaluedContext(R_i).
　　　　　　　　tvc := dependencyContext(mvc).
　　　　　　　　dl := dependencyLattice(tvc).
　　　　　　　　refineAllFunctions(dl, nil, mvc).
　　　　　　　　dSet := dSet ∪ dl]
　　　　　　if nestedDomains(R_i) = ∅
　　　　　　　then [return(dSet)]
　　　　　　　else [functionaldependencies(nestedDomains(R_i),dSet)]]

Explanation 5.8 *In the initial call of the function the parameter setOfRelationInstances is set to R and the dependency set is set ∅. Generally, the algorithm iterates
over all input relation instances and distinguishes between $[R] \in [\mathcal{DRC_2}]$ and
$[R] \notin [\mathcal{DRC_2}]$. If the first condition is true, the binary classification algorithm
typeRefinement is called, otherwise a multivalued context mvc is computed and
from that the dependency context tvc is derived. Application of dependencyLattice
leads then to the dependency lattice dl. All functional dependencies represented
in the dependency lattice are then refined using the procedure refineAllFunctions.
The refined dependency lattice is then added to the dependency set dSet. If there
are no further subrelations anymore the algorithm terminates, otherwise it is recursively called for nestedDomains and the dependency set dSet that has been built
so far.*

To illustrate how the algorithm works consider the two different March relation schemata we have used as the opening examples of this section. The first schema is nested and all nested subcomponents are themselves binary relations. This means that, independently of the relation instance, the first 'else' -case in the algorithm above is never entered and thus only the type refinement algorithm for binary relation classification is applied. In other words binary relation classification is embedded in the more general n-ary classification case. In case of the second March relation schema that is not nested the 'else' -case is immediately entered and a multivalued context, as in Figure 5.18 is calculated. For this context the dependencies are obtained as in Figure 5.19. A further refinement of dependencies is not possible with respect to the binary Relation Type Lattice.

5.2.4 Summary of n-ary Relation Classification

The goal of this section was to describe the structure of n-ary relations by means of the dependencies established between the involved domains. As in the last section, we have distinguished between the class level where relations are schematically specified and the instance level where a relation may show more specific properties. We distinguished two types of regularities: (horizontal) functional dependencies are those that describe the dependencies on the same level of nesting by means of unique mappings established between two domains. (Vertical) nested dependencies are those that describe the dependencies between consecutivelevels of nesting as unique mappings between the corresponding domains.

The classification result of horizontal dependencies can be represented as a concept lattice that integratively represents the dependencies between all pairs of domains. This has the advantage that we do not only have a pairwise view on the dependencies between the domains but also obtain a global dependency structure from which we may easily read transitive functional dependencies as well as the weaker set-valued mapping relationships. This may be algorithmically exploited to detect more specfic regularities, e.g., surjective functional relationships, by applying the binary relation algorithm for further type refinement. In the case we find even one-to-one correspondences, we interpret this as a strong correlation between two domains, which allows us to compose the two domains to form an instance-based nested subrelation.

5.3 Classification of Object Networks

The classification of object networks may be seen as a generalisation of the classification of n-ary relations, since it aims at describing how a given set of n-ary relations may be characterised at the same time. It is therefore the top-level, and thus a natural extension, of the hierarchic classification model including binary relation classification on the bottom level and n-ary relation classification on the intermediary level. An advantage of this hierarchic classification model is that it allows for the formulation of a uniform hierarchic classification algorithm for object networks which we will discuss at the end of this section. Since object networks are instances of a given set of relation schemata, the basic algorithmic paradigm we apply is a divide and conquer approach decomposing a given object network into its relational subcomponents that are separately analysed using the n-ary classification component. The major problem that occurs in this context is to find out data redundancies, e.g., objects shared by a set of relations, since these may lead to conflicts in the graphical resource allocation process. The aim of this section is therefore to provide the means for controlling 'shared domain dependencies' (cf. chapter 4). Besides that, expressive graphical mappings must reflect the share of a given relation that is part of the object network to be displayed. Therefore, we will also discuss a simple method quantifying the share of a relation in an object network.

5.3.1 Shared Domain Dependencies

Obviously, we may model domain dependencies on the schema level by representing the involved relations as the objects and their domains as the attributes of a 2-valued context, which we call the 'network dependency context'. We will formally introduce the dependency context and the corresponding dependency lattice next.

Definition 5.10 (Network Dependency Context and Lattice) *Let* $\mathcal{N}^* := \{[R_1]$ $, \ldots, [R_n]\}$ *for* $[R_i] \in \mathcal{R}$ *and* $1 \leq i \leq n$ *be an object network schema in which each* $[R_i]$ *is defined on the domain sets* $\mathcal{D}_i := \{[D_{1i}], \ldots, [D_{mi}]\}$ *for* $[Dji] \in \mathcal{C}$ *where* $1 \leq j \leq m$. *Then the network dependency context is given by*

$$C_{\mathcal{N}^\bullet}(\mathcal{N}^*, \bigcup [D] \in \mathcal{D}_i, I_{\mathcal{N}}) \tag{5.12}$$

where $I_{\mathcal{N}^\bullet}$ *denotes the binary relation* '$[R_i]$ *is defined on domain* $[D] \in \mathcal{D}_i$' *and we call*

$$B_{\mathcal{N}^\bullet}(\mathcal{N}^*, \bigcup [D] \in \mathcal{D}_i, I_{\mathcal{N}}) \tag{5.13}$$

the network dependency lattice.

To illustrate these concepts we use an extension of example F in chapter 4 which contains the following relation schemata:

> EvolvedFrom(Profession,Profession)
> PerformedByAt(Profession,Person,School)
> Duration(Profession,DurationPeriod)
> DurationPeriod(Date,Date)
> LifeSpan(Person,LifePeriod)
> LifePeriod(Date,Date)

The resulting network dependency context is straightforwardly constructed as presented in Figure 5.20 and the corresponding network dependency lattice is given in Figure 5.21.

	profess	durPeriod	date	person	lifPeriod	school
duration	X	X	X			
durationPeriod			X			
lifeSpan			X	X		
lifePeriod			X			
performedByAt	X			X		X
evolvedFrom	X					

Figure 5.20: *Network dependency context for the relation schemata above.*

From the dependency lattice we may read the following information: the relations LifeSpan and PerformedByAt share the persons as their common domain, whereas the relations PerformedByAt, Duration, and EvolvedFrom have the professions in common. The relations LifeSpan, LifePeriod, Duration, and DurationPeriod have the dates as a common domain. However, in this case there is a difference to the shared domains before, because both Duration and LifeSpan are nesting relations, containing LifePeriod and DurationPeriod, respectively, as nested parts. This is reflected by the fact that the last two relations occur once as objects and another time as attributes of the context (and thus in the lattice). As we already know, we find the shared domains for a given set of relation schemata in the lattice by applying the lattice operator *sup* (lowest upper bound) to the corresponding object concepts. As we will see, the dependency lattice, processed top-down, will be an effective means in the resource allocation process, in which it has to be decided how the different domains are graphically encoded. To give some clue in advance,

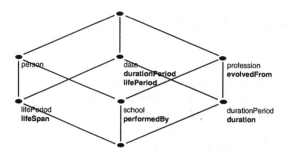

Figure 5.21: *Network dependency lattice corresponding to the context in the Figure above. Data relations are displayed in bold type face and domains in normal typeface. Reading the diagram in the way explained in section 5.1 we find that the relation PerformedByAt is defined on the domains Person School and Profession.*

it is very likely to encode those domains that are shared by many relation schemata (those lying further up in the lattice) as first class graphical objects, whereas others are only realised as attributes of these objects (cf. 6.3.9).

Before we go on defining the classification algorithm for object networks, we need to specify a ranking of the involved relations assigning each a number that expresses its quantitative share in the overall object network. This is also important for the resource allocation process, since a quantitative ranking of importance is a good foundation (but not the only source) for assigning the most effective graphical resources to the most significant data relations. We will next present the definition of the ranking, which is essentially a real value computed from the number of tuples of a relation, its arity, and a user-defined weight reflecting, e.g., user defined inportance rankings (preferences) for particular portions of the data:

Definition 5.11 (Relation Ranking) *Let $\mathcal{N}$ be an object network instance composed of the relations $R_1, \ldots, R_n$ and let $\omega : \mathcal{N} \mapsto [0,1]$ be a weight. Then, the function $f : \mathcal{N} \mapsto [0,1]$, defined by*

$$f(R_i) := \frac{|R_i| arity(R_i) \omega(R_i)}{s} \tag{5.14}$$

for $s := \sum_{i=0}^{n} |R_i| arity(R_i) \omega(R_i)$ is called the quantitative rank of R_i in N. In the remainder we will use the denotation $f_{qr}(i)$ to refer to the quantitative rank of the relation $R_i \in \mathcal{N}$.

Given the function *quantitativeRanking(R)* that returns the rank value of the relation instance R we may now proceed to formulate the classification algorithm for object networks. At this point, we have to mention, however, that the network dependency lattice is computed in analogy to the Relation Type Lattice and the domain dependency lattices if the network dependency context was constructed according to formula 5.10. Therefore, we skip the description of the lattice generation process here again .

Algorithm 5.10 (Classification of Object Networks) *Let networkDependencyLattice(N) be the operation computing the network dependency lattice $C_N \cdot (N^*, \bigcup[D] \in D_i, I_N)$ from the network dependency context $B_N \cdot (N^*, \bigcup[D] \in D_i, I_N)$.*

Input: an object network N

Output: the most specific description of each relation $R \in N$ and a
*   shared domain dependency lattice $B_N \cdot (N^*, \bigcup D \in D_i, I_N)$*

> *function sharedDomainDependenciesFor(N)*
> *local variables: relDescriptions, R, qr, fD, sdd.*
>
> *relDescriptions := $\emptyset$.*
> *forall $R \in N$ do:[*
> *   qr := quantitativeRanking(R).*
> *   fD := functionalDependencies(R).*
> *   relDescriptions := relDescriptions $\cup$ (R,qr,fD)]*
> *sdd := networkDependencyLattice(N).*
> *return(sdd,relDescriptions)*

Proof 5.2 *The function iterates over all $R \in N$ and computes for each a quantitative ranking. Then, the functional dependencies are computed and stored in the variable fD. The procedure nestedDependencies(R) computes nestings from bijective functions analysed for R. It refines the instance relation R and has therefore no return value. The set relDescriptions stores triples containing the relation instance R and the corresponding ranking value as well as the functional dependencies of R. After the loop the shared domain dependencies are computed and stored in sdd. Finally the tuple containing the classification result, that is, the shared domain dependencies and the relation descriptions is returned and the algorithm terminates.*

According to this algorithm an object network conforming to the example schema introduced above is decomposed into its constituent parts, each of which is separately analysed using the n-ary classification algorithm *refineAllFunctions* and assigned an importance ranking value. Then this is the input to the graphical resource allocation process that is discussed in the next chapter.

5.4   Summary of Relation Classification

In this chapter, we have introduced a hierarchic classification framework for semantic object relations in which the categories classification of binary relation, classification of n-ary relations (where $n > 2$), and classification of object networks are distinguished.

In section 5.1 we have shown how binary data relations may be classified using relation types. The types were defined by relational properties and only such properties were chosen that promised to be visually realisable. The relation types together with their logical interdependencies were modelled as a formal concept lattice, called the Relation Type Lattice. To provide as much genericity in the construction of the TypeLattice, which is important with respect to updates of its structure, we have discussed how the lattice may be interactively constructed using the program 'Interactive Attribute Exploration'. Then, it was discussed how to implement the Type Lattice by modelling binary relation types as 'data types' being connected to their subtypes. Each type may then be used to qualify a given data relation and the classification operations may be applied to check whether all relational properties defining a relation type are true for a given binary relation instance that is subject to classification. In this case the relation instance is set to this type, even if it is on the schema level defined to be of a more general type. We have demonstrated how instance-based relation type refinement may be effectively performed by making use of this principle.

In section 5.2 we have demonstrated how n-ary relations may be classified with respect to horizontal functional dependencies as well as vertical functional dependencies established between the domains on which the given relation is defined. We have shown how a dependency lattice may be generated from the given relation instance and how horizontal dependencies are represented in it. We have further shown how nested subrelations may be defined for a given subset of the domains on which the relation is defined if bijective dependencies between these domains can be found for the given relation instance. Moreover, an n-ary relation classification algorithm embedding the binary classification method was introduced. In section 5.3 we have introduced the overall classification algorithm for object networks. It decomposes a given network into its relational subcomponents and classifies each separately. Since shared domain dependencies may lead to conflicts in the graphical resource allocation process, it was also necessary to generate an explicit representation of these dependencies. They are represented in a network dependency lattice which is computed from the relation schemata included in the network schema. In addition to the network dependency lattice, a ranking of the network's relation components is calculated. The classification algorithm returns the classified object network instance, which is the input to the resource allocation process.

Chapter 6

Graphical Mapping

In chapter 5 we have outlined a hierarchic classification framework for object networks. The latter were considered to be composed of object relations of arbitrary arity, and the classification was performed along well defined data characteristics so that we could introduce classification algorithms computing instance-based refinements of the data to determine their most specific description. For the classification of binary relations we have introduced the Relation Type Lattice. Binary relations represent an important class of relations, since higher-arity relations ($n >$ 2) may be decomposed and represented by means of their binary functional and set-valued-functional components — generally, as we know, in form of a Mixed Dependency Lattice. The impact on the visualisation process is the following: we will introduce a set of relation type specific graphical binary relations. In this way we will achieve an expressive graphical mapping for a data relation whenever a graphical relation is chosen that matches the relation type of the data relation. The graphical realisation of n-ary relations in general becomes then a matter of graphical binary relation composition (cf. section 6.3). However, since graphical relations are not arbitrarily combinable we need to find combinations that suit all involved components at the same time. Moreover, as we have argued in chapter 5, the assignment of graphical relations to the relation types is not unique and thus the composition process must select the most effective graphical resource among the different choices defined at the particular type or at any of its super types. In chapter 5 we have further outlined that effectiveness is determined by quantitative data aspects, reader tasks, perceptual aspects and by graphical aspects. The graphical composition process will therefore be designed as a discrete optimisation process that performs expressive graphical mappings while taking the different aspects of effectiveness into consideration[1] in order to visualise a given object network.

---

[1] In subsection 6.3.1 we will outline what aspects we integrate in our approach.

This chapter is organised as follows: in section 6.1 we will introduce the visual vocabulary, that is, graphical elements connected by graphical binary relations. The latter will be subject to classification again. The major part of this section will thus be dedicated to a discussion of the different types of graphical binary relations among which we will distinguish. At the end of this section we will introduce the binding of graphical binary relations at the Relation Type Lattice which is a prerequisite for expressive graphical encoding of binary and higher-arity data relations. The last topic of this subsection will be a discussion of effectiveness criteria.

In section 6.3 we will outline algorithmic strategies for the encoding of n-ary relations. The result will be an abstract description of the visualisation of a given object network. Our approach will be to partition this problem into subproblems that can be treated separately. We will thus investigate strategies for functional dependencies in section 6.3.1, set-valued-functional dependencies in section 6.3.3, mixed-dependencies in section 6.3.5, nested dependencies in section 6.3.7, and for object networks in section 6.3.9. The order of the topics is not arbitrarily chosen, though. Instead, we will start with the functional encodings as the simplest encoding strategy, develop a resource allocation algorithm for this case, and show how this algorithm may be generalised to cover also the more difficult cases. The aim of this section will be the development of a uniform algorithm for the graphical encoding of nested n-ary relations. For the encoding of object networks we will not provide a detailed algorithm here. Instead, we will only discuss the problems occurring in this case and indicate possible approaches for their solution.

6.1   Graphical Binary Relations

We discriminate graphical elements into primitive elements (rectangles, diamonds, circles, triangles, lines, text etc.) and complex elements composed of these primitives. The composition may be described by means of graphical binary relations (binary predicates) which we classify into 'attribute relations' , 'element-element relations' , and 'constraint relations' .

Figure 6.1: *A primitive graphical element set.*

Attribute relations set the internal attributes of a graphical element, e.g., the width of a box, to a valid value or add other graphical elements as external attributes. We may thus discriminate *internal attribute relations* using the visual properties of the graphical elements and *external attribute relations* attaching graphical elements to other graphical elements so that the latter become first class elements and the former their attachments. In chapter 4 we have discussed several examples where text string elements were used as attachments to encode the name of data objects. Another differentiation of attributes can be made with respect to their range values which may be *quantitative*, that is, sets of numeric values such as heights or lengths, or *qualitative*, that is, sets of non-numeric values such as textures or fonts.

Element-element relations, unlike , e.g., attachments, relate two graphical elements in such a way that their visual salience, expressed in terms of ratios of their internal attributes, is the same. For instance two rectangles of about the same size, connected by a line will appear to be equivalent in visual salience. This is not the case if one of the two rectangles is significantly larger than the other.

Constraint relations essentially restrict the internal attribute values of graphical elements. If this happens with respect to the internal attribute values of other graphical elements we will speak of *relative constraints*. Thus a graphical element may be required to be positioned below or right of another element, or the height of an element must be the same as that of another element. If an element's attribute is set to some fixed value without reference to another element's attribute value we call this an *absolute constraint*.

Before we may introduce the graphical relations, however, we first need to provide some definitions concerning the graphical element sets on which the relations are defined.

Let [Rectangle], [Diamond], [Circle], [Triangle], [Line], and [Text] denote the respective sets of graphical elements. We presume each of these elements to be assigned a bounding box which is the smallest rectangle including the element. Let $E := \{r \mid r \in [Rectangle]\} \cup \{d \mid d \in [Diamond]\} \cup \{c \mid c \in [Circle]\} \cup \{t \mid t \in [Triangle]\} \cup \{l \mid l \in [Line]\} \cup \{tx \mid tx \in [Text]\}$
be the union of all primitive graphical elements and let E_1, E_2, E_3, E_4 be subsets of E defined as follows:

$$E_1 := E \setminus \{l \mid l \in [Line]\}$$

$$E_2 := E \setminus (\{l \mid l \in [Line]\} \cup \{tx \mid tx \in [Text]\})$$

$$E_3 := E \setminus (\{c \mid c \in [Circle]\} \cup \{tx \mid tx \in [Text]\})$$

$$E_4 := E \setminus (\{c \mid c \in [Circle]\} \cup \{tx \mid tx \in [Text]\} \cup \{l \mid l \in [Line]\})$$

We will denote the class of bounding boxes by $[Bounding Box] \in [\mathcal{GOC}]$, the class of possible fonts by $[Font] \in [\mathcal{GOC}]$, the class of textures by $[Texture] \in [\mathcal{GOC}]$ the class of possible colours by $[Colour] \in [\mathcal{GOC}]$, and the set LineStyle $:= \{normal, dashed, dotted\}$. To describe colours more accurately we will distinguish their hue, saturation, and brightness components as separate attributes in the remainder. In addition, we introduce the Euclidean distance between two vectors $x = (x_1, \ldots x_n) \in \mathbf{R}^n$ and $y = (y_1, \ldots y_n) \in \mathbf{R}^n$ in the usual way as $\|x, y\|_2 := \sqrt{\sum_{i=1}^{n} (x_i - y_i)^2}$. Clearly, $\|x\|_2 := \|x, 0\|_2$ denotes then the length of vector x. We may now go on defining qualitative attributes:

Qualitative Attribute Relations:

Let Hue $:= \{h_0, \ldots, h_{255}\}$ denote the set of hues available in the visualisation system.

hue: $E \mapsto Hue$ (int)
$\forall e \in E : \exists i \in [0, 255] \; s.t. \; hue(e) = h_i.$
$\forall e \in E, \forall i, j \in [0, 255]:$
$hue(e) = h_i \land hue(e) = h_j \implies h_i = h_j.$

texture: $E_2 \mapsto [Texture]$ (int)
$\forall e \in E_2 : \exists t \in [Texture] \; s.t. texture(e) = t.$
$\forall e \in E_2 : \forall t, t^* \in [Texture]:$
$texture(e) = t \land texture(e) = t^* \implies t = t^*.$

attachment: $E_1 \mapsto E$ (ext)
$\forall e_1, e_2 \in E_1 : attachment(e_1, e_2) :\Leftrightarrow \|(position(e_1), position(e_2))\|_2 < \epsilon$
for some $\epsilon \in [0, 1]$ and $visualSalience(e_1) < visualSalience(e_2).$

font: $[Text] \mapsto: [Font]$ (int)
$\forall t \in [Text] : \exists f \in [Font] \; s.t. \; font(t) = f.$
$\forall t \in [Text], \forall f, f^* \in [Font]:$
$font(t) = f \land font(t) = f^* \implies f = f^*.$

typeFace: $[Font] \mapsto T := \{normal, bold, italic, boldItalic\}$
$\forall f \in [Font] : \exists t \in T \; s.t. \; typeFace(f) = t.$
$\forall f \in [Font], \forall t, t^* \in T:$
$typeFace(f) = t \land typeFace(f) = t^* \implies t = t^*.$

firstArrow: $[Line] \mapsto: \{true, false\}$ (int)

$\forall l \in [Line] : firstArrow(l) = true \lor firstArrow(l) = false$

secondArrow: $[Line] \mapsto: \{true, false\}$ (int)
$\forall l \in [Line] : secondArrow(l) = true \lor secondArrow(l) = false$

lineStyle: $[Line] \mapsto: LineStyles$ (int)
$\forall l \in [Line] : \exists l \in LineStyles \; s.t. \; lineStyle(e) = l.$
$\forall l \in [Line], \forall l, l^* \in LineStyles:$
$lineStyle(e) = l \land lineStyle(e) = l \Longrightarrow l = l^*.$

firstValue: $[Line] \mapsto E$ (ext)
$\forall l \in [Line]: \exists e \in E \; s.t. \; firstValue(l) = e$

secondValue: $[Line] \mapsto E$ (ext)
$\forall l \in [Line]: \exists e \in E \; s.t. \; secondValue(l) = e$

borderLineStyle: $E_2 \mapsto LineStyles:$ (int)
$\forall e \in E_2 : \exists l \in LineStyles \; s.t. \; borderLineStyle(e) = l.$
$\forall e \in E_2, \forall l, l^* \in LineStyles$
$borderLineStyle(e) = l \land borderLineStyle(e) = l^* \Longrightarrow l = l^*.$

borderLineColour: $E_2 \mapsto Hue:$ (int)
$\forall e \in E_2 : \exists h \in Hue \; s.t. \; borderLineColour(e) = h.$
$\forall e \in E_2, \forall h, h^* \in Hue$
$borderLineColour(e) = h \land borderLineColour(e) = h^* \Longrightarrow h = h^*.$

The definitions above show that each element must have a hue, but only for those elements with a 2-D extension textures are required. In the same way it must be ensured that for each text element a font value is set and lines may or may not have arrows at either end. Moreover, element attachments are defined in such way that the Euclidean distance between the elements falls under some threshold ϵ which ensures that they are positioned close to one another. Additionally, it is required that the visual salience of the attributed element is lower than that of the element to which it is attributed. Throughout this book we will essentially distinguish 'shapeAttachments' and 'textAttachments' .

Next, we will present the list of quantitative attribute relations we consider. We will presume the unit coordinate space $[0, 1] \times [0, 1]$ with origin in the left upper corner to represent a two-dimensional screen. Moreover, we will further presume the position of an element to be defined in the element's midpoint.

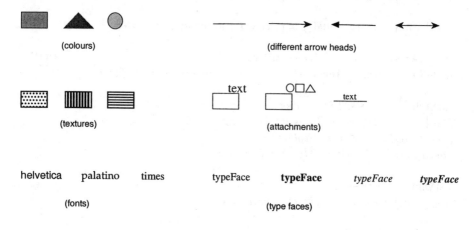

Figure 6.2: *Use of qualitative attributes.*

Quantitative Attribute Relations:

position: $E \mapsto [0,1] \times [0,1]$ ⠀⠀⠀⠀⠀⠀⠀⠀⠀⠀⠀⠀⠀⠀⠀⠀⠀⠀⠀⠀⠀⠀⠀(int)
$\forall e \in E : \exists p := (x,y) \in [0,1] \times [0,1] \; s.t. \; position(e) = p.$
$\forall e \in E, \forall p, p^* \in [0,1] \times [0,1]:$
$position(e) = p. \wedge position(e) = p^* \Longrightarrow p = p^*.$
We use $position_x$ and $position_y$ to denote the x and y coordinates
of the element's position.

The left, right, top, and bottom extents of a bounding box are numbers
denoting the horizontal and vertical distances between its midpoint and the
outer edges.

rightExtent: $[BoundingBox] \mapsto [0,1]$ ⠀⠀⠀⠀⠀⠀⠀⠀⠀⠀⠀⠀⠀⠀(int)
$\forall b \in [BoundingBox] : \exists r \in [0,1] \; s.t. \; rightExtent(b) = r.$
$\forall b \in [BoundingBox], \forall r, r^* \in [0,1]:$
$rightExtent(b) = r \wedge rightExtent(b) = r^* \Longrightarrow r = r^*.$

leftExtent: $[BoundingBox] \mapsto [0,1]$ ⠀⠀⠀⠀⠀⠀⠀⠀⠀⠀⠀⠀⠀⠀(int)
$\forall b \in [BoundingBox] : \exists r \in [0,1] \; s.t. \; leftExtent(b) = r.$
$\forall b \in [BoundingBox], \forall r \in [0,1]:$
$leftExtent(b) = r \wedge leftExtent(b) = r^* \Longrightarrow r = r^*.$

topExtent: $[BoundingBox] \mapsto [0,1]$ ⠀⠀⠀⠀⠀⠀⠀⠀⠀⠀⠀⠀⠀⠀(int)

$\forall b \in [BoundingBox] : \exists r \in [0,1] \ s.t. \ topExtent(b) = r.$
$\forall b \in [BoundingBox], \forall r \in [0,1]:$
$topExtent(b) = r \land topExtent(b) = r^* \Longrightarrow r = r^*.$

bottomExtent: $[BoundingBox] \mapsto [0,1]$ (int)
$\forall b \in [BoundingBox] : \exists r \in [0,1] \ s.t. \ bottomExtent(b) = r.$
$\forall b \in [BoundingBox], \forall r \in [0,1]:$
$bottomExtent(b) = r \land bottomExtent(b) = r^* \Longrightarrow r = r^*.$

length: $[Line] \mapsto [0,1]$ (int)
$\forall l \in [Line] : length(l) := leftExtent(l) + rightExtent(l).$

width: $E_3 \mapsto [0,1]$ (int)
$\forall e \in E_3 : width(e) := leftExtent(l) + rightExtent(l).$

height: $E_4 \mapsto [0,1]$ (int)
$\forall e \in E_4 : height(e) := topExtent(l) + bottomExtent(l).$

radius: $[Circle] \mapsto [0,1]$ (int)
$\forall c \in [Circle] : radius(c) := rightExtent(l).$

Let Brightness $:= \{b_0, \ldots, b_{255}\}$ denote the set of brightness values.
brightness: $E \mapsto Brightness$ (int)
$\forall e \in E : \exists i \in Brightness \ s.t. \ brightness(e) = i.$
$\forall e \in E :, \forall i,j \in [0,255]:$
$brightness(e) = b_i. \land brightness(e) = b_j \Longrightarrow b_i = b_j.$

Let Saturation $:= \{b_0, \ldots, b_{255}\}$ denote the set of saturation values.
saturation: $E \mapsto Saturation$ (int)
$\forall e \in E : \exists i \in Saturation \ s.t. \ saturation(e) = i.$
$\forall e \in E :, \forall i,j \in [0,255]:$
$saturation(e) = s_i. \land saturation(e) = s_j \Longrightarrow s_i = s_j.$

fontsize: $\{[Font]\} \mapsto [1, \ldots, n]$ (int)
$\forall f \in [Font] \ \exists i \in [1, \ldots, n] \ s.t. \ fontsize(f) = i$
$\forall f \in [Font], \forall i,j \in [1, \ldots, n]:$
$fontsize(f) = i \land fontsize(f) = j \Longrightarrow i = j.$

Clearly, all internal attributes must be set to some valid value, since an element must have, e.g., a hue or a position. This is different for external attributes, because attachments need not necessarily be used. We also see from the definitions that all quantitative attributes are at the same time internal attributes, but not all qualitative

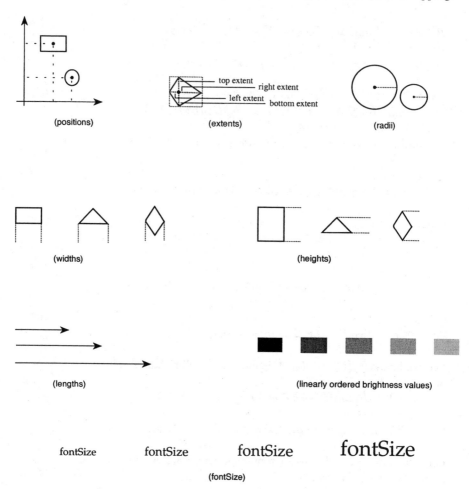

Figure 6.3: *Use of quantitative attributes* .

attributes are external attributes. As we have mentioned above, colours comprise the three aspects hue, saturation, and brightness. Therefore, we formally understand a colour to be a vector composed of a hue, a saturation and a brightness value. This interpretation of colours refers to the user-oriented HSB colour model (Hue, Saturation, Brightness) as opposed to the hardware-oriented RGB (Red, Green, Blue) or CMY (Cyan, Magenta, Yellow) colour models ([Smi78] and [FDFH90]). The HSB model is schematically presented in the form of the hexcone in Figure C.1.

We formally define the colour value attribute next:

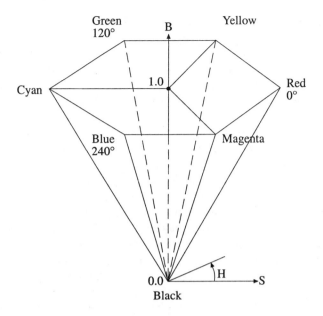

Figure 6.4: *The HSB colour model.*

colourValue: $E \mapsto Hue \times Saturation \times Brightness$ (int)
$\forall e \in E : \exists c := (h, s, b)$ where $h \in Hue, s \in Saturation, b \in Brightness$
s.t. $colourValue(e) = c$.
$\forall e \in E : \forall c, c^* := (h^*, s^*, b^*)$ where $h^* \in Hue, s^* \in Saturation, b^* \in$
$Brightness$: $colourValue(e) = c \wedge colourValue(e) = c^* \implies c = c^*$

In our approach we distinguish 256 hue values, saturation values, and brightness
values. Therefore, we obtain 256^3 different colour values corresponding to a "true
colour" display.
Next, we will introduce the two attributes, *hueClasses* and *orderedHue* concerning
other aspects related to the use of colour. The first imposes a grouping of colours
allowing, e.g, to speak of the red, the green, or the blue colours:

Let HueClasses be a disjoint partition of the set Hue s.t.
hueClass: $Hue \mapsto HueClasses$ (int)
$\forall h \in Hue \, \exists c \in HueClasses$ s.t. $hueClass(h) = c$.
$\forall h \in Hue \, \forall c_1, c_2 \in HueClasses$:

$$hueClass(h) = c_1 \land hueClass(h) = c_2 \Longrightarrow c_1 = c_2.$$

The second attribute reflects the fact that colours may be used in an ordered fashion. As we will see, this is, however, not always possible. To explain this problem we refer in the subsequent discussion again to the HSB colour model introduced above.

Since we are interested in ordered hues, we will ignore the B-dimension of the hexcone at this point and focus rather on the polygonal face representing the base of the cone. The fact that the hue of a colour is measured by the angle around the vertical B-axis indicates the circularity of the hue spectrum. Moreover, given a constant saturation value, the Euclidean distance between the colour values of Magenta, Cyan, and Yellow is in this model equally 2, whereas the distance between the values Blue, Magenta, and Red is not equal. It is 2 between Blue and Red and 1 between the two other distances. Yet, this difference is responsible for the fact that the sequence of colour values (Blue, Magenta, Red) is perceived as a sequence, whereas the colour sequence (Magenta, Cyan, Yellow) is not perceived sequentially (cf. [NA93]). If the perception of a colour sequence is desired the solution to this problem is to pick an interval of the colour spectrum that is small enough so that, given a constant saturation value, a perceivable sequence of colour values may be selected [2]. In addition, the used graphical elements must be positioned in the corresponding order. Let $k \in [0, 255]$ be the starting index of the hue value interval then we define the ordered hue attribute as:

orderedHue: $E \mapsto I := [h_k, h_{(k+50)mod256}]$ (int)
$\forall e \in E : \exists i \in I \ s.t. \ orderedHue(e) = i.$
$\forall e \in E, \forall i, j \in I:$
$orderedHue(e) = h_i \land orderedHue(e) = h_j \Longrightarrow h_i = h_j.$
$\forall e, e^* \in E, \forall i, j \in I \ for which \ j > i:$
$orderedHue(e) = h_i \land orderedHue(e^*) = h_j \Longrightarrow$
$position_x(e^*) > position_x(e) \lor position_y(e^*) > position_y(e)$

As we have outlined before, element-element relations, unlike attribute relations, relate two equally salient graphical elements to form a composite element. The 'line' relations defined below ensure this by introducing additional line segments graphically connecting two elements and thus representing a relation tuple. Spatial grouping defines, similarly to attachments, a threshold value ϵ for the maximum distance between two elements below which they appear to be spatially grouped. Nesting of elements graphically realises tuples by including rectangles in other

---

[2] As a result of the implementation of the visualisation system proposed in this book, we have found that an interval length of 50 is sufficient, given 256 different hue values.

rectangles. This resource therefore needs constraint relations to fully graphically realise the data relation tuples.

Let $f(t) = [(x(t), y(t)]$ be the *parametric representation* of a curve in $\mathbf{R}^2$ for $t \in [0, 1]$, then we call $f(t) = f(t^*)$ a *join point* of the curve. If f(t) has exactly one join point we speak of a *closed curve*. The class of closed curves is referred to by [ClosedCurve] in the sequel. Let Pixels denote the number of screen pixels and let $pixels : E \mapsto Pixels$ be the function returning the set of pixels of an arbitrary graphical element $e \in E$ at a given position $p_0 \in [0, 1]^2$. Moreover, let $b : E \mapsto [BoundingBox]$ be the mapping uniquely assigning each element its bounding box. Then we define for $e_1, e_2 \in E_2$ the list of element-element relations in the following way:

Element-Element Relations:

lineWithOneArrow $\subseteq E_2 \times E_2$
$\quad \forall e_1, e_2 \in E_2 :$
lineWithOneArrow $(e_1, e_2) :\Leftrightarrow \exists l \in [Line]$, s.t. $(firstArrow(l) = true$
$\wedge secondArrow(l) = false) \vee (firstArrow(l) = false \wedge secondArrow(l)$
$= true) \wedge (firstValue(l) = e_1 \wedge secondValue(l) = e_2).$

lineWithOneOrTwoArrows $\subseteq E_2 \times E_2$
$\quad \forall e_1, e_2 \in E_2 :$
lineWithOneOrTwoArrows $(e_1, e_2) :\Leftrightarrow \exists l \in [Line]$, s.t. $(firstArrow(l) = true$
$\vee secondArrow(l) = true) \wedge (firstValue(l) = e_1 \wedge secondValue(l) = e_2).$

lineWithTwoArrows $\subseteq E_2 \times E_2$
$\quad \forall e_1, e_2 \in E_2 :$
lineWithTwoArrows $(e_1, e_2) :\Leftrightarrow \exists l \in [Line]$, s.t. $(firstArrow(l) = true$
$\wedge secondArrow(l) = true) \wedge (firstValue(l) = e_1 \wedge secondValue(l) = e_2).$

lineWithNoArrows $\subseteq E_2 \times E_2$
$\quad \forall e_1, e_2 \in E_2 :$
lineWithTwoArrows $(e_1, e_2) :\Leftrightarrow \exists l \in [Line]$, s.t. $(firstArrow(l) = false$
$\wedge secondArrow(l) = false) \wedge (firstValue(l) = e_1 \wedge secondValue(l) = e_2).$

spatiallyGroupedElements $\subseteq E_2 \times E_2$
$\quad \forall e_1, e_2 \in E_2 :$
spatiallyGroupedElements $(e_1, e_2) :\Leftrightarrow \exists \epsilon$ s.t. $\|position(e_1), position(e_2)\|_2 < \epsilon$

nestedElements (inclusion) $\subseteq [Rectangle] \times [Rectangle]$
$\quad \forall r_1, r_2 \in [Rectangle] :$

nestedElements $(r_1, r_2) :\Leftrightarrow pixels(r_2) \subset pixels(r_1)$

frameCurve $\subseteq [ClosedCurve] \times [Rectangle]$
   $\forall c \in [ClosedCurve] \land \forall r \in [Rectangle] :$
   frameCurve $(c, r) :\Leftrightarrow pixels(r) \subset pixels(c)$

indentation $\subseteq [Text] \times [Text]$
   $\forall t_1, t_2 \in [Text]$
   indentation $(t_1, t_2) :\Leftrightarrow$
         $(position_x(t_2) := position_x(t_1) + c_1) \lor$
         $(position_y(t_2) := position_y(t_1) + c_2)$ for some $c_1, c_2 \in [0, 1]$
For an illustration of element-element relations see Figure 6.5.

The constraint graphical relations used to define the nestedElements relation above
will be specified next. They restrict the positions of two graphical elements on a
2D-screen by means of constraining the positions of their bounding boxes relative
to one another.
Let $D := \{left, right, top, bottom\}$ be the set of boundaries of an element. Moreover, let $boundary : [BoundingBox] \times D \mapsto [0, 1]^2$ such that $\forall e \in E$ and
$\forall d \in D$

$$boundary(b(e), d) := position(e) \begin{cases} -(leftExtent(e), 0) & if\ d = left \\ +(rightExtent(e), 0) & if\ d = right \\ -(0, topExtent(e)) & if\ d = top \\ +(0, bottomExtent(e)) & if\ d = bottom \end{cases}$$

$$(6.1)$$

Based on this definition we may introduce the set of relative position constraints
categorised into free and fixed constraints.

Free Relative Position Constraints:

leftOfRightBoundary $\subseteq E \times E$
   $\forall e_1, e_2 \in E :$ leftOfRightBoundary(e_1, e_2)
         $:\Leftrightarrow boundary(b(e_1), right) < boundary(b(e_2), right)$

rightOfRightBoundary $\subseteq E \times E$
   $\forall e_1, e_2 \in E :$ rightOfRightBoundary(e_1, e_2)
         $:\Leftrightarrow boundary(b(e_1), left) > boundary(b(e_2), right)$

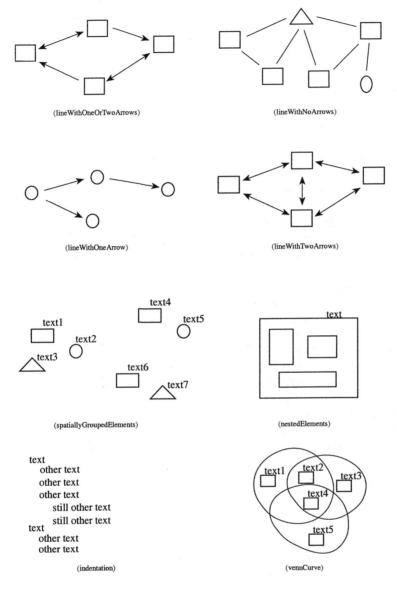

(lineWithOneOrTwoArrows)

(lineWithNoArrows)

(lineWithOneArrow)

(lineWithTwoArrows)

(spatiallyGroupedElements)

(nestedElements)

(indentation)

(vennCurve)

Figure 6.5: *Use of element-element graphical relations.*

leftOfLeftBoundary $\subseteq E \times E$
    $\forall e_1, e_2 \in E :$ leftOfLeftBoundary(e_1, e_2)
        $:\Leftrightarrow boundary(b(e_1), right) < boundary(b(e_2), left)$

rightOfLeftBoundary $\subseteq E \times E$
    $\forall e_1, e_2 \in E :$ rightOfLeftBoundary(e_1, e_2)
        $:\Leftrightarrow boundary(b(e_1), left) > boundary(b(e_2), left)$

belowTopBoundary $\subseteq E \times E$
    $\forall e_1, e_2 \in E :$ belowTopBoundary(e_1, e_2)
        $:\Leftrightarrow boundary(b(e_1), top) < boundary(b(e_2), top)$

aboveTopBoundary $\subseteq E \times E$
    $\forall e_1, e_2 \in E :$ aboveTopBoundary (e_1, e_2)
        $:\Leftrightarrow boundary(b(e_1), bottom) > boundary(b(e_2), top)$

belowBottomBoundary $\subseteq E \times E$
    $\forall e_1, e_2 \in E :$ belowBottomBoundary (e_1, e_2)
        $:\Leftrightarrow boundary(b(e_1), top) < boundary(b(e_2), bottom)$

aboveBottomBoundary $\subseteq E \times E$
    $\forall e_1, e_2 \in E :$ aboveBottomBoundary (e_1, e_2)
        $:\Leftrightarrow boundary(b(e_1), bottom) > boundary(b(e_2), bottom)$

leftAlignment $\subseteq E \times E$
    $\forall e_1, e_2 \in E :$ leftAlignment(e_1, e_2)
        $:\Leftrightarrow boundary(b(e_1), left) = boundary(b(e_2), left)$

rightAlignment $\subseteq E \times E$
    $\forall e_1, e_2 \in E :$ rightAlignment(e_1, e_2)
        $:\Leftrightarrow boundary(b(e_1), right) = boundary(b(e_2), right)$

topAlignment $\subseteq E \times E$
    $\forall e_1, e_2 \in E :$ topAlignment(e_1, e_2)
        $:\Leftrightarrow boundary(b(e_1), top) = boundary(b(e_2), top)$

bottomAlignment $\subseteq E \times E$
    $\forall e_1, e_2 \in E :$ bottomAlignment(e_1, e_2)
        $:\Leftrightarrow boundary(b(e_1), bottom) = boundary(b(e_2), bottom)$

parallelXPositions $\subseteq E \times E$

$\forall e_1, e_2 \in E$: parallelXPositions(e_1, e_2)
$\quad :\Leftrightarrow$ rightOfLeftBoundary(e_1, e_2) $\wedge$
$\quad$ position$_x(e_1) = c_1 \wedge$ position$_x(e_2) = c_2$,
$\quad$ for some constants $c_1, c_2 \in [0, 1]$ s.t. $c_1 > c_2$

parallelYPositions $\subseteq E \times E$
$\quad \forall e_1, e_2 \in E$: parallelYPositions(e_1, e_2)
$\quad\quad :\Leftrightarrow$ belowBottomBoundary(e_1, e_2) $\wedge$
$\quad\quad$ position$_y(e_1) = c_1 \wedge$ position$_y(e_2) = c_2$,
$\quad\quad$ for some constants $c_1, c_2 \in [0, 1]$ s.t. $c_1 > c_2$

Let $R := (\{r_1, \ldots, r_n\}$ be a linearly ordered set of discrete radii around
the coordinate origin $(0, 0)$ for a finite number $n \in \mathbf{N}$, then

concentricSuccessors $\subseteq E \times E$
$\quad \forall e_1, e_2 \in E, \forall r_i, r_j \in R$: concentricSuccessors$(e_1, e_2)$ $:\Leftrightarrow$
$\quad\quad ||position(e_1)||_2 = r_i \wedge ||position(e_1)||_2 = r_j$ for $r_i > r_j$

Using the constraints introduced above it is computationally more efficient to replace the definition of the element-element relation nestedElements given above

nestedElements (inclusion) $\subseteq [Rectangle] \times [Rectangle]$
$\quad \forall r_1, r_2 \in [Rectangle]$:
$\quad$ nestedElements $(r_1, r_2) :\Leftrightarrow pixels(r_2) \subset pixels(r_1)$

by the following definition

nestedElements (inclusion) $\subseteq [Rectangle] \times [Rectangle]$
$\quad \forall r_1, r_2 \in [Rectangle]$:
$\quad$ nestedElements $(r_1, r_2) :\Leftrightarrow leftOfRightBoundary(b(r_1), b(r_2)) \wedge$
$\quad rightOfLeftBoundary(b(r_1), b(r_2)) \wedge belowTopBoundary(b(r_1), b(r_2))$
$\wedge aboveBottomBoundary(b(r_1), b(r_2))$

because it is easier to check the four cases than to compare the rectangles pixel-wise.

From the definitions above we see that relative position constraints are expressed as linear and non-linear equations and inequalities. Fixed relative position constraints form a specific case of free relative position constraints in that an element is assigned a constant position $p \in [0, 1]^2$ relative to the position of another element. We will distinguish horizontal and vertical constraints fixing the distance relative to the left, right, top, and bottom edges of an element's bounding box as well as arbitrary constraints that determine the position of an element relative to

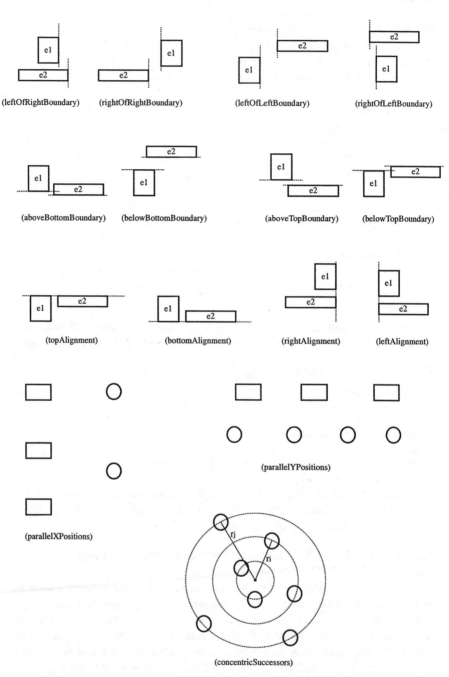

Figure 6.6: *Using relative position constraints.*

another element by adding an arbitrary vector to the position of the latter. We will formally introduce fixed constraints next.

Fixed Relative Position Constraints:

$\forall e_1, e_2 \in E, \forall k \in [0, 1]$,
$\forall d \in D \cup \{arbitrary\}$, and $\forall p \in \{(x, y) \in [0, 1]^2 \mid \|position(e_2) - (x, y)\|_2 = k\}$

$fixedDistance_d \subseteq E \times E$
$\quad fixedDistance_d(e_1, e_2) :\Leftrightarrow$

$$
position(e_1) = \begin{cases} boundary(b(e_2), d) - (k, 0) & if\ d = left \\[2mm] boundary(b(e_2), d) + (k, 0) & if\ d = right \\[2mm] boundary(b(e_2), d) - (0, k) & if\ d = top \\[2mm] boundary(b(e_2), d) + (0, k) & if\ d = bottom \\[2mm] position(e_2) - p & if\ d = arbitrary \end{cases} \tag{6.2}
$$

The definitions above show our distinction into such fixed constraints specifying horizontal or vertical distances between the corresponding boundaries of the elements' bounding boxes and such constraints establishing Euclidean distances between element positions. We obtain a specific form of fixed relative position constraints for linearly ordered sets of graphical elements. In this case we may wish to establish equidistant positions between the elements. We may define such constraints as follows.

Let $E^* := \{e_1, \ldots, e_n\}$ be a linearly ordered set of graphical elements $e_i \in E$, then

$\quad$ equidistance $\subseteq E^* \times E^*$
$\quad \forall e_i \in E^* :$ equidistance(e_i, e_{i+1})
$\quad\quad :\Leftrightarrow \|position(e_i), position(e_{i+1})\|_2 = c$ for some constant $c \in [0, 1]$.

An even more specific type of fixed constraints are the *absolute position constraints* 'absolutePosX' and 'absolutePosY' . They set the x-coordinate $position_x(e)$, or the y-coordinate $position_y(e)$, or both coordinates of an element $e \in E$ to constant values $c \in [0, 1]$. Absolute position constraints are thus defined without reference to the positions of other graphical elements.

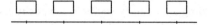

Figure 6.7: *Equidistant positioning of linearly ordered elements.*

As mentioned before, besides the important group of position constraints we will consider an additional group of constraint relations which we call *relative non-positional constraints*. They restrict the values of other internal attributes such as the height, the radius, or the colour of an element depending on the internal attribute value of another element. We will further classify these constraints in analogy to the distinction of attributes into *qualitative* and *quantitative* constraints.

Non-Positional Qualitative Constraints:

$sameColour \subseteq E \times E$
$\quad \forall e_1, e_2 \in E : sameColour(e_1, e_2) :\Leftrightarrow$
$\qquad colourValue(e_1) = colourValue(e_2)$

$sameTexture \subseteq E_2 \times E_2$
$\quad \forall e_1, e_2 \in E : sameTexture(e_1, e_2) :\Leftrightarrow$
$\qquad texture(e_1) = texture(e_2)$

$sameFont \subseteq [Text] \times [Text]$
$\quad \forall e_1, e_2 \in E : sameFont(e_1, e_2) :\Leftrightarrow$
$\qquad font(e_1) = font(e_2)$

Non-Positional Quantitative Constraints:

$samePosition \subseteq E \times E$
$\quad \forall e_1, e_2 \in E : samePositions(e_1, e_2) :\Leftrightarrow$
$\qquad position(e_1) = position(e_2)$

$sameRightExtent \subseteq [BoundingBox] \times [BoundingBox]$
$\quad \forall e_1, e_2 \in E : sameRightExtent(e_1, e_2) :\Leftrightarrow$
$\qquad rightExtent(e_1) = rightExtent(e_2)$

$sameLeftExtent \subseteq [BoundingBox] \times [BoundingBox]$
$\quad \forall e_1, e_2 \in E : sameLeftExtent(e_1, e_2) :\Leftrightarrow$
$\qquad leftExtent(e_1) = leftExtent(e_2)$

$sameTopExtent \subseteq [BoundingBox] \times [BoundingBox]$
$\qquad \forall e_1, e_2 \in E : sameTopExtent(e_1, e_2) :\Leftrightarrow$
$\qquad\qquad topExtent(e_1) = topExtent(e_2)$

$sameBottomExtent \subseteq [BoundingBox] \times [BoundingBox]$
$\qquad \forall e_1, e_2 \in E : sameBottomExtent(e_1, e_2) :\Leftrightarrow$
$\qquad\qquad bottomExtent(e_1) = bottomExtent(e_2)$

$sameLength \subseteq [Line] \times [Line]$
$\qquad \forall e_1, e_2 \in E : sameLength(e_1, e_2) :\Leftrightarrow$
$\qquad\qquad length(e_1) = length(e_2)$

$sameWidth \subseteq E_3 \times E_3$
$\qquad \forall e_1, e_2 \in E : sameWidth(e_1, e_2) :\Leftrightarrow$
$\qquad\qquad width(e_1) = width(e_2)$

$sameHeight \subseteq E_4 \times E_4$
$\qquad \forall e_1, e_2 \in E : sameHeight(e_1, e_2) :\Leftrightarrow$
$\qquad\qquad height(e_1) = heigth(e_2)$

$sameSaturation \subseteq E \times E$
$\qquad \forall e_1, e_2 \in E : sameSaturation(e_1, e_2) :\Leftrightarrow$
$\qquad\qquad saturation(e_1) = saturation(e_2)$

$sameBrightness \subseteq E \times E$
$\qquad \forall e_1, e_2 \in E : sameBrightness(e_1, e_2) :\Leftrightarrow$
$\qquad\qquad brightness(e_1) = brightness(e_2)$

$sameFontSize \subseteq E \times E$
$\qquad \forall e_1, e_2 \in E : sameFontSize(e_1, e_2) :\Leftrightarrow$
$\qquad\qquad fontSize(e_1) = fontSize(e_2)$

In analogy to the position constraints we have formally expressed relative non-positional constraints above. Apparently, also in the case of non-positional constraints we may conceive *absolute* constraints to be those assigning a constant, i.e. a texture value, to an element's corresponding attribute.

In the remainder, we will understand diagrams to be composed of graphical elements in which each internal attribute is set to a constant value, that is, all visual elements must be absolutely constrained. How this may be achieved will be outlined later in the resource allocation process and in the final layout process. We will further presume that element-element relations as well as attachments will create complex graphical elements.

In this section, we have introduced the primitive graphical elements as the 'words' and the binary graphical relations as the primitive 'sentences' of a graphical language. We have distinguished between attribute relations, element-element relations and constraint relations. Attribute relations were categorised along the dimensions internal / external as well as qualitative / quantitative. Internal attributes use an element's genuine properties such as position, colour, texture etc. to graphically communicate a binary data relation, whereas external attributes are graphical elements attached as dependents to a first class element. Element-element relations use two graphical elements of equal visual salience to visualise data relations, and constraint relations restrict the internal attributes of graphical elements, either relative to other graphical elements or absolutely, by assigning constant values to the element's attributes.

6.2   Graphical Binding

In this section, we will describe how graphical relations may be combined and bound as visual resources at the types of the Type Lattice introduced in chapter 5. Before we can do this, we need to define how graphical relations may encode data relations in principle. According to our distinction between attribute and element-element relations we will differentiate between element-element encoding and attribute encoding. A formal introduction of these concepts follows next:

Let 'encodesObject' be the mapping uniquely assigning graphical elements to data objects, that is, $encodesObject : [\mathcal{DOC}] \mapsto [\mathcal{GOC}]$, then we may give the following definitions for element-element encodings and attribute encodings:

Definition 6.1 (element-element encoding) *Let $[R] \in [\mathcal{DRC}_2]$ be a binary data relation defined on the data domain $[D] \in [\mathcal{DOC}]$, let R be a data relation instance conforming to [R], let $[G] \in [\mathcal{GRC}]$ be a graphical element-element relation defined on the set of graphical elementclasses*

$$E := \{r \mid r \in [Rectangle]\} \cup \{d \mid d \in [Diamond]\} \cup \{c \mid c \in [Circle]\} \cup \{t \mid t \in [Triangle]\} \cup \{tx \mid tx \in [Text]\}.$$

Then the mapping $encodesRelation : R \mapsto G$ defined by

$$encodesRelation(r(d_1, d_2)) = g(e_1, e_2) :\Leftrightarrow \qquad (6.3)$$

$$encodesObject(d_i) = e_i \wedge encodesObject(r) = g \qquad (6.4)$$

for $i \in \{1, 2\}$, $\forall r \in R$, $\forall g \in G$, $\forall d_i \in D$, and $\forall e_i \in E$ is called an element-element encoding of the data relation R. If the two objects are assigned the same graphical element, that is

$$encodesRelation(r(d_1, d_2)) = e :\Leftrightarrow encodesObject(d_i) = e \qquad (6.5)$$

for $i \in \{1, 2\}$, $\forall r \in R$, $\forall d_i \in D$, *and* $\forall e \in E$ *we call this an identical element encoding of the relation R.*

Definition 6.2 (attribute encoding) *Let* $[R] \in [\mathcal{DRC}_2]$ *be a binary data relation defined on the data domains* $[D], [D^*]$ *in* $[\mathcal{DOC}]$*, let R be a data relation instance conforming to* $[R]$*, and let* $[A] \in [\mathcal{GRC}]$*be a graphical attribute relation defined on E. Then, the mapping* $encodesRelation : R \mapsto G$ *defined by*

$$encodesRelation(r(d, d^*)) = (e, a(e)) :\Leftrightarrow \qquad (6.6)$$

$$encodesObject(d) = e \quad \wedge \quad encodesObject(d^*) = a(e) \qquad (6.7)$$

for $\forall r \in R$, $\forall a \in A$, $\forall d \in D$, $\forall d^* \in D^*$*, and* $\forall e \in E$ *is called an attribute encoding of the data relation R.*

Clearly, these encoding functions must be implemented as operations at the relation type classes for each type-specific combination of graphical resources. We will discuss this in greater detail in the next section. Next, we will assign all relation types of the Type Lattice valid graphical binary relations. Combinations of graphical relations will be described by unbound logical formulae in disjunctive normal form. Each of the conjunction terms represents one complex graphical relation that cannot be further decomposed at this type. Thus, it is, e.g., not possible to use the graphical relation 'concentricSuccessors' alone if the relation type is 'antisymmetricTreeType'. Instead, it works only in combination with the relation 'lineWithOneArrow' . If the disjunction contains more than one conjunction term we impose a discrete precedence order on the set of resources to rank them. The order is indicated by integers set in parentheses.

UnqualifiedRelationType
  lineWithOneOrTwoArrows

AcyclicRelationType
  lineWithOneOrTwoArrows ∧ concentricSuccessors

AntisymmetricRelationType
  lineWithOneArrow

SymmetricRelationType
  lineWithNoArrows ∨ lineWithTwoArrows

EquivalenceRelationType

spatiallyGroupedElements (1) ∨ colour (2) ∨ texture (3)

AntisymmetricTreeType
 lineWithOneArrow ∧ concentricSuccessors

SymmetricTreeType
 lineWithNoArrows ∧ concentricSuccessors (1)∨
 lineWithNoArrows ∧ lineWithTwoArrows (2)

BipartiteRelationType
 lineWithOneOrTwoArrows ∧ parallelXPositions (1)∨
 lineWithOneOrTwoArrows ∧ parallelYPositions (2)

SetValuedMappingRelationType
 attachments (1)∨
 frameCurve (2)∨
 lineWithOneArrow ∧ parallelXPositions (3) ∨
 lineWithOneArrow ∧ parallelYPositions (4)∨
 indentation (5)

UniqueMappingRelationType
 attributeEncoding (1))∨
 nestedRectangles (2)

BijectiveMappingRelationType
 identicalElementEncoding

StrictOrderRelationType
 lineWithOneArrow ∧ belowTopBoundary (1) ∨
 lineWithOneArrow ∧ rightOfLeftBoundary (1) ∨
 lineWithOneArrow ∧ leftOfRightBoundary (2)∨
 lineWithOneArrow ∧ aboveBottomBoundary(2)

CompleteLatticeType
 lineWithOneArrow ∧ belowTopBoundary ∧ parallelLines (1)∨
 lineWithOneArrow ∧ rightOfLeftBoundary ∧ parallelLines(1) ∨
 lineWithOneArrow ∧ leftOfRightBoundary ∧ parallelLines (2)∨
 lineWithOneArrow ∧ aboveBottomBoundary∧ parallelLines (2)

TreeOrderType
 nestedElements

DiscreteLinearOrderType

belowBottomBoundary ∧ equiDistance ∧ leftAlignment (1) ∨
rightOfRightBoundary ∧ equiDistance ∧ topAlignment (1)∨
aboveTopBoundary ∧ equiDistance ∧ leftAlignment (2)∨
leftOfLeftBoundary ∧ equiDistance ∧ topAlignment (2)∨
colourValue (3)∨ brightness (4)∨ saturation (5)

RealValuedLinearOrderType

quantitativeAttributes

SetType

qualitativeAttributes

Since we require all graphical elements to have pairwise distinct positions we assign the global 'differentPositions' constraint at all types. For the sake of simplicity we have not indicated this at the types.

Moreover, as we have pointed out before, internal attributes must be set to some value to fully specify the graphical elements. It may occur, though, that some of the attributes are not used to communicate data, in which case we must ensure that these attributes will be set to the same value. This will make these attributes visually insignigficant which is important with respect to expressiveness aspects. Recall that we have argued in chapter 4 that we must not communicate information that cannot be derived from the data. To guarantee this we will apply non-positional 'sameAttributeValue' constraints introduced before. Remember that the bars in Figure 4.7, for instance, were set to the same height value, because height was not used as an attribute.

6.2.1 Expressiveness and Effectiveness of Graphical Binary Relations

The implementation of graphical resources at the types of the Type Lattice as introduced above ensures expressive graphical mappings of binary data relations in the sense of [Mack86], because data relations and graphical resources share, by definition of the types, the same relational data charactersistics. This means that all graphical resources defined at the types visually encode the type's relational properties. For instance, a data relation that is a strict order may be graphically communicated by the resource "lineWithOneArrow ∧ belowTopBoundary", because this combined graphical relation is obviously irreflexive, antisymmetric, and transitive. Whenever the most specific type of a relation instance is determined after type refinement the relation may use the resources defined at this type. These are then the most specific resources for this relation with respect to the type lattice. Since the resources at each type are also ranked, the most specific resource is uniquely determined. Example encodings are presented in Figure 6.8.

A selection of the most specific resource is, of course, only possible if there are no other relations competing for the same resource. In case of a conflict one of the two data relations must be graphically communicated using another resource. The choice is, however, not restricted to the resources defined at the given relation type. Instead, the object-oriented inheritance mechanism conveniently allows the use of resources defined at the supertypes too. How the selection problem may be solved generally will be the topic of the graphical resource allocation process the discussion of which will start in the next section.

The ranking of the resources at each type reflecting our notion of effectiveness is based on the following principles: first, we have adopted Mackinlay's model of effectiveness (see chapter 2), in which position resources should generally be given priority. Then, we have considered aspects of graphical complexity, for instance, lineWithNoArrows is stronger than lineWithTwoArrows, because the latter needs arrow heads as additional resources. The third criterion is concerned with established conventions. Thus, "lineWithOneArrow ∧ belowTopBoundary" and "lineWithOneArrow ∧ rightOfLeftBoundary" are in accordance with the traditional top-down and left-to-right reading orders established in the European culture. This may, of course, be changed if the cultural context is different.

6.3   Visualisation Strategies for n-ary Relations

In the last section we have formalised the visualisation principle for binary relations: the basic paradigm was to encode the domain objects of a relation as well as the tuples that bind the domain values together using graphical elements and their attributes. This is, of course, not different in the more general case of n-ary relations. Here, also the domain objects as well as the tuples connecting them must be graphically represented. The major difference between the visualisations of binary relations and those of n-ary relations results, however, from the fact that n-tuples consist of a generally non-trivial structure reflecting the dependencies between the relation domains as we have described it in section 5.2. The impact on the visualisation is as follows: whereas in the case of binary relations graphical realisations may be defined descriptively (as in the last section), this is no longer possible in the case of n-ary relations, since their dependency lattice may take arbitrary shapes. Consequently, the graphical communication of n-tuples requires an algorithmic implementation of non-trivial visual encoding strategies. However, a dependency lattice describes a relation by means of its binary components (recall that each arc of the lattice, read from bottom to top, represents a function from one domain into another). We will exploit this circumstance to design the visualisation

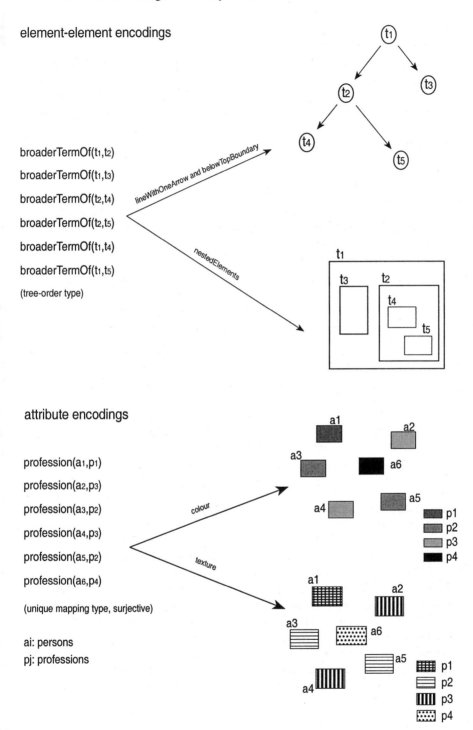

Figure 6.8: *Binary relation encodings.*

strategies as compositions of graphical binary relations respecting the topology of
the lattice.

In this section, we will focus on visualisation strategies for functional dependencies, set-valued functional dependencies, mixed functional and set-valued functional dependencies, and for nested dependencies. For each class of dependencies
we will discuss example visualisations in which the principles become transpar-
ent. Eventually, we will introduce an algorithmic visualisation strategy for each
dependency type.

6.3.1   Visualisation of Functional Dependencies

If we consider a sequence of functional dependencies established between the n
domains $[D_1], \ldots, [D_n]$ of an n-ary relation instance R conforming to the relation
schema $[R] \in [\mathcal{DRC}]$ then the corresponding dependency lattice DL_F may generally be given as in Figure 6.9.

Figure 6.9: *General lattice representing functional dependencies.*

Principally, we may select any of the n domains to represent its objects as first class
graphical elements. Suppose we select D_i, for $1 \leq i \leq n$, then we may realise the
sequence of unique mappings $f_i : D_i \mapsto D_{i+1}, \ldots, f_{n-1} : D_{n-1} \mapsto D_n$ using
the graphical relations defined at the UniqueMappingRelationType and its super
types. In this case, however, we have to realise the remaining functions $f_1 : D_1 \mapsto
D_2, \ldots, f_{i-1} : D_{i-1} \mapsto D_i$ by means of their converse relations. Since these are
generally not functions themselves we cannot apply the graphical relations defined
at the UniqueMappingRelationType, but instead, we have to use the graphical relations defined at its supertypes. This is, of course, in contradiction to the effectiveness criteria we have formulated above, saying that we should use the most
specific graphical resources possible. Therefore, the preferred domain objects to
be realised as first class graphical elements should be those of domain D_1, since

only in this case we may ensure all domains to be encoded using the most specific resources in a bottom-up visualisation process. That is, we presume the encoding process to realise the functions in the following way: $encodesRelation_1 (f_1 : D_1 \mapsto D_2), \ldots, encodesRelation_{n-1}(f_{n-1} : D_{n-1} \mapsto D_n)$. From now on we will refer to D_1 as the *basic domain*.

In the remainder of this subsection we will illustrate the bottom-up visualisation approach using the ternary relation extracted from our example database (see Figure 5.9 in section 5.2) presented in Figure 6.10 whose dependency lattice, displayed in Figure 6.11, is of the linear form introduced above.

	Person	Profession	School
g1	Gropius	Architect	Bauhaus
g2	Breuer	Architect	Bauhaus
g3	Johnson	Architect	Harvard
g4	Mies v.d. Rohe	Architect	Harvard
g5	Moholy-Nagy	Urban Planner	IIT
g6	J. Albers	Designer	BMC
g7	Le Corbusier	Architect	Bauhaus
g8	A A.lbers	Designer	BMC
g9	Bartning	Architect	Bauhaus
g10	Hilberseimer	Architect	Bauhaus
g11	Schawinsky	Urban Planner	IIT
g12	Peterhans	Urban Planner	IIT

BMC: Black Mountain College
IIT: Illinois Institute of Technology

Figure 6.10: *Multivalued context representing persons, professions and schools.*

Figure 6.11: *Dependency lattice corresponding to the context displayed in Figure 6.10.*

In the design presented in Figure 6.12, we have chosen the graphical element rectangle together with a text attachment to represent the persons as the basic domain, and hues and hue classes, respectively, to represent the double classification of the persons by the schools and the professions. Regarding the legend, we see that such encodings may lead to a visual aggregation of coloumns. In this example we represent schools and professions using one hue, e.g., 'Harvard architects' using a red hue and 'Bauhaus architects' using a different red hue in order to express the fact that these persons have the same profession. Noteworthy about the design below is also that we have applied spatialGrouping constraints to redundantly reinforce the colour groupings. In this way, we may easily identify the different professions as the coloured clusters, but also within the clusters we may identify the red architect clusters fast, because they are located next to one another. Without this redundant measure the graphic would have been correct, but certainly not as clear. Therefore, redundant use of graphical relations must also be seen as an important aspect of effectiveness, since it pronounces certain aspects of the data more saliently.

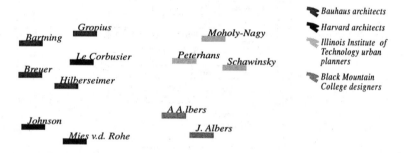

Figure 6.12: *Visualisation using classified colours (see appendix D for a coloured illustration).*

A second design for the same data is presented in Figure 6.13. Here, we have encoded the person objects in the same way as before using rectangles (and text string attachments). In contrast to the design before, though, the first function, mapping persons into schools, was realised using the nestedRectangle resource. Since the nesting (surrounding) rectangles are graphical elements themselves, we could use their internal attribute hue to realise the consecutive functions.

In the visualisation displayed in Figure 6.14 we have applied the nestedRectangle resource twice to encode the two consecutive functions. Thus, we have selected no internal attributes at all. The same is true for the visualisation presented in Figure 6.15 where we have used indentations to realise the functions. In addition, we have encoded the domains by applying different type faces to the elements repre-

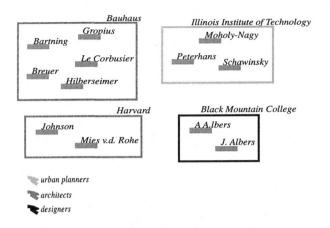

Figure 6.13: *Visualisation using nested rectangles and colours (see appendix D for a coloured illustration).*

senting domain objects of different domains.

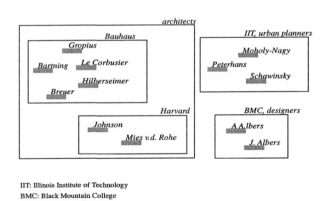

IIT: Illinois Institute of Technology
BMC: Black Mountain College

Figure 6.14: *Visualisation using nested rectangles.*

The last visualisation of the data is a line diagram which is presented in Figure 6.16. There, we have represented each domain object by a text element and the consecutive functions were realised using lineWithNoArrow and parallelLeftToRightPosition constraints.

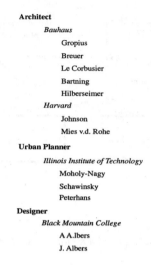

Figure 6.15: *Visualisation using relative position constraints.*

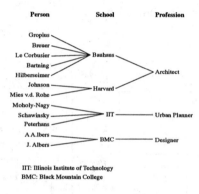

Figure 6.16: *Line diagram visualisation of the the facts.*

So far, we have described five different designs as the possible outcome of a sequential visualisation process. We will next discuss these visualisations with respect to effectiveness aspects.

The first example visualisation extensively uses internal attributes. These are in the case of functional relations the most specific graphical relations (recall, that we have defined the graphical resources at the UniqueMappingRelationType according to the following precedence order: internalAttributes, nestedRectangles, indentedList). However, this example shows also that the use of internal attributes may lead to a comparatively large legend so that legend look-ups are necessary to understand the graphic. This reduces the strength of effectiveness of internal attributes to some extent. The second diagram makes besides internal attributes also use of the element-element relation nestedRectangles. As a result, the legend appears less prominent compared with the main part of the diagram. The third and the fourth visualisation only apply the element-element relations nestedRectangles and indentedList, respectively, to encode the functions and use no internal attributes at all. Thus, they need no legend at all. Finally, the last diagram uses graphical relations defined at the supertype (SetValuedMappingRelationType) of the UniqueMappingRelationType. The graphical complexity of this diagram, measured in the number of graphical elements used, is clearly the highest, since it needs 35 graphical elements versus 16 in the first, 19 in the second, 19 in the third, and 19 in the fourth diagram (including legend elements).

Above we have shown that the use of internal attributes as the most specific graphical means is relative. Its relative strength is reflected by the quantitative ratio that is obtained by dividing the number of graphical elements representing the legend and the number of graphical elements encoding the actual graphic. We call this value the *legend ratio*.

Besides these aspects *qualitative-perceptual aspects*, *graphical complexity of the diagram* and *quantitative-perceptual aspects* are important factors of effectiveness. Qualitative perceptual aspects refer to the order of graphical resource assignments at the relation types (cf. page 111). Quantitative perceptual aspects will be discussed next.

We distinguish three different influence factors by which the use of graphical relations is constrained: the first factor, called the *grouping number*, addresses their limited recursive power, that is, the possibility to define attributes recursively. Internal attributes as the most specific graphical resources for functional dependencies are, for instance, rather constrained. Some internal attributes like hue or font allow for further attributations, e.g., by subsequently applying the attribute hueClass that is defined on hues or by applying the attribute typeFace after font. However, in these cases the depth of the recursion is limited to one further attributation. Other attributes such as texture cannot be further attributed at all. Consequently, we may only encode functional dependencies up to three domains deep using internal attributes alone. For $n > 3$ we must use other graphical resources as well. Nested rectangles can, for instance, be applied a number of times, and indentation even arbitrarily often.

The second factor, called the *capacity*, addresses limitations concerning the number of data objects that may be encoded by a graphical relation in one design. For example, aesthetic consideration suggest the use of only two different fonts to encode data objects or classes of data objects, and perhaps up to eight colours, but we may use a larger number of spatial groupings.

The third factor, called the *frequency*, is concerned with the frequency by which a graphical relation may be applied in one graphical design. Whereas we may apply, e.g., texture only once we may apply text attachments several times to encode data objects of different domains.

As we will see later, the implementation of the three influence factors as resource selection rules represents quantitative -perceptual aspects of effectiveness. Their implementation is besides qualitative relation type information responsible for flexibility in the designs. We will therefore incorporate them into a discrete optimisation process for the encoding of the domains. To this purpose, we must, however, define constant upper bounds for the three factors. We will refer to them by the terms *grouping limit*, *capacity limit*, and *frequency limit* respectively. A more formal introduction of the three encoding limitations is given next.

Let $G \in \mathcal{G}$ be an arbitrary graphical relation defined at a given relation type and let $capacity : \mathcal{G} \mapsto \mathbf{N}$ denote the current number of encoded objects and $capacityLimit := const$ be a constant value of this function. Let furthermore $frequency : \mathcal{G} \mapsto \mathbf{N}$ denote the current number of assignments of a graphical relation in a given design and $frequencyLimit := const$ the corresponding maximum. Finally, we define $groupingNumber : \mathcal{G} \mapsto \mathbf{N}$ to be the current number of groupings and $groupingLimit := const$ the maximum number of groupings . Based on these definitions we may specify the following selection rules:

$$\text{capacity}(D_i) \leq \text{capacityLimit}(G)$$
$$\text{frequency}(G) \leq \text{frequencyLimit}(G)$$
$$\text{groupingNumber}(G) \leq \text{groupingLimit}(G)$$

In appendix C we list the concrete specifications of limitation constants for the graphical relations as we consider them useful.

Next, we will present a resource allocation algorithm that aims at optimising the discussed aspects of effectiveness for the production of effective designs. Given the Type Lattice the algorithm tries to maximise the use of internal attributes while taking into account the qualtitative-perceptual ordering of graphical resources and the quantitative-perceptual limitations that determine the use of the graphical resources. The graphical complexity value measuring the complexity of the design and the legend ratio value cannot be part of the generation process, because they can only be the result of a-posteriori evaluations of the design which we will not discuss in this work.

6.3.2   Resource Allocation Algorithm for Functional Dependencies

An object-oriented implementation of the resource allocation algorithm for functional dependencies may now be designed in the following way: all graphical elements will be represented as objects conforming to graphical resource classes such as [Rectangle],[Circle], [Text] $\in \mathcal{C}$ etc, at which the internal attributes, defined in section 6.1, are defined. This implies a distinction of quantitative, qualitative, and constraint relations that are assigned to the graphical element classes. Moreover, any graphical element, with the exception of text, is presumed to be added a specific text string attachment representing the name of the data object that is encoded by the graphical element.

To realise a sequence of functions we implement a recursive resource allocation algorithm that consists of three nested subroutines: *encodeLattice*, *encodeDomains*, and *encodeDomain*.

The operation *encodeLattice* takes as input a functional dependency lattice DL_F and assigns the basic domain a first class graphical resource depending on the domain type. Since domains can be interpreted to establish relations [3] as well, the domain type is specified by means of the Type Lattice. A default first class graphical element must therefore be specified at each relation type. As the default for all relation types we propose rectangles, except for the RealValuedLinearOrderType, in which case we prefer points. The operation *encodeLattice* calls the operation *encodeDomains* with the parameter setOfEncodings storing the first domain encoding and the parameter domain that stores D_2. Finally, *encodeLattice* determines the complexity of the graphic by computing the ratio between the number of graphical relations and the number of tuples to be encoded. This ratio is stored at the dependency lattice.

The operation *encodeDomains* recursively walks up the lattice DL_F and calls for each domain D_i the operation *encodeDomain* to encode it. If the return value of *encodeDomain* is not nil, the encoding is added to the current set of encodings. Otherwise, *encodeDomains* calls *encodeDomain* defined at the supertype to encode D_i and the encoding is then added to the current set of encodings.

The operation *encodeDomain* has as input parameters the current domain D_i to be encoded, and the setOfEncodings. It checks if the ranked graphical relations defined at the UniqueMappingRelationType (internalAttributes, nestedRectangles, indentation) are applicable to the given domain. The first graphical relation meeting the above mentioned quantitative encoding limitations is returned. The decision for a concrete attribute must, however, be drawn in the context of the given domain type. If, for instance, the domain type is the SetType, then we need to select qualitative internal attributes, whereas if the domain type is the DiscreteLinearOrderType we need to select relative position relations or ordered hues. The decision depends, however, also on the first class element that was encoded last. If this was, e.g., rectangle, the qualitative attributes are hue, texture etc., whereas if the element was text, then qualitative attributes are font, typeFace, hue etc. The operation ensures also that a domain is assigend its graphical resource once it is found. A schematic overview of the internal attribute encoding mechanism is pre-

---

[3] even a plain set of values can be taken as a unary relation, cf. chapter 3

sented in Figure 6.17 and a formal algorithmic description of the resource allocation process follows after that.

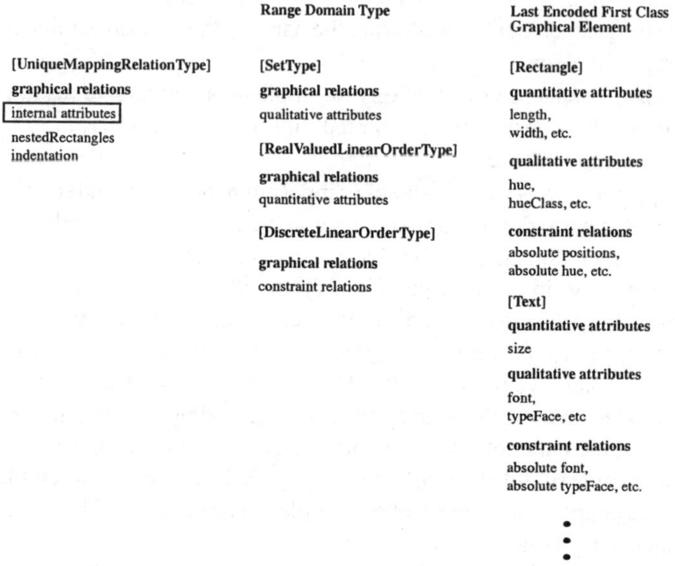

Range Domain Type		Last Encoded First Class Graphical Element
[UniqueMappingRelationType]	[SetType]	[Rectangle]
graphical relations	graphical relations	quantitative attributes
internal attributes	qualitative attributes	length, width, etc.
nestedRectangles		
indentation	[RealValuedLinearOrderType]	qualitative attributes
	graphical relations	hue,
	quantitative attributes	hueClass, etc.
	[DiscreteLinearOrderType]	constraint relations
		absolute positions,
	graphical relations	absolute hue, etc.
	constraint relations	
		[Text]
		quantitative attributes
		size
		qualitative attributes
		font, typeFace, etc
		constraint relations
		absolute font, absolute typeFace, etc.

⋮

Figure 6.17: *Schematic display of the attribute encoding mechanism.*

To guide the resource allocation process we introduce a resource allocation object that is an instantiation of the class [ResourceAllocation] which is defined next.

Definition 6.3 (Resource Allocation) *A resource allocation will be represented
as an object conforming to the class* $[ResourceAllocation] \in C$. *This class stores
the set of encoded graphical resources in its attribute currentEncodings: [Resource
Allocation]* $\mapsto \mathcal{G}$. *In addition, it implements the operations encodeLattice, encode-
Domains, encodeDomain, and graphicalRelations defined below.*

Moreover, we let DL_F be an instance conforming to the class $[DependencyLat-
tice] \in C$ which will, in addition to the attribute domains, that was defined in sub-
section 5.2.3), implement the attribute $basicDomain : [DependencyLattice] \mapsto
[\mathcal{DOC}] \cup [\mathcal{DRC}]$ storing the basic domain of the lattice. Let furthermore D_i for
$1 \leq i \leq n$ be an object conforming to $[D_i] \in [\mathcal{DOC}] \cup [\mathcal{DRC}]$ for which we
specify the attribute $resource : [D_i] \mapsto [\mathcal{GOC}] \cup [\mathcal{GRC}]$ as well [4]. For the as-

---

[4]remember that $[\mathcal{GOC}]$ denotes the set of graphical object classes and $[\mathcal{GRC}]$ denotes the set of
graphical relation classes

signment of default graphical elements to the Types we introduce the type attribute
$defaultElement : Types \mapsto E$

Algorithm 6.1 (Functional Dependency Encoding)

Input: *a functional dependency lattice DL_F.*

Output: *an encoding of DL_F in such a way that the encoding of the binary
functions using internal attributes is maximised.*

encodeLattice(DL_F)
    local variables : gD.

        $D_1 := basicDomain((DL_F)).$
        $gD := resource(D_1) := defaultElement(relationType(D_1)).$
        $encodeDomains(\{gD\}, D_2, UniqueMappingRelationType).$

Let superType be defined as in chapter 5, and let encodeDomain be defined as below. Then the subroutine encodeDomains may be given as follows:

encodeDomains(currentEncodings, D_i, relType)
    local variables : set, domType, superType.

        set := currentEncodings.
        domType := relationType(D_i).
        resource(D_i) := encodeDomain(D_i, set, domType, relType).
        if resource(D_i) $\neq$ nil
            then [set := set $\cup \{resource(D_i)\}$]
            else [
                superType := superType(relType).
                if superType $\neq$ nil
                      then [(resource(D_i):= encodeDomains(set, D_i, superType).
                      (set := set $\cup \{resource(D_i)\}$)]].
        if ($D_{i+1} \neq$ nil)
            then [(encodeDomains(set, D_{i+1}, relType))]

The subroutine encodeDomain may be modelled in the following way:

encodeDomain(D_i, currentEncodings, domType, relType)
    local variables : possibleRelations.

        possibleRelations := graphicalRelations(domType, relType).

forall $G \in possibleRelations$ *do:[*
  if $(capacity(D_i) \leq capacityLimit(G) \wedge frequency(G) \leq frequencyLimit(G)$
  $\wedge groupingNumber \leq groupingLimit(G))$
    then $[resource(D_i) := G$. $return(G)]$.
return(nil)

Let *gRelations(t)* return the graphical resources defined at an arbitrary relation type *t* of the Type Lattice. Then the operation *graphicalRelations* may be defined in the following way:

$graphical Relations(domType, relType)$
  if $(relType = UniqueMappingRelationType)$
    then $[return(gRelations(domType))]$
    else $[return(gRelations(relType))]$.

Explanation 6.1 *The function encodeLattice only encodes the first domain by selecting a graphical element depending on the relation type of* D_1. *It then calls the function encodeDomains with the parameters currentEncodings storing the allocated graphical element,* D_i *storing the actual domain to be encoded, and relType storing the given relation type. The result of this call is returned. The initial call contains the following parameter settings: currentEncodings* $:= \emptyset$, $i := 2$, *and relType* $:=$ *UniqueMappingRelationType.*

The function encodeDomains recursively iterates over the ordered domains and calls encodeDomain for each domain D_i. *If the result of this call, stored in the variable resource, is not nil, then the resource is added to the currentEncodings. Otherwise, the relation type is set to the supertype and encodeDomains defined at the supertype is called. This procedure terminates when the UnqualifiedRelationType is reached. The function encodeDomains is linear in the number of domains.*

EncodeDomains retrieves the possible graphical relations depending on the domain type of D_i *by calling the operation graphicalRelations that returns the graphical relations of the domain type if the relation type is the UniqueMappingRelationType and the graphical relations of the relation type otherwise. It further checks for the first resource to meet the quantitative encoding criteria. If it finds one, the graphical resource attribute of* D_i *is set to this resource and the resource is returned, otherwise, nil is returned.*

The overall algorithm maximises the application of internal attributes, since internal attributes are tried before any other graphical relation. This is guaranteed, because the UniqueMappingRelationType defines internal attributes as its preferred graphical resources that are selected before any other graphical relation is considered. Since the different resources are also sensitive with respect to the quantitative encoding limits introduced above, different designs are produced dependending both on the domain type information as well as on the quantitative information. Because the more general graphical resources tend to have less quan-titative limitations, these are selected when the number of domains or the number of elements in the domains increase. Since some graphical resources such as in-dented lists have no quantitative restrictions at all, the algorithm will always find an encoding. ◇

To illustrate the algorithm, let us have a look at the examples presented in Figure 6.18. There we have first considered a 4-ary relation for which we have varied the number of elements in the domains five times. This has led to the selection of dif-ferent graphical means of expression depending on the quantitative changes. The result were five different designs. Then we have considered two ternary relations with different domain types and this has led to type-specific selections of graphical resources and thus type-dependent designs.

The realisation of these decisions is the task of procedural layout techniques (see chapter 7) that know how to concretely realise the selected graphical relations in accordance with the definitions given in section 6.1.

Example	Data				Graphical Encoding			
	D_1	D_2	D_3	D_4	D_1	D_2	D_3	D_4
	SetType	SetType	SetType	SetType				
1	100	100	100	100	text	indent	indent	indent
2	100	7	5	2	text	nestedR	txtAttach	font
3	100	8	5	3	rect	nestedR	txtAttach	typeF
4	5	5	5	5	rect	hue	hueClass	texture
5	8	8	8	5	rect	nestedR	nestedR	hue
	SetType	SetType	RLOType(p)					
6	8	7	6		rect	hue	absXPos	
	SetType	SetType	DLOType					
7	8	7	6		rect	hue	bBB & equiD	

column numbers: number of distinct domain objects

bBB: belowBottomBoundary constraints

equiD: equiDistance constraints

absXPos: absoluteXPosition constraints

RLOType(p): RealValuedLinearOrderType

DLOType: DiscreteLinearOrderType

Figure 6.18: *Resource allocation decisions for different data.*

6.3.3   Visualisation of Set-Valued Functional Dependencies

The dependency lattice DL_N for set-valued functional dependencies may generally be given as in Figure 6.19.

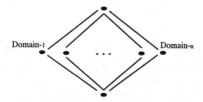

Figure 6.19: *General lattice representing set-valued-functional dependencies.*

The problem is that here, in contrast to the functional dependencies, the order of encoding of the domains cannot be derived directly from the lattice structure, since all n domains of the relation are equal. They are, however, only equal in so far as the type of the pairwise relationships (SetValuedMappingRelationType) is concerned. They are not equal with respect to quantitative aspects such as the number of elements each domain contains. We will exploit this for the definition of an artificially imposed horizontal ordering of the domains with respect to their cardinalities.

Let $Domains := \{D_1 \ldots D_n\}$ be the set of domains on which the n-ary relation $[R] \in [\mathcal{DRC}]$ is defined. In this case we define the encoding order as a linear order relation:

$$\forall D_i, D_j \in Domains \; for \; 1 \leq i, j \leq n \quad E(D_i, D_j) :\Leftrightarrow |\,D_i\,| \geq |\,D_j\,| \quad (6.8)$$

The idea behind this cardinality ordering is that the data objects of the largest domain become encoded as first class graphical elements, similar as in the case of functional dependencies. We may thus construct a left-to-right encoding approach producing many graphical elements of low visual complexity. We prefer this over the processing of the converse order of encoding in which case we obtained less, but generally much more complex graphical elements, because the use of internal attributes is not possible in this case.

Presuming a left-to-right realisation of the encoding order E we describe the visualisation principle in the following way: as in the case of functional dependencies we graphically encode the relation by assigning resources to its linearly ordered binary components (they are all qualified by the SetValuedMappingRelationType). Formally, we will describe the encoding in analogy to that of the last subsection as a sequence of encodings of set-valued mappings: $encodesRelation_1(f_i : D_1 \mapsto D_2) \ldots encodesRelation_{n-1}(f_{n-1} : D_{n-1} \mapsto D_n)$. The objects of the first domain D_1 will be encoded using first class graphical elements, whereas the data objects of the subsequent domains D_i will be assigned the graphical resources defined at the SetValuedMappingRelationType (attachments). If all these resources are consumed we may use the resources defined at the UniqueMapping RelationType to further qualify the used attachments.

In the same way as in the case of functional dependencies we must take into account the quantitative restrictions constraining the use of the graphical resources. It may thus turn out that the resource allocation, as we have described it so far, fails. In this case the strategy is, in analogy to the functional dependencies, to exploit the Type Lattice by making use of the graphical resources defined at the supertypes of the SetValuedMappingRelationType.

To illustrate this strategy we will next discuss example visualisations. To this purpose, we consider the data extractions presented in Figure 6.20 for which the dependency lattice is displayed in Figure 6.21.

	Person	Profession	School
g1	Gropius	Architect	Bauhaus
g2	Gropius	Architect	Harvard
g3	Breuer	Architect	Bauhaus
g4	Breuer	Urban Planner	Harvard
g5	A. Albers	Designer	Bauhaus
g6	J. Albers	Urban Planner	Bauhaus
g7	Le Corbusier	Architect	Bauhaus
g8	Peterhans	Urban Planner	Bauhaus
g9	Van Brunt	Architect	Harvard
g10	Johnson	Architect	Harvard
g11	Bartning	Architect	Bauhaus
g12	Mies v.d. Rohe	Urban Planner	Harvard

Figure 6.20: *Facts concerning performed artistic professions.*

For these facts we compute the following encoding order E: (Person, Profession, School) according to which we first realise the persons using rectangles as the default graphical elements (see Figure 6.22). Then we encode the schools using text attachments. Counting the different values of text attachments in the graphic we obtain twelve attachments which is the total number of data relation tuples. This is not just a mere coincidence. It rather shows that attachments, unlike internal attributes, do not reduce the amount of graphical encoding. Instead, we need to generate a graphical element (in this case a letter) to encode each tuple. Thus, we may see each attachment to establish a graphical representative of a tuple. Our in-

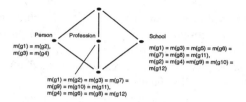

Figure 6.21: *Dependency Lattice for the facts in Figure 6.20.*

terpretation of this circumstance is to have realised the dependency lattice infimum which represents a *virtual domain*, that is, a dependency lattice node with no data semantics, emerging only by construction of the lattice (in contradistinction to the conception of a virtual domain we speak of a *real domain* if a lattice node represents a domain instance D conforming to $[D] \in [\mathcal{DOC}]$). This is the reason why we may apply the resources of the subtype — the UniqueMappingRelationType — given we have encoded attachments before. Concretely, in the graphic we have further qualified the text attachments using different hues. The spatial groupings only amplify this grouping and the result is thus a Venn-diagram like representation.

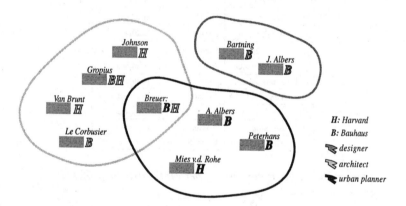

Figure 6.22: *Visual representation of set-valued-functionally dependent facts (for a coloured illustration see appendix D).*

As in the case of functional dependencies, this encoding strategy may fail, because of the quantitative restrictions concerning capacity, frequency, and grouping number of the graphical resources. In such cases more general visualisations such as the one presented in Figure 6.23 may be computed using the graphical relations defined at the supertypes of the SetValuedMappingRelationType. Note that in this graphic we had to encode some domain objects, e.g., 'Breuer', more than once, which was not the case in the visualisation before. The indented list visualisation cannot avoid the double encoding of domain elements and this is an objective reason why it is less effective than the visualisation before. In the same way a multivalued context itself can be seen as a trivial visualisation. The triviality results from the fact that it does not realise any regularities of the data. This is at the same time the reason why it is always applicable.

Bauhaus:

      architects: Gropius, Breuer, Le Corbusier

      designer: A. Albers, Bartning

      urban planner: J. Albers, Peterhans

Harvard:

      architect: Gropius, Van Brunt, Johnson

      urban planner: Breuer, Mies. v.d. Rohe,

Figure 6.23: *Visual representation of set-valued-functionally dependent facts.*

6.3.4 Resource Allocation Algorithm for Set-Valued Functional Dependencies

The resource allocation algorithm for set-valued-functional dependencies is not much different from that of functional dependencies. In fact, it is a generalisation of it. The operations *encodeLattice* and *encodeDomains* must be modified so that functional and set-valued functional encodings can be performed, whereas the operations *encodeDomain*, and *graphicalRelations* remain the same.

The generalisation consists of a check for the type of dependency lattice. If it is a set-valued functional lattice and the second domain is already encoded as an attachment (according to the strategy outlined above) the encoding will be performed according to the functional strategy outlined in the previous subsection. Otherwise a set-valued functional encoding strategy is applied.

Let the set of domain instances $\{D_1, \ldots D_n\}$ be cardinality ordered according to formula 6.3.3 and let the VirtualRelationType $\in \mathcal{T} \setminus \{t \mid t \in TypeLattice\}$ be stored in the relation type attribute of a virtual domain, then we may define the following encodeDomains routine:

1st Extension of Algorithm 6.1

encodeLattice(DL)
        local variables : gD, relType.

        $gD := resource(D_1) := defaultElement(relationType(D_1)).$
        if (relType(basicDomain(DL)) = VirtualRelationType)
            then [relType := SetValuedMappingRelationType]
            else [relType := UniqueMappingRelationType]
        encodeDomains($\{gD\}, D_2, relType).$

encodeDomains(currentEncodings, D_i, relType)
        local variables : set, domType, superType.

        $set := currentEncodings.$
        $domType := relationType(D_i).$
        if ((relType = SetValuedMappingRelationType) $\land$ | set |> 1))
        then [relType := UniqueMappingRelationType].
        $resource(D_i) := encodeDomain(D_i, set, domType, relType).$
        if resource(D_i) $\neq$ nil
            then [set := set $\cup\{resource(D_i)\}]$
            else [
                $superType := superType(relType).$
                if superType $\neq$ nil
                    then [(resource(D_i):= encodeDomains(set, D_i, superType).
                    $(set := set \cup \{resource(D_i)\})]].$
        if ($D_{i+1} \neq$ nil)
            then [(encodeDomains(set, D_{i+1},relType))]

Explanation 6.2 *In contrast to the functional encoding in the previous subsection encodeLattice checks for the relation type of the basic domain and sets the local variable relType to SetValuedMappingRelationType if the basic domain's relation type is the VirtualRelationType. Otherwise it sets relType to UniqueMappingRelationType. It calls encodeDomains with the resource assigned to D_1, D_2, and relType. The operation encodeDomains must be modified in such a way that it is checked if D_2 is already encoded given relType stores the SetValuedMappingRelationType. In this case relType is set to the UniqueMappingRelationType. In the case the dependency lattice represents a functional dependency between the domains the algorithm encodes the domains in the same way as the functional dependency encoding algorithm 6.1 so that the given algorithm is indeed a generalisation of the latter.*

In Figure 6.24 we present resource allocation results for set-valued-functional domain dependencies as the algorithm computes them. In analogy to the resource algorithm for functional dependencies the examples show the algorithm's sentitivity to type-information and quantitative data aspects.

Example	Data				Graphical Encoding			
	D_1	D_2	D_3	D_4	D_1	D_2	D_3	D_4
	SetType	SetType	SetType	SetType				
1	100	8	8	5	text	indent	indent	hue
2	100	5	5	3	text	shpAttach	txtAttach	indent
3	7	5	5		rect	shpAattach	hue	
4	100	5	5	5	text	shpAttach	hue	hueClass
5	5	5	5	5	rect	shpAttach	hue	hueClass
	SetType	SetType	SetType	DLOType				
6	5	5	5	5	rect	shpAttach	hue	orderedHue

DLOType: DiscreteLinearOrderType

Figure 6.24: *Resource allocations for data relations with varying type information and quantitative aspects.*

6.3.5 Visualisation of Mixed Functional and Set-Valued Functional Dependencies

So far, we have discussed visualisation strategies for two rather extreme types of domain dependencies. Typically however, data sets may not embody such pure types of data regularities alone. Instead, they will rather contain combinations of both types of dependencies so that the topology of the dependency lattice must be presumed to take arbitrary shape. This implies that we cannot provide a lattice diagram (as in the two subsections before) illustrating this general domain dependency case. Nevertheless, we will again show how even arbitrary dependency lattices can be visualised.

Since a general dependency lattice incorporates both functional and set-valued functional dependencies (this is why we call it also a 'mixed dependency lattice' in the remainder) the problem is to find an allocation strategy integrating both aspects. Such a strategy will then result in a uniform allocation algorithm for n-ary relations.

Given a mixed dependency lattice DL_M with domains $D_1, \ldots, D_m$ we may distinguish two different cases again: first, the basic domain D_1 (again, the global

lattice infimum which always exists for concept lattices, cf. theorem 5.1) is a real
domain instance (real domain), that is, a data object class instance D conforming
to $[D] \in [\mathcal{DOC}]$, and second, it is a virtual domain, that is, a dependency lattice
node with no data semantics emerging by construction of the lattice.

In the first case, we may identify the basic domain objects with the tuples of
the given relation, since the cardinality of the set of tuples and that of the set of
domain objects is identical (see section 6.3.1). In this case, we may proceed with
the allocation process functionally. That is, we encode all super domains in the
way we have done it for pure functional dependencies. In this attempt we have to
take two problems into consideration, though.

The first problem refers to the fact that a general dependency lattice DL_M may
contain more than one virtual domain, because of the lattice construction principles
outlined in section 5.2. Virtual domains do not represent data. Therefore, they will
not be assigned any graphical resources. Therefore, we must consider only real
domains as *direct superdomains*. We will next formalise the computation of the
direct superdomains and illustrate that graphically in Figure 6.25.

Let $D_k \in DL_M$ be one of the domains of a mixed dependency lattice DL_M,
then the set of its direct superdomains $S(D_k)$ is constructed as:

$$S(D_k) := \{D_j \mid D_j \in superDomains(D_k) \wedge$$

$$relationType(D_j) \neq VirtualRelationType\}$$

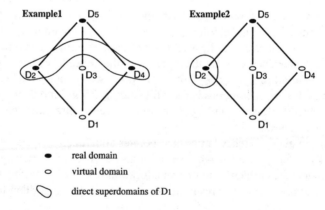

Figure 6.25: *Illustration of the construction principle for a set of direct superdomains.*

We apply this construction principle to define linearly ordered *domain levels* L_k ($1 \leq k \leq m - 1$) on DL_m in the following way:

$$L_0 := D_1, \; L_1 := S(D_1).$$

$$L_k := \{D_j \mid D_j \in \bigcup_i S(D_i) \; for \, D_i \in L_{k-1} \wedge 1 \leq i, j, \leq n, \} \tag{6.9}$$

The second problem relates to the fact that the level elements are in a set-valued-functional dependency with one another. Therefore, they must be encoded 'orthogonally' which means in this context, we have to avoid an allocation of recursively defined resources to two direct super domains of a given domain. To explain this we consider the following example: if we have encoded domain $D_r \in L_{k-1}$ using rectangles, we may not encode one of its direct superdomains, say $D_i \in L_k$, using hue and another one, say $D_j \in L_k$, using hueClass, because hue and hueClass are functionally dependent, whereas the two super domains are not. A positive formulation of this argument, namely, to encode functionally depending domains using recursively defined resources, is desired, because in this way only one resource class (e.g., the hue class) is used to encode more than one domain.

Apart from the virtual domain problem concerning the computation of the direct superdomains and the orthogonal encoding, there are essentially no differences to the allocation process specified for pure functional dependencies. Thus, we only need to extend this algorithm to solve also the more general problem. We will discuss this, however, later in this subsection.

The second case indicated above was that the basic domain is a virtual domain, which means the allocation process must follow a set-valued functional approach. Thus, we compute the real, direct superdomains of the basic domain in the same way as we have proposed it above, and perform a cardinality ranking for the domain objects in level L_1. Then, we allocate first class graphical elements for the domain with the highest rank and attachments as well as attributes of these attachments for the subsequent domains of L_1. The following levels L_k are realised in a similar way, except that all domains must be encoded either as internal attributes of the chosen graphical elements or as element-element relations, e.g. nestedRectangles, or frameCurve. The selection of the latter means the introduction of closed curves as new first-class elements in the design.

Before we go on outlining the changes of the algorithms discussed so far and their integration into a uniform resource allocation routine for n-ary relations, we will discuss some example visualisations illustating the encoding principle next.

To this purpose, we consider the PerformedProfession facts presented in Figure 5.13 and their dependency lattice which we display here again together with possible domain encodings.

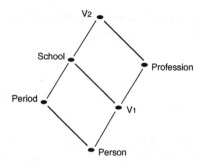

Figure 6.26: *Dependency lattice corresponding to the multivalued context presented in Figure 5.13.*

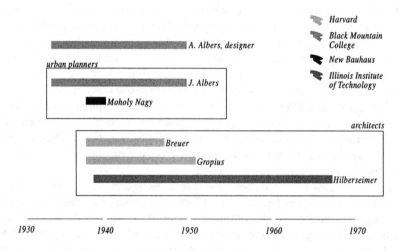

Figure 6.27: *Visualisation of PerformedProfession facts (see appendix D for a coloured illustration).*

The diagram in Figure 6.27 is a possible visualisation of these data. Since the basic domain is a real domain we have encoded its objects using rectangles as first class graphical elements (plus the required name attachments). The first level of super concepts L_1 consists of the set $\{period, profession\}$. Since the periods represent themselves a recursively defined binary relation defined on the real-valued domain Date, we encode them using the absoute x-position attribues leftBound and right-Bound of the rectangles [5]. The professions are represented using nestedRectan-

---

[5] At this point, we have to anticipate the encoding of recursive structures. This topic will, however, be discussed at length in the next subsection

gles. The second level L_2 contains only the domain School which is realised by applying the qualitative hue attribute of the rectangles. The second design, presented in 6.27, is similar to that in Figure 6.28. The difference is that the same graphical resources are applied to different domains.

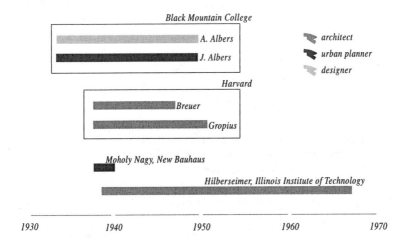

Figure 6.28: *Alternative visualisation of PerformedProfession facts (see appendix D for a coloured illustration).*

6.3.6 Resource Allocation Algorithm for Mixed Dependencies

In this subsection we will introduce a resource allocation algorithm for mixed dependencies which is a further generalisation of the allocation algorithm introduced so far. Major changes will affect the operations *encodeLattice* and *encodeDomains* with respect to the concepts of superdomain levels introduced above.

Let *S(D)* be the routine that computes the set of superdomains of an arbitrary domain $D \in DL_M$ as defined in formula 6.3.5 and let *cardOrd(L_k)* be the operation that returns a cardinality ordered set of elements of each level according to formula 6.3.3, then we may formulate the modified resource allocation algorithm for mixed dependencies as follows:

2nd Extension of Algorithm 6.1

encodeLattice(DL)
        local variables : gD, D_1, relType.

$gD := resource(D_1) := defaultElement(relationType(D_1)).$
$if (relType(basicDomain(DL)) = VirtualRelationType)$
$\quad then [relType := SetValuedMappingRelationType]$
$\quad else [relType := UniqueMappingRelationType]$
$L_1 := S(D_1):$
$encodeDomains(\{gD\}, L_1, relType).$

$encodeDomains(currentEncodings, L_k, relType)$
$\quad local\ variables : set, domType, superType.$

$\quad set := currentEncodings.$
$\quad L_{k+1} := \emptyset.$
$\quad if ((relType = SetValuedMappingRelationType) \wedge \mid set \mid > 1))$
$\quad then [relType := UniqueMappingRelationType].$
$\quad for\ i = 1\ to \mid cardOrd(L_k) \mid do:[$
$\quad\quad domType := relationType(D_i).$
$\quad\quad resource(D_i) := encodeDomain(D_i, set, domType, relType).$
$\quad\quad if\ resource(D_i) \neq nil$
$\quad\quad\quad then [set := set \cup \{resource(D_i)\}.\ L_{k+1} := L_{k+1} \cup S(D_i)]$
$\quad\quad\quad else [$
$\quad\quad\quad\quad superType := superType(relType).$
$\quad\quad\quad\quad if\ superType \neq nil$
$\quad\quad\quad\quad\quad then [(resource(D_i):= encodeDomains(set, D_i, superType).$
$\quad\quad\quad\quad\quad (set := set \cup \{resource(D_i)\}).\ L_{k+1} := L_{k+1} \cup S(D_i)]]]$
$\quad if (L_{k+1} \neq nil)$
$\quad\quad then [(encodeDomains(set, L_{k+1}, relType))]$

Explanation 6.3 *Instead of calling encodeDomains with the second domain D_2, as was the case in algorithm 6.3.4, encodeLattice calls encodeDomain here with the second level L_1 (the first is L_0). The operation encodeDomains has been changed in such a way that each domain of a given level L_k is encoded while level L_{k+1} is constructed as the union of superdomains of the $D_i \in L_{k+1}$. Thus, the algorithm described above represents indeed a generalisation of the resource allocation process we have introduced so far, since it extends the algorithm by the processing of superdomain levels. Worth to mention at this point is that the complexity of the algorithm has not increased. It is still linear in the number of domains to be processed, since each domain D_i is visited only once.*

As a result, we present in Figure 6.29 a graphically enriched mixed-dependency lattice showing how the domains of the example visualisations in Figure 6.27, discussed earlier in this subsection, are encoded. The dotted arrows additionally indicate the linear encoding process.

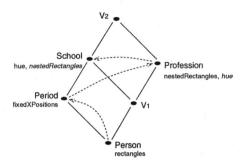

Figure 6.29: *Dependency lattice with encoded domains.*

Constructing the algorithm in this way, we ensure, of course, also that the quantitative encoding restrictions lead to a manifold of designs for the same lattice topology. Thus, quantitative modifications of the data above will, in the same way as before, lead to different domain encodings. Also larger lattices are conceivable. However, there are certainly limits for the encoding. They result primarily from the limited capabilities of the human perceptual system distinguishing too many items at the same time. A graphic must therefore not become arbitrarily complex. One way to resolve this problem might be that the visualisation system gives response to the user if this is the case so that the user is able to reduce the amount of input data to be visualised. Such interactive strategies are, however, out of the scope of this work.

6.3.7 Visualisation of General (Nested) n-ary Relations

The visualisation problem as we have discussed it so far ignored two facts: first, domains may themselves be relations, and second, dependency lattice representations may model the functional and set-valued-functional dependencies of n-ary relations for n ≥ 2, but it is not possible to specify directed graphs (defined on one domain) by means of dependency lattices. To construct a general encoding strategy, the goal must be to improve the allocation process by integrating the two aspects mentioned above. To this purpose, the basic encoding paradigm we propose will be the following:

Given an n-ary relation instance R, we obtain a dependency lattice DL_i describing the functional dependencies established between the domains of level i if either the arity of R is greater than 2 or the binary relation type of R is the SetValuedMappingType (or one of its subtype, see Figure 5.7). In this case, R is encoded using the strategy we have described in the previous subsection. Otherwise, if R represents a graph instance, the resource allocation process is provided with R's relation type information and a graph encoding mechanism is triggered.

Besides the data distinction into graphs and non-graphs we need to address the impact of nested (relational) domains on the encoding process. Relational domains will, in contrast to non-relational domains, be encoded recursively in a top-down process by walking down the nesting tree and encoding its leaves using graphical elements and attributes. After that the chosen elements are composed into a uniform whole in a bottom-up process. As a consequence, relational domains will be graphically represented as composed graphical elements.

We will illustrate the composition process using the March relation schema introduced in chapter 5. There we have defined:

$$March :\subseteq Troop \times Move$$

$$Move :\subseteq LocDate \times LocDate$$

$$LocDate :\subseteq Location \times Date$$

Considering the facts below, in which the recursion is indicated using parentheses, the classification process finds that the March relation constitutes a unique mapping from the moves into the troops, whereas the relation Move itself represents a connected, directed tree and the relation LocDate constitutes a set-valued mapping relation instance.

(Napoleon,((Paris,November1801),(Luxemburg,April1802))),
(Napoleon,((Luxemburg,May1802),(Koblenz,May1802))),
(Napoleon,((Koblenz,June1802),(Cologne,June1802))),
(Napoleon,((Cologne,July1802),(Leipzig,August1802))),
(Napoleon,((Leipzig,November1802),(Berlin,December1802))),
(Napoleon,((Berlin,March1803),(Warsaw,June1803))),
(Prussia1,((Magdeburg,August1802),(Leipzig,August1802))),
(Prussia2,((Dresden,August1802),(Leipzig,August1802)))

In addition to these facts, we presume we have another set of facts describing the locations on a more detailed level as binary tuples conforming to the schema: *Location* : ⊆ *Longitude* × *Latitude*. The visualisation process then starts on the top-level encoding the functional dependency between the moves and the troops. This happens in the way we have described it in subsection 6.3.5. Consequently, the moves must be graphically realised before the troops. To this purpose, the resource allocation process has to step one level down in the recursion. Since the move tuples represent a directed tree both its domains, the locDates, are encoded in the same way. Because LocDate is again a relational domain the allocation process must step one further level down in the recursion. At this point, we have to realise the set-valued mapping relation established between the locations and the dates. As Location is a nested domain as well, the algorithm needs to step down in the nesting tree again. Longitude and Latitude are not nested anymore. This is the point where the first encoding starts. The binary relation type established between Longitudes and Latitudes is the BijectiveMappingRelationType. The resource defined at this type is identicalElementEncoding, that is, both domains may share one graphical element. The graphical element picked to encode the domains are circles, and because Longitude values and Latitude values are numbers of a real-valued domain the resulting graphical relations will be $position_x$ and $position_y$ so that we obtain a 2D coordinate space in which each circles is positioned at its respective (longitude,latitude) coordinate. This situation is displayed in Figure 6.30 a).

So far the visualisation is expressive but not as effective as if we knew about the semantics of locations that allow to place them on an empty geographical map, which is in fact a 2D-coordinate space as well, enriched however, by geographical information on country borders etc. In the presented visualisation we presumed this information to be given. [6].

Now, the allocation process has arrived at the bottom level of the recursion and it must walk up the nesting tree again to encode the remaining domains and to link the chosen elements. To realise Date we need to encode the set-valued functional dependency that holds between the locations and the dates. As the graphical resource we select text attachments and assign them to the circles. In this way, we may see the locDates to be represented as compositions of circles and text attachments. Since the locDates are the domains of the moves we may classify them into 'from'-locDates and 'to'-locDates and exploit this additional information to further encode the text attachments using their typeFace attribute. Such a classification is always possible in case a domain represents a directed graph defined on one domain. The result is displayed in Figure 6.30 b). As the moves relate the locDates in the form of an antisymmetric tree, the circle/text attachment composites may be connected using arrows, because this is the preferred graphical resource for the encoding of the tuples of antisymmetric trees. We have to be careful however, when connecting them, because we may in fact only connect the attachments of the circles, because the attachments represent the 'from'-locDates and the 'to'-locDates and not the whole composite. This situation is illustrated in Figure 6.30 c). On the top-level, we finally realise the troops as the functional dependents of the moves using different line attributes to distinguish the arrows. The last step is important to discriminate the march of different troops. As a layout decision we

---

[6] This discussion shows that our rather formal visualisation approach may well be extended with semantic information to become more powerful

may place the date strings along the arrows. The final diagram is presented in Figure 6.30 d).

The second example by which we illustrate the recursive allocation process is concerned with a completely different kind of relational data, as they may, e.g., be the output of scientific experiments. Nevertheless, we will show how the recursive allocation process introduced above can be used to graphically realise also such data. To this purpose, we consider the following data relation schema:

$$f : U \times V \mapsto W, \quad for \quad U, V, W \subset \mathbf{R}$$

The function may, e.g., describe melting points of a material depending on changes of temperature and pressure. Its tuples are, of course, of the form ((u,v),w), for $u \in U$, $v \in V$, $w \in W$ and it consists of two levels of recursion. The top-level contains as its domains the Cartesian product $U \times V$ and the set W. According to the encoding principles for functional dependencies we first realise the nested domain $U \times V$ and then W. To this purpose, we must step one level down in the recursion entering f's bottom level which contains the (u,v)-tuples. Presuming the binary relation between the u and v values has the SetValuedMappingRelationType then the resource allocation process for set-valued-functional dependencies, as we have outlined it in subsection 6.1, performs a cardinality ordering for the two involved domains. Since the most effective graphical resource defined at the Real-ValuedLinearOrderType is $position_x$ the first domain is assigned this resource and the second is assigned $position_y$ (absolute y positions). In this way the algorithm will create 2-D Cartesian coordinate system in which the potential (u,v) tuples may be encoded as circles residing at the corresponding (x,y)-positions of the coordinate space. This is demonstrated in Figure 6.31 a)). Now the algorithm has arrived at the bottom level of the recursion and the domain of the top-level is graphically realised. To encode also the depending domain W we may even use the third dimension $position_z$, but alternatively also brightness values. We have illustrated this in Figure 6.31 b) and c).

This example is particularly interesting, since we may compare on the one hand the structural affinity to the March example before, since both data relations are nested relations. On the other, we may relate this example to the examples presented in Figure 6.30 to show the domain-type-based affinity between these examples. There, we have presented a 3-D curve and a solid. Solid, curve and surface are commonly related under the term '3D objects' and their commonality results from the fact that all three data relations are defined on real-valued domains. Their difference in appearance, however, results from the different dependency structures of the involved domains. These are displayed in the form of dependency lattices in Figure 6.32.

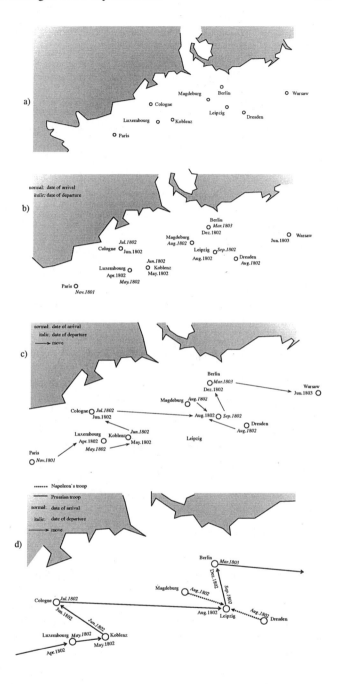

Figure 6.30: *Napoleon's march.*

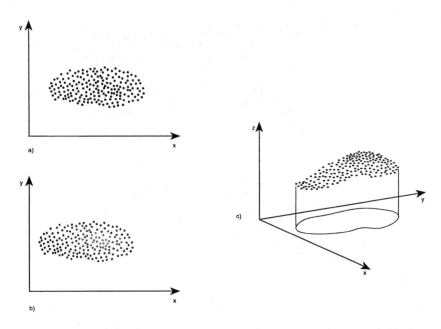

Figure 6.31: *Scientific data visualisation. The base line (diagram c)) only under-lines the border of the space surface. It is not part of the visualisation itself.*

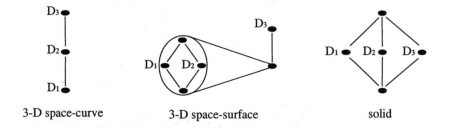

Figure 6.32: *Geometric objects and their dependency structures.*

6.3.8   Resource Allocation Algorithm for Nested n-ary Relations

As we have mentioned earlier in the previous subsection, the resource allocation algorithm for nested dependencies is a generalisation of the allocation algorithm for non-nested domains, outlined in subsection 6.3.5. If a given relation instance represents a binary relation defined on one domain the *resourceAllocation* routine calls the encoding operation *encodeGraph*, which we will be introduced below, it calls the operation *encodeLattice* otherwise.

To allow for nested encodings, we need to modify the code of *encodeDomains* to include if-statements checking whether a domain is nested or not. If this is the case, *resourceAllocation* is recursively invoked with the relational domain and the already encoded resources as input parameters. If this is not the case, the operation proceeds as if it was not modified. In the same way we must provide nesting checks for the operation *encodeGraph*.

This situation is schematically modelled next in the diagram in Figure 6.33. After that, the generalised resource allocation routine is presented using pseudo-code.

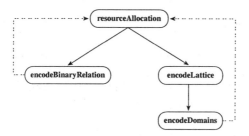

Figure 6.33: *Schematic presentation of the resource allocation process.*

Algorithm 6.2 (Resource Allocation Algorithm for Nested n-ary Relations) *Let mappings* : [*ResourceAllocation*] $\mapsto$ [*TypeConcept*] *be the attribute storing the set of subtypes of the SetValuedMappingRelationType in the TypeLattice. Moreover, let* [*D*] $\in$ *Domains* := [*DOC*]$\cup$[*DRC*] *and nestedDomains* : [*D*] $\mapsto$ *Domains be the attribute storing the nested domains of a domain.*

Input: *a possibly nested n-ary relation instance R conforming to* [*R*] $\in$ [*DRC*].

Output: *a graphical encoding of R assigning resources to itself and to its (nested) domains.*

resourceAllocation(R, currentEncodings)
      local variables: DL_M, relType.

      relType := relationType(R).
      if relType $\in$ mappings

then
 DL_M := *dependencyLattice(R)*.
 return(encodeLattice(DL_M, currentEncodings))
else "the graph case"
 $return(encodeGraph(R, currentEncodings, relType))$

$encodeGraph(R, currentEncodings, relType)$
local variables: set, D, D_i, superType.

 set := currentEncodings.
 $D :=$ *domain(R)*.
 superType := superType(relType).
 resource(R) := encodeDomain(R, set, relationType(R)).
 if resource(R) = nil
  then [resource(R) := encodeGraph(R, set, superType))]
 if nestedDomains(D) = $\emptyset$
 then[
  if (set = $\emptyset$)
   then [resource(D) := defaultElement(relationType(D))]
   else [resource(D) := encodeDomain (set, relationType(D))].
  set := set $\cup$ resource(R)]
 else [
  for all $D_i \in$ nestedDomains(D) do:[
   resourceAllocation(D_i, set)]

$encodeLattice(DL, currentEncodings)$
 local variables : gD, D_1, relType.

 set := currentEncodings.
 if set = $\emptyset$
  then [gD := resource(D_1) := defaultElement(relationType(D_1))]
 if (relType(basicDomain(DL)) = VirtualRelationType)
  then [relType := SetValuedMappingRelationType]
  else [relType := UniqueMappingRelationType]
 $L_1 := S(D_1)$:
 encodeDomains(set, L_1, relType).

$encodeDomains(currentEncodings, L_k, relType)$

local variables : set, domType, superType.

$set := currentEncodings.$
$L_{k+1} := \emptyset.$
$if\ ((relType = SetValuedMappingRelationType) \wedge | set | > 1))$
$then\ [relType := UniqueMappingRelationType].$
$for\ i = 1\ to\ |\ cardOrd(L_k)\ |\ do:[$
　　$domType := relationType(D_i).$
　　$if\ nestedDomains(D_i) = \emptyset$
　　　$then[$
　　　　$resource(D_i) := encodeDomain(D_i, set, domType, relType).$
　　　　$if\ resource(D_i) \neq nil$
　　　　　$then\ [set := set \cup \{resource(D_i)\}.$
　　　　　$L_{k+1} := L_{k+1} \cup S(D_i)]$
　　　　　$else\ [$
　　　　　　$superType := superType(relType).$
　　　　　　$if\ superType \neq nil$
　　　　　　　$then\ [(resource(D_i) := encodeDomains(set, D_i, superType).$
　　　　　　　$(set := set \cup \{resource(D_i)\}).$
　　　　　　　$L_{k+1} := L_{k+1} \cup S(D_i)]]]]$
　　　$else\ [resourceAllocation(D_i, set)]$
$if\ (L_{k+1} \neq nil)$
　$then\ [(encodeDomains(set, L_{k+1}, relType))]$

Explanation 6.4 *The algorithm takes any relational input and applies encodeLattice, which we have explained before, in case the relation R is given in the form of a dependency lattice. It applies encodeGraph in case R is not a mapping type of relation. Graphs follow an element-element encoding strategy in which both data objects of a data tuple must be encoded by first class graphical elements and the tuples by an element-element relation, cf. formula 6.1. The operation encodeGraph implements such a strategy by first encoding the relation R itself. If it cannot be encoded by the graphical relations of the given relation type encodeGraph is called for the supertype if it exists. Then the algorithm checks wether R's domain is nested or not. If this is not the case, the domain is encoded depending on the domain type, as was the case in the encoding strategies described above. If this is the case, the operation resourceAllocation is called in a loop with the nested domains as the parameters.*
Both operations, encodeGraph and encodeDomains, recursively invoke the top operation resourceAllocation if a nested domain is encountered. This ensures the desired interplay between graph encoding and lattice encoding in case a data relation is composed of both types of data structure. In order to achieve this it was,

however, necessary to extend encodeDomains for the additional "if nestedDomain"
statement that checks whether a domain is nested or not. ◇

6.3.9   Visualisation Strategies for Object Networks

As we have argued in chapter 5 section 5.3, networks of relations are the most general type of data structure we consider. In this book we will not provide a general solution to the resource allocation problem, and thus, we will not provide a general encoding algorithm. Instead, we will only discuss the problems we are confronted with and point out possible ways in which they may be tackled. In fact, we have already adressed them in the introduction to our approach in chapter 4. However, we will recall them at this point to discuss them anew in the context of the theory and the algorithms we have developed so far.

The first problem we will address is related to the fact that we have to graphically realise different data relations at the same time. Presuming all data relations should be encoded by the most effective graphical relations, resource allocation conflicts might occur, because different data relations may compete for the same graphical resources.

This problem was partially solved by [RKG95] who proposed an importance ranking of data relations using a weighted sum of instance based, quantitative rankings (similar to what we have introduced in formula 5.11 section 5.2) and predefined relation type based ranking values, reflecting the fact that more specific relation types organise the data more effectively than more general types. [RKG95] used this importance ranking to assign graphical resources to binary data relations starting with the most important data relation, that is, the most important data relation is assigned the best graphical relations in case there is a conflict.

The second problem is caused by the circumstance that the data relations may involve shared domain dependencies (see chapter 5). If there are no such dependencies for a given data instance, this implies that the different relations are completely disjoint, and then the encoding is no problem, because the program may generate an independent graphical output for each involved data relation. However, since this is generally not the case a resource allocation algorithm for networks that is able to handle such dependencies is desired. To illustrate the impact of such dependencies on the encoding process we will next discuss a concrete example.

Considering the network dependency context discussed in section 5.3 containing six different relations as its objects and six different domains as its attributes we will focus on the relation PerformedByAt, a ternary relation defined on the domains Profession, Person and School, as well as on the binary relation LifeSpan, which is a mapping from the Person domain to the nested domain LifePeriod. Given the facts extracted from our example database presented in Figure 6.34 and

	Person	Profession	School
g1	Breuer	Urban Planner	Harvard
g2	Breuer	Architect	Harvard
g3	Kandinsky	Painter	Bauhaus
g4	Schlemmer	Sculptor	Harvard
g5	Bartning	Designer	Bauhaus
g6	Kandinsky	Painter	Harvard

	Person	Birth	Death
g1	Breuer	1897	1972
g2	Kandinsky	1866	1944
g3	Schlemmer	1888	1943
g4	Bartning	1883	1959

Figure 6.34: *Contexts for the relations PerformedByAt and LifeSpan.*

presuming an importance ranking, defined as in section 5.3, formula 5.11, we may find that PerformedByAt gets the higher rank and is thus encoded first. Let us further presume that the relation instances of PerformedByAt and LifePeriod are described by the functional dependency lattices displayed in Figure 6.35 and that the cardinality of the set of persons is greater than that of the set of schools.

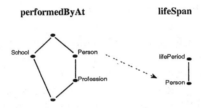

Figure 6.35: *Dependency lattices for the relations PerformedByAt and LifeSpan.*

Then a possible allocation algorithm for object networks could first realise the PerformedProfessionAt facts, because the ranking function (formula 5.11 would compute a higher value for this relation. Since the encoding of each relation component of the network would happen according to the encoding policy for (nested) n-ary relations we have described in the previous section the allocation algorithm would encode the professions as first class graphical elements (mixed encoding), say rectangles, the schools, e.g., as shape attachments, and the persons as internal attributes of the rectangles, for instance, hues. The problem we encounter realising the second data relation is the following: the persons depend functionally on the professions in case of the PerformedProfessionAt relation and at the same time they are the basic domain in case of the LifeSpan relation. This circumstance is responsible for the impossibility to display the two data relations in one diagram if we follow the encoding policy outlined above. A possible solution for the example discussed above would be, however, to encode the LifeSpan relation in the legend. In this case the visualisation may look like the one presented in Figure 6.36. Such

a solution is, however, not general enough, since the situation becomes even worse
if the network contains more than two relation components. In this case we would
have to generate legends of legends and so forth and this is certainly not desired.

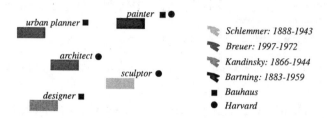

Figure 6.36: *Visualisation of the PerformedByAt and the LifeSpan relation (for a
coloured illustration see appendix D)* .

Another possibility to handle such data would be to encode the persons, as the
domain that is shared by both relations, as the first class graphical elements. However, this would force the encoding of the professions as attachments, instead of
the more effective internal attributes . The lifeSpan relation could still be visualise
using the x-extent attributes of the rectangles. Such an approach had the advantage that we could integrate both data relations into the actual diagram, instead of
unnecessarily extending the legend. The corresponding diagram is presented in
Figure 6.37. Note that the relation LifeSpan cannot be treated as a nested relation
of PerformedByAt, because lifePeriod, School, and Profession are not necessarily semantically related. Instead, the two relations must be taken as two separate
semantic units.

Such a solution can be generalised to an approach that takes the relation with the
highest rank and checks for the domain that it most shares with other relations.
This domain should become visualised using first class graphical elements. In this
way the data problem outlined above can be handled. However, if the shared domain dependency structure becomes too complex such a solution is certainly not
sufficient.

6.4   Summary of Graphical Mapping

In this section, we have discussed the principles of the graphical encoding approach
we follow in this book.

In section 6.1 we have first outlined the graphical vocabulary we use in this
approach. There, we distinguish primitive graphical elements such as different
shapes or text elements and the graphical binary relations that may be defined on

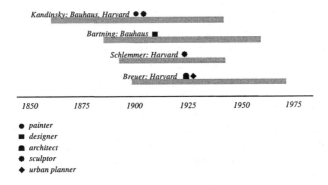

Figure 6.37: *Alternative visualisation of the PerformedByAt and the LifeSpan relation (for a coloured illustration see appendix D).*

such elements. We have classified graphical binary relations into attributes that are further distinguished into internal (colour, texture) and external (shape or text attachments), but also qualitative (hue, texture) or quantitative (width, height) attributes. Then we have identified element-element relations (lineWithOneArrow, indentation) connecting first class graphical elements, and constraint relations defining the position or other internal attributes, either relative to those of other graphical elements or absolutely. We have then demonstrated the use of the Type Lattice (which systematically models the logical implications of the formal relational properties of interest) to bind graphical binary relations at its relation type nodes. In this way we achieve expressive graphical encodings for a given binary data relation by choosing a graphical relation that is defined either at the data relation's type or at any of its supertypes. However, we have argued that a graphical design representing a given data set using the most specific graphical resources possible is desired to satisfy effectiveness criteria. Since effectiveness relies also on quantitative data aspects such as the number of times a graphical resource is used in one design, or the number of elements that can be encoded by it we have included such criteria into the resource selection process as well. This implies that the most specific graphical relation might not always be taken, because a quantitative selection criterion would be violated. Since the quantitative restrictions correlate with the generality of the graphical resource with respect to the position where it is defined in the Type Lattice, large data sets tend to be encoded using more general graphical means than data sets moderate in size.

The encoding of (possibly nested) n-ary relations , described in subsection 6.3.1, 6.3.3, and 6.3.5, is based on a differentiation between binary relations and relations with arity greater than 2. For binary relations the encoding policy described above is applied. For non-binary relations the dependency lattice is the basic data structure upon which the visualisation relies. A dependency lattice systematically describes an n-ary relation instance by means of the functional and set-valued-functional dependencies established between its domain sets. This means that the topology of an n-ary relation instance is generally not 'flat'. Instead, it may take the shape of an arbitrary lattice and we can exploit this for the encoding of the domain objects. The principle behind the encoding is rather simple: since functional and set-valued-functional dependencies both represent binary relations, we may encode a relation instance by means of its binary components. The complexity of the dependency lattice structure requires, however, the introduction of an algorithmic encoding strategy performing the graphical resource allocation. In this chapter, we have demonstrated how such a strategy may be systematically derived from the basic encoding strategies for functional and set-valued-functional dependencies. Functional dependencies are encoded bottom-up assigning the data objects of the lattice infimum first class graphical elements and using the graphical relations defined at the UniqueMappingRelationType or at its supertypes to encode the objects of the remaining domains. The encoding process for set-valued-functional dependencies assigns the domain objects belonging to the largest domain first class graphical elements and uses the resources defined at the SetValuedMappingRelationType or at its supertypes to encode the remaining domain objects. Both strategies are combined into a uniform algorithm for the encoding of n-ary relation instances. In subsection 6.3.7 we have presented a further generalisation of the resource allocation algorithm that allows the encoding of nested domains – in dependency lattice structures and in graph structures – in a top-down encoding process in which the encoded nesting tree represents the domain's graphical representation.

Finally, in section 6.3.9 we have discussed the problems that occur while graphically encoding networks of relations. They essentially result from the complex dependency structure between data relations sharing domains.

Chapter 7

Layout and Implementation

7.1 Layout

In the previous chapter we have described how data relations of arbitrary arity and nesting structure may be graphically encoded. We have designed a resource allocation process in which graphical relations were used to encode the relation domains as well as the tuples binding the domain objects together. We have, however, not addressed the question on how to realise the encoding decisions made to concretely generate the designs. This will be the subect of this chapter.

Here, we will distinguish between two different aspects: the first is concerned with the processing of the encoding structure that was produced by the resource allocation algorithm, be it a graphically encoded nested dependency lattice, a graphically encoded nested directed graph, or a combination of both. The second aspect is concerned with the procedural layout techniques that concretely realise a given design decision. Hence, we will structure the discussion in this section with respect to the two topics.

7.1.1 Processing the Encoding Structure

The processing of the encoding structure essentially follows the way it was constructed, that is, a mixed dependency structure needs to be laid out bottom-up and left-to-right, nested domains must be realised before the remaining domains on the same level of nesting are laid out, and graphs are laid out according to the graphical relations assigned during the allocation phase. Consequently, we must design a layout process whose task comprises the realisation of the computed encoding structure. In the remainder of this section we will provide the pseudo-code adequate for this task. A schematic presentation of the layout process showing the recursive interplay between the three main operations *layout*, *latticeLayout*, and *graphLayout* is displayed in Figure 7.1.

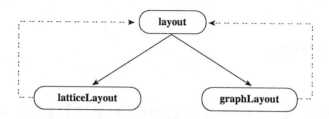

Figure 7.1: *Schematic presentation of the layout process.*

Algorithm 7.1 (Layout Process)
Input: *a graphical encoding of R assigning resources to its (nested) domains.*

Output: a layout following the decisions defined in the encoding structure

*Let R be an arbitrary, possibly nested, relation instance , and let 'basicDomain'
be defined as in algorithm 6.1. Let furthermore $\mathcal{G}$ denote the set of 'directed graph
types', that is, $\mathcal{G} := Types \setminus \{t \mid t\ is\ subtype\ of\ SetValuedMappingRelation-
Type\}$. Then we may specify the operation 'layout (R)' in the following way:*

layout(R)
local variables: Domains, D.

>   *if $R \in \mathcal{G}$*
>   *then*
>   *graphLayout (R)*
>   *else*
> $Domains := \emptyset.$
> $D := basicDomain(dependencyLattice(R)).$
> $Domains := Domains \cup D.$
>   *latticeLayout(Domains)*

*Input to the procedure graphLayout is a binary relation R defined on a single do-
main D. Let 'domainResource' as well as 'tupleResource' be the functions returning the resources allocated for these data elements. Let furthermore 'draw' be a
procedural layout technique determined by the parameters 'domainResource' and
'tupleResource' (for example draw may create rectangles and connect them using*

arrows, because domainResource stores the value 'rectangle' and tupleResource stores 'lineWithOneArrow'). Then we may define the procedures 'graphLayout' and 'latticeLayout' in the following way:

graphLayout(R)
local variables: D.

$D := domain(R)$.
$if\,(nestedDomains(D) = \emptyset)$
    then[
        $resource_d := resource(D)$.
        $resource_t := resource(R)$.
        $draw(R, resource_d, resource_t).]$
    else [layout(D)]]

latticeLayout(Domains)
    local variables: D_i

$forall\,D_i \in Domains\ do:[$
    $if\,(nestedDomains(D_i) = \emptyset)$
        then[
            $resource_d := domainResource(D_i)$.
            $draw(D_i, resource_d)$.
            $if\,(successors(D_i) = \emptyset)$
                then[return]
                else[layout(successors(D_i))]]
        else [layout(D_i)]]

Explanation 7.1 *The layout process consists of the operation 'layout' , the operation 'graphLayout' and the operation 'latticeLayout' . The operation 'layout' controls the layout process. It takes any graphically encoded relational structure as its input and decides to call 'graphLayout' if the given input is a graph and 'latticeLayout', otherwise. Both subroutines either layout the graphically encoded domains and tuples performing procedural layout techniques, or they recursively invoke 'layout' in case a given domain is nested.*

7.1.2 Procedural Layout Techniques

As we have outlined in the last section, the layout process recursively walks through the given encoding structure to call the appropriate procedural layout techniques. Procedural layout techniques are the means the layout process uses to set the attributes of the selected graphical elements, be it first class elements or only attachments, to constant values, since only in this case a design is completely specified. There are, however, as many techniques as there are graphical resources, and since the invention of new resources is not limited, the potential number of layout techniques is not bounded. This is the reason why we will not discuss all possible techniques in depth at this point. Instead, we will discuss the role they play in the automatic diagram design tool we are describing and we will categorise them with respect to complexity aspects.

The Role and Complexity of Procedural Layout Techniques
The role procedural layout techniques play in our approach is to provide an algorithmic implementation of graphical relations. Since different graphical relations have different impacts on the assignment of attribute values, they require more or less sophisticated algorithms for their realisation. The complexity of the layout technique essentially depends, however, on how much a given attribute's value space is restricted by constraint graphical relations assigned in the Encoding Process. Thus, we may roughly come up with three categories of complexity: attributes that are not constrained at all, attributes whose value space is restricted by relative constraints, and attributes whose values are constants.

In the first case we need to define additional aesthetic criteria according to which the layout routine sets the values of the given attribute. These criteria need sometimes to be implemented using sophisticated optimisation strategies. The second case requires aesthetic criteria to work in combination with the imposed constraints, which may lead to constraint optimisation problems, and the third case does not require an algorithmic strategy at all, since the attribute values are given in the form of constants. We will next discuss some examples to illustrate the distinction.

Example 7.1 *Let us consider a data relation, qualified by the AntisymmetricRelationType, that is to be realised using 'lineWithOneArrow', and suppose the domain of the relation has to be encoded using rectangles. In this case we cannot derive any statements about the positioning of the rectangles from the graphical resource assignments, which means the positions are not constrained at all. Therefore, we need to define aesthetic criteria for the layout of the graph in the plane. In chapter 2 we have discussed graph layout techniques that can be employed to solve this problem. One of those was the spring-model algorithm proposed by [Ead84]. It computes the positions in a unit coordinate space starting with random coordinates for the rectangles. The aesthetic principle it adopts is to map the topological distance between the nodes in the graph (the shortest path between two nodes in a graph) into the Eucledian distance between the corresponding rectangles.*

Example 7.2 *We obtain a slightly different, but closely related problem to the one in the previous example, if we are given a data relation that is characterised by the* *more specific StrictOrderRelationType. Let us suppose the graphical resource by which the data relation has to be encoded is 'lineWithOneArrow' ∧ 'belowBottomBoundary'. In comparison with the example before we addition-ally need to realise a constraint graphical relation that restricts possible value spaces for each rectangle's position to a two-dimensional semi-plane. Still, the positions of the rectangles remain insufficiently specified. To compute the final po-sitions we may apply a modification of algorithm [Ead84], proposed by [KKR95], that accepts linear constraints.*

Example 7.3 *The third example we consider is rather straight forward. Suppose we are given temporal data as was the case in some of the examples presented in chapter 6. If the encoding process decides to use absolute x, y, or z positions for the graphical realisation of the data there is not much to do for the layout engine apart from setting the position values of the graphical elements to the correspond-ing values in the unit coordinate space in which we calculate the positions.*

These examples have shown how the computation of positions may be more or less difficult depending on the restriction imposed on the value space defining the valid positions.

We encounter a similar problem if we consider other attributes, e.g., the assign-ment of qualitative hues to encode the range of a function. In this case we expect the layout to compute the same hue values for those first class graphical elements representing data objects of the same aggregation (see section 5.2.1) and differ-ent values for those representing data objects of different aggregations. However, there is no guideline according to which these values have to be set. In this context, we interpret the attribute 'different' to imply that all hue pairs must have equal dis-tance in the circular hue spectrum to avoid pronounciation of particular graphical elements. This is in the same way a functionally motivated aesthetic criterion as those defined for the layout of line diagrams.

A more sophisticated question in this context, which goes beyond the pure func-tional approach introduced in this book, is to ask for the most appropriate colours in a given application context. It is, for instance, not advisable in our opinion to use brilliant colours in the context of diagram layout, because colour is a means that is used to explain a complex circumstance and brilliant colours may distract the reader from his task. This is the reason why we have used pastel colours which are characterised by comparatively low brightness and saturation values. How-ever, this is only an ad-hoc assumption for which there is no empirical evidence. Nevertheless, these arguments suggest the need to develop aesthetic rules also for the appropriate use of colours.

We consider the selection of colours to be a difficult, but interesting problem for which we will not discuss a solution here, since this goes beyond the scope of this book. We will only cite [NA93] who propose a systematisation for the use of colours that is based on human perceptual aspects. We think, however, that particularly the use of colours depends to a large extent on the spirit of the age, and thus, on fashion which is in our opinion very difficult to systematise.

7.2 Implementation

In this section, we will describe the implementation of the Extended Automatic Visualisation Engine (EAVE).

In subsection 7.2.1 we will explain some basic concepts of the VisualWorks/Smalltalk ([Par92]) programming language and give general remarks on the implementation of classes and types. In subsection 7.2.2 we will discuss the modelling of the input data structure as we have defined it in chapter 3. In subsection 7.2.3 we will sketch the internal implementation of the input data structure in EAVE and the implementation of dependency lattices as well as type lattices. In subsection 7.2.4 we will outline the implementation of relation types. In subsection 7.2.5 we will discuss the implementation of graphical elements, and finally, in subsection 7.2.6 we will describe the implementation of the process model.

7.2.1 Object-Oriented Design

Since we gave an object-oriented specification of the visualisation algorithm in the chapters above an object-oriented implementation suggests itself. In the remainder of this section we will thereofore discuss our object-oriented implementation. In Smalltalk objects may be instantiated from classes. A class defines a class-specific attribute set, called *class variables*, and operations that apply to the class, called *class methods*. In addition, it defines instance-specific attributes, called *instance variables* and instance-specific methods, called *instance methods*. Each class defines exactly one super class from which it inherits both the class variables and the class methods. Analogously, the instantiated objects inherit the instance variables and the instance methods from the superclass. The resulting class structure, expressed by the binary relation 'is superclass of' (or dually by 'is subclass of') forms a tree order, since it is a strict order (irreflexive, transitive, antisymmetric) whose intransitive kernel is, due to the definitions in appendix A, a tree. Therefore the class structure is called *class tree* from now on. The root of the class tree is the class Object. We should mention that Smalltalk is a weakly typed programming language, because variables may be declared without reference to the value sets on which they are defined.

The classes, introduced in chapter 5, 6, and 7, may directly be mapped into Smalltalk classes. In the remaining subsections we will show how the Smalltalk inheritance model may be exploited to achieve an effective implementation of the visualisation system. At this point, we note, however, that the implementation of the TypeLattice is not as straight forward. This is due to the fact that the information stored at the types (e.g., graphical resources) must be kept persistent (cf. chapter 5.1). In the Smalltalk programming language, however, there exists no such concept as an abstract data type as we have specified it in chapter 3 for the purpose of representing relation types. In subsection 7.2.4 we will show how the persistent information stored at the relation types may be stored at type classes connected by an instance-based type lattice that is computed (in a set-up routine) each time when the visualisation algorithm is started.

7.2.2   Data Object Classes and Data Relation Classes

A requirement imposed by the application context — visualising subsets of the Dictionary of Art object network — has been that data objects and data relations are modelled in the way described in chapter 3. To this purpose, we have defined the Smalltalk class DoADataObject, a subclass of Object, and assigned it a name attribute that is stored in a class variable. The class DoADataObject itself is never instantiated and as such it represents an *abstract class*. Instead, subclasses of DoA-DataObject such as DoAPerson (Dictionary of Art Person), or DoAProfession become *concrete classes* whose objects (instantiations of the class) are elements of the data relation domain instances.

Data relations are modelled analogously by defining the abstract Smalltalk class DoADataRelation specifying the commonalities of all concrete data relation classes obtained by subclassing. Commonalities represent in this case such attributes that are important with regard to the contents, e.g., name, $domain_i$ etc. (they are defined in chapter 5), but also "housekeeping" attributes such as the one storing the Smalltalk module to which the class is assigned. We have not mentioned them before, because they pertain only to the given implementation and do not add any value to the visualisation approach. Both, the data object classes and the data relation classes are seen as external data structures for which a specific input interface has been built that allows the visualisation System EAVE their import.

7.2.3   Context and Lattice Representations

Next, we will discuss the *internal representation* of the input data as 2-valued contexts and multivalued contexts as they are used by the visualisation algorithm. An internal model of the input data is not only important, because we have designed the algorithms in chapter 5, 6, and section 7 to operate on them, but also, becauseit makes EAVE independent of the external data structures. In other words, if the external data structures are stored in another format (e.g., another object-oriented database format or a relational database format) we only need to change the input interface, in this case algorithm 5.5 that converts the input data into the internal representation. The internal input data structures we consider for EAVE are the class EAVEMultiValuedContext, the class EAVETwoValuedContext and the class EAVEDomain.

TwoValuedContexts, MultiValuedContexts and RelationTypeContexts

The class EAVEMultivaluedContext is a subclass of the abstract class EAVEContext and the class EAVETwoValuedContext, in turn, is a subclass of EAVEMultivaluedContext. In chapter 5 we have outlined that 2-valued contexts internally represent binary data relations, whereas multivalued contexts represent n-ary data relations (when $n > 2$). To ensure independence of the external data structure such attribute values as the name of the external relation or the relation type of a given binary data relation are defined at the corresponding attributes of the particular contexts. They belong to the interface attributes supported by EAVE. Important to mention at this point is that in case the relation type attribute is not set in the external data structure, EAVE assigns the representing 2-valued context the attribute value 'UnqualifiedRelationType' as a default value. In this way it is guaranteed that also untyped binary relations may be analysed by means of the typeRefinement algorithm described in chapter 5.

As we will show in subsection 7.2.4, also the class RelationTypeContext is a subclass of EAVEContext. This allows the implementation of common operations, e.g., the generation of the concept list or the generation of the concept lattice itself, at the common superclass. It is then the repsonsibility of the sublasses to perform specific adaptations necessary for the different kinds of lattices.

Domains

The class EAVEDomain, a subclass of Object, is the internal analog to the class DoADataObject. Each subclass of DoADataObject is internally represented by a set of instantiated objects conforming to the class EAVEDomain. Thus, there is only one instance of EAVEDomain that represents all DoADataObjects. To be able to still distinguish the different kinds of DoA-objects, all EAVEDomain objects store the class name of the particular DoA-object in the instance variable *internalDomain*. In this way both DoAPerson objects and DoAProfession objects are internally represented by objects of the same class EAVEDomain, but their internalDomain attribute stores two different values.

DependencyLattices and RelationTypeLattices

For the two kinds of lattices — type lattices and dependency lattices — there exists no external analog. Thus, they represent genuine data structures of the visualisation algorithm. In the same way as the contexts they are organised in a class hierarchy in which the abstract class EAVELattice, a subclass of Object, models the properties common to both types of lattices. Its subclasses EAVEDependencyLattice and RelationTypeLattice model the specific properties of the particular type of lattice. As outlined in sections 5.1 and 5.2, both types of lattices connect different kinds of nodes. A dependency lattice connects instantiations of the class EAVEDependencyLatticeNode, whereas a type lattices connects objects conforming to the class RelationTypeNode. Dependency lattice nodes store, in contrast to relation type nodes, the redundancy information found during the classification process (what context objects store the same value of one context attribute, cf. section and 5.2). Both classes, EAVEDependencyLatticeNode and RelationTypeNode are subclasses of the common abstract superclass EAVEConcept, that is itself a subclass of Object.

The class hierarchy for contexts, lattices and concepts are presented in Figure 7.2. The Figure shows a Smalltalk hierarchy browser on the class EAVEContext. The left subwindow contains the class tree, the subwindow in the middle shows method categories, in this case only one, and the subwindow on the right shows the methods contained in the category. The buttons 'instance' and 'class' toggle. In this case, we see the reimplementation of the instance method nextClosure, which is an interface method to the actual implementation of the algorithm *nextClosure-ForLatticeType:andNodeType:* in the class EAVEContext that computes arbitrary concept lists from a 2-valued context. Figure 7.3, shows a hierarchy browser on the class EAVELattice. The method category 'computation' contains in this case several methods among which we find the implementation of the typeRefinement algorithm discussed in section 5.1. Figure B shows a hierarchy browser on the class EAVEConcept. It also shows that the class RelationTypeNode owns the instance variable relationType that stores the type class to which a given type node corresponds.

7.2.4 Relation Types and Relation Type Lattice

In subsection 7.2.1 we have already mentioned the problem of representing the types of the TypeLattice that store persistent information (e.g., graphical relations). Since there exists no concept of an abstract data type in Smalltalk, a pragmatic way to represent these data is by means of abstract type classes that are generated from the relation type lattice instance during the first time the visualisation system is started. Each time when the visualisation system is invoked anew, it is ensured (using name attribute value matchings) that the relation type nodes are in

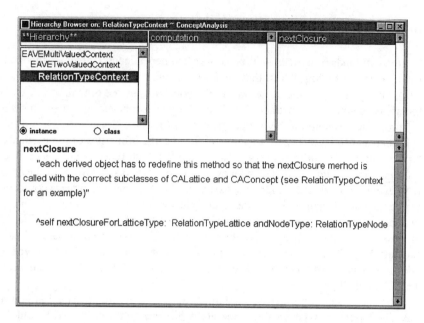

Figure 7.2: *Hierarchy browser on EAVEContext*

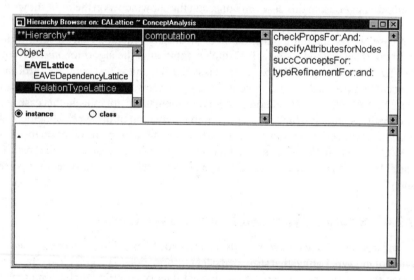

Figure 7.3: *Hierarchy browser on EAVELattice*

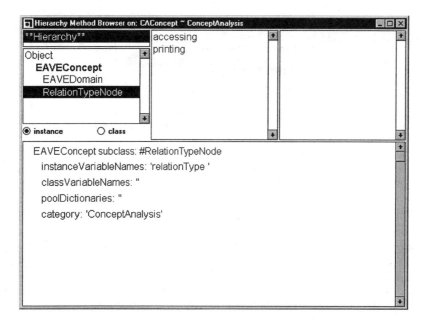

Figure 7.4: *Hierarchy browser on EAVEConcept*

a one-to-one correspondence with the type classes. In this way the operations *superTypes* and *subTypes* can be realised by walking up and down the instance-based type lattice. After having generated the type classes in the first run the persistent knowledge needs to be defined manually. This implies the definition of the corresponding relational properties at the type classes. In addition, algorithms checking whether these properties are true for a given data relation instance are implemented at the types. Eventually, ranked graphical relations are stored as ordered sets of arrays of length 2 in class variables (ordered sets and arrays are instantiations of the Smalltalk standard classes OrderedSet, and Array) Figure 7.5 presents a Smalltalk System Browser showing a subset of the relation type classes implemented.

7.2.5 Graphical Elements

In this subsection we will discuss the different types of graphical elements we have implemented. The superclass of all graphical elements is the class EAVEGraphicalElement which is itself a direct subclass of the class Object.

The abstract class EAVEGraphicalElement is further subclassed into the classes EAVE2DElement (also an abstract class), EAVECurve, and EAVEText. The class EAVE2DElement, in turn, further contains the classes EAVECircle, EAVEEllipse,

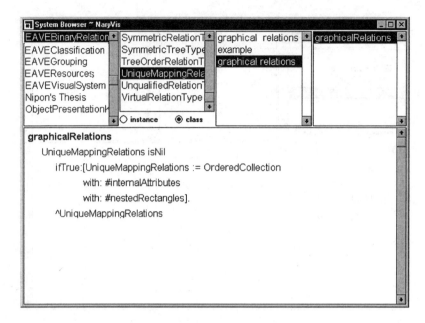

Figure 7.5: *The Figure shows a Smalltalk System Browser that that contains in the left subwindow an additional category for classes. Here, we have selected the UniqueMappingRelationType class. The method graphicalRelations is implemented analogously in all relation type classes.*

and EAVERectangle as its concrete subclasses. The class EAVECurve, instead, is not abstract and its subclass EAVELine is only more specific. The class EAVEText is not further subclassed.

In general, graphical elements implement their internal attributes as the graphical resources themselves, because internal attributes are element-specific and may thus not be implemented at the type classes. This works well with the assignment of the resource 'internal attributes' defined at the UniqueMappingRelationType, since each time an element has to encode an internal attribute it should do that depending on the given type of element. As is shown in Figure 7.6, internal attributes are further differentiated into positional, qualitative, and quantitative attributes.

7.2.6   The Three Phases of the Visualisation Algorithm

This section is dedicated to the description of the overall visualisation process. Above we have identified three phases of the visualisation algorithm: a data analysis and classification phase, a graphical resource allocation phase, and a layout phase. Since these phases represent consecutive subprocesses of the overall, lin-

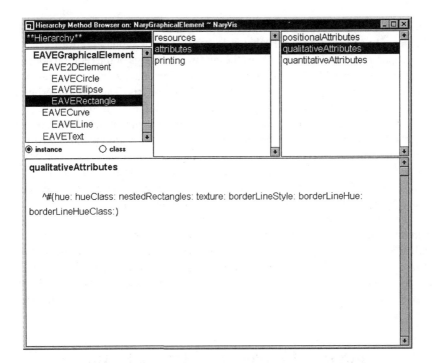

Figure 7.6: *The hierarchy browser on NaryGraphicalElement shows the ranked internal attributes the class EAVERectangle implements. The highest rank is assigned to hue, than hueClass etc.*

ear visualisation process, we have decided to let each phase be controlled by a corresponding object. Thus, the first phase is controlled by an *analysis object* conforming to the Smalltalk class EAVEAnalysis, the second phase is controlled by a *resourceAllocation object* conforming to the Smalltalk class EAVEResourceAllocation, and the third phase is controlled by a *layout object* conforming to the Smalltalk class EAVELayout. All three classes are direct subclasses of the class Object. A commonalitiy of the instances of these classes is that they store the relevant information computed during each phase, particularly for the purpose of handing the results over to the next phase.

The dataAnalysis object stores either the top dependency lattice or the top graph of the input data structure, because all nested lattices or graphs are accessed top-down and other classification results such as the most specific type of a binary relation are directly stored either at the corresponding lattice or at the corresponding graph. In addition to storing information, dataAnalysis objects implement an instance method, called *analysis*, that coordinates the different steps of the analysis process. This method is the analog of the operation *sharedDomainDependencies-For* described in algorithm 5.10 that triggers all classification operations.

The resourceAllocation object stores the current encodings of the relation domains in the instance variable currentEncodings and implements the instance method *resourceAllocation*, that is called by the method dataAnalysis. The method resource-Allocation guides the resourceAllocation in the way described in section 6.3, algorithm 6.2. It passes the variable currentEncodings on to the layout phase. Eventually, the layout object implements the instance method *layout* that walks down the nesting tree as described in the previous section and triggers adequate procedural layout techniques. For EAVE we have implemented a number of such techniques, among them: constraint-based graph drawing algorithms, constraint-based nestedRectangle positioning algorithms and colouring algorithms.

The control over the entire process has the instance method *visualise*, implemented in the class EAVELauncher, that takes the external input data structures, calls the conversion method, and passes the converted results on to the analysis phase. The result of the analysis phase is then returned to the method visualise which is responsible for the provision of the resource allocation process with the analysis results. In the same way it passes the results of the resource allocation phase to the layout phase.

7.3   Summary of Layout and Implementation

In section 7.1 of this chapter we have discussed the nested processing of the graphically encoded relational structure which is the input into the layout process. The task of the layout process is the concrete production of a diagram layout. To this purpose, it uses procedural layout techniques that implement graphical relations algorithmically. The goal is in this context to set all internal attributes of the graphical elements to constant values, since only in this case the layout is completely specified. In this context we have identified different degrees of algorithmic complexity depending on the restrictions of the value space on which the attributes are defined.

In section 7.2 we have discussed the implementation of the EAVE visualisation system in VisualWorks/Smalltalk. We have first introduced basic concepts concerning the programming language. This was followed by a description of the classes by which we consider the external input to be specified. Then we have outlined the way in which EAVE represents the input data internally to be independent of the external input data format. After that we have discussed the representation of relation types using Smalltalk classes that are in a one-to-one correspondence with an instance-based type lattice. This was followed by a discussion of the implementation of graphical elements, and finally, we have sketched the implementation of the three step linear visualisation process.

Chapter 8

Conclusions

In this chapter, we will first give a summary of the diagram visualisation approach underlying the Extended Automatic Visualisation Engine (EAVE). Then, we will discuss our results and compare them with the state of the art. This is followed by an outline concerning commercial applications of the EAVE system, other than using it in a publishing environment, as proposed in the introduction. Finally, we will delineate interesting open problems to be solved in the future.

8.1   Summary and Results

In this thesis we have proposed a constructive theory for automatic diagram visualisation and its algorithmic implementation. As a result, we obtained a generation process comprising three consecutive phases: a *data classification phase*, a *graphical resource allocation phase*, and a *layout phase*.

In chapter 3 we have identified networks of possibly nested n-ary relation instances as the most general type of input to the visualisation system.

Due to our distinction of schematic definitions of relations on the one side, and instances conforming to such definitions on the other, we could design an instance-based classification algorithm in chapter 5, in which the input undergoes a systematic analysis to detect the most specific properties of the data, with respect to the employed classification criteria. This, in turn, is a necessary condition for the graphical communication of the data using the most specific graphical resources. The analysis is based on a formal distinction of the input into binary relations, n-ary relations (for n> 2), nested relations, and networks of nested relations.

For binary relations we have introduced a *Relation Type Lattice* whose nodes – *the types* – were defined as visually sensible aggregations of binary relation properties, and whose tuples establish a "subtype" relation on these types modelling the logically correct implications between the aggregated properties. We have shown that these types can be used to qualify the data relations on the schema level. In this way, a data relation may, e.g., schematically be assigned the "StrictOrderRelation-Type" which, in turn, implies that an instance conforming to this relation schema may be more specific with respect to the Relation Type Lattice. To take this circumstance into account, we have designed a *type refinement algorithm* whose task is the detection of the most specific type of a given binary relation instance. To this purpose, the algorithm walks down the lattice starting at the given type and checks whether the subtypes are valid descriptions of the data. If no type is assigned, the algorithm presumes the lattice supremum, that is, the top type, to be the valid type. Due to the mathematical properties of the Relation Type Lattice the refinement algorithm could be designed in a computing time-effective way, which means, in the order of $O(m)$, if m denotes the number of types on the shortest path between the given type and the most specific type detectable .

For the classification of n-ary relations (for n>2) we have introduced dependency lattices modelling the pairwise relationship between a relation's domains by means of *functional*, *set-valued functional*, and *mixed dependencies*. For the detection of such dependencies we have developed a classification algorithm which may in certain cases also detect *nested dependencies*. At the end of chapter 5 we have modelled a uniform, hierarchical classification algorithm for object networks that computes *shared-domain dependencies* for the involved network and represents them in the form of a *network dependency lattice*. It further performs a classification of each involved (possibly nested) n-ary relation instance as well as an importance ranking of the relations in which quantitative aspects and user preferences are taken into account. The complexity of the overall classification algorithm is essentially linear except for the function *multivaluedContext* for which we obtain the complexity $O(\frac{m(m-1)}{2}n)$ if m denotes the number of relation tuples and n the number of domains.

The classification result is the input to the graphical resource allocation phase that is described in chapter 6. Based on a systematic classification of graphical binary relations, discriminating on the top level *attribute relations*, *element-element relations*, and *constraint relations*, we have defined *expressive graphical mappings* as those assignments of *(combined) graphical binary relations* to *binary data relations* in which both data and graphical relation are of the same relation type. This implies, of course, that also graphical relations are typed by means of the type lattice's nodes. Unlike data relations, however, graphical relations as well as the type lattice represent persistent knowledge of the visualisation system.

We have further defined *effective graphical mappings* as those expressive mappings satisfying *data and task requirements*, but also *graphical and perceptual requirements*. Data and task requirements impact, as indicated above, on the ranking of data relations in a network, whereas graphical requirements aim at the reduction of graphical complexity by selection of the most specific resource type possible. *Quantitative-perceptual requirements* are met by first imposing an ordering on the graphical resources defined at the types in the way [Mac86] has proposed, and second, by restricting their allocation to those meeting quantitative criteria such as the frequency by which a graphical resource may be applied in one design. For instance, "qualitativeHue" and "position" may only be applied once in a design, whereas "textAttachments" may be assigned multiply.

The graphical encoding of n-ary data relations (for n>2) is based on the encoding of binary relations, particularly on the encoding of set-valued mappings and their subtypes. We began this discussion in section 6.3.1 with the encoding of functional dependencies as the strongest form of domain dependencies we consider. There, we have formulated the encoding objective to be the maximisation of the use of internal attributes, since those represent the most specific graphical means of expression for the communication of functional dependencies. To this purpose, we have introduced a resource allocation algorithm processing the functional dependency lattice bottom-up while taking the effectiveness criteria outlined above into account. As a result, we have shown how, given the same lattice topology, the designs vary depending on quantitative changes in the data. Since we only compute the most effective design with respect to the formulated effectiveness criteria the complexity of the encoding algorithm is linear in the number of domains.

In section 6.3.3 we have demonstrated how set-valued-functional dependencies may also be encoded by applying similar encoding techniques. An important difference compared to the functional encoding was that the domains are not a-priori ranked, and therefore, we have artificially imposed a *cardinality ranking* on the domains which allowed, similar to the functional case, a left-to-right encoding beginning with the largest domain. Its objects are assigned first class graphical elements, whereas the objects of the remaining domains may use external attributes and internal attributes of these attributes respectively. For the more general case, where both types of dependencies occur together, we have again adapted the allocation algorithm to combine the bottom-up approach with the left-to-right approach (see section 6.3.5). An important feature of this algorithm is to exploit the hierarchic structure of the type lattice for the assignment of graphical resources by allowing for recursive use of the resources defined at the supertypes. This is necessary in case all resources at the given type fail, because a (non-graphical) effectiveness criterion prevents that. This feature is justified, because all supertypes are by definition expressive for the given data relation. Also, this generalised resource allocation algorithm works in linear time.

In section 6.3.7 we have introduced the last generalisation of the resource allocation algorithm which is able to encode also nested n-ary relations in linear time. To this purpose, we have distinguished the encoding of dependency lattices from that of graphs. In both cases, however, the strategy is to perform a *depth-first encoding*, by which a nested subrelation is processed immediately when encountered, rather than a *breadth-first encoding* where the domains on the same level of nesting are given processing preference.

In section 6.3.9 we have discussed how shared domain depencies impact on the resource allocation process, but we have, however, only indicated possible directions for the solution of the network encoding problem, instead of presenting a concrete solution.

In chapter 7 we have demonstrated how to further process the graphically enriched (possibly) nested n-ary relations. The algorithm distinguishes, in the same way as before, depth-first processing for enriched dependency lattice structures, for nested graph encodings and for combinations of such encoding structures. Since it visits each encoded domain only once it works in linear time as well.

In this chapter, we have further shed light upon the role and complexity of procedural layout techniques as the algorithmic means by which the graphical decisions are turned into concrete layouts.

In summary we can say that we have modelled a fast visualisation algorithm that constructively designs diagrams essentially depending on the analysed data characteristics, but also on perceptual aspects, graphical aspects, and user-preferences.

8.2   Comparison with the State of the Art

We see the work presented here in the tradition of the visualisation approaches discussed in chapter 2 although we have put emphasis on data classification, rather than focussing on the modelling of user-preferences and task knowledge and how this may influence the visual design process.

The most salient difference compared with the work in the state of the art results from the classification mechanism that does not accept the input data as they are, but instead tries to uncover implicitly available facts by applying instance-based data refinement techniques. This results first in the creation of a persistent classification data structure for binary relations – the Relation Type Latttice – by which both data relations as well as graphical relations may be classified, and second, in the creation of instance-based classification structures for n-ary relations (n>2) – generally mixtures of graphs and dependency lattices. Since such a classification functionality is missing in all other approaches also EAVE's graphical encoding mechanism is different. Instead of encoding the original input data the system may encode the more expressive classification structures whose generality allow for a flexible resource allocation process that is not restricted to the visualisation of a certain type of relational data such as quantitative functional data on the one side or qualitative graph data on the other.

8.3 More Application Areas for EAVE Components

A further advantage of putting more emphasis on a systematic data classification is that the application of the classification techniques is not limited to the use in a graphical output generation system. Instead, the classification structures may also be used to guide text generation processes. For instance, [MRK95] and [Sha95] have shown how fact aggregation techniques, similar to the tuple-based data object redundancy detection we have presented in section 5.2.1, may be used to generate concise summaries. This is in the context of the multi-modal presentation system sketched in the introduction an important issue, since such textual constructions as 'Gropius taught architecture at the Bauhaus, and Breuer taught architecture at the Bauhaus' as they may be generated from the facts presented in Figure 5.10 may be avoided in favour of the more condensed sentence: 'Gropius and Breuer taught architecture at the Bauhaus' if the aggregations presented in Figure 5.11 are exploited. Moreover, the dependency lattice structures themselves may directly guide the transformation of abstract facts into natural language text. For instance, the functional lattice presented in Figure 5.11 may textually be expressed, e.g., in the following form: "the artists taught at four different schools: at the Bauhaus, at Harvard, at the IIT, and at the BMC. The ones who taught at the Bauhaus and those who taught at Harvard were architects". In this context we should also mention that text generation facilities are at some point inevitable for a diagram visualisation system, because diagrams are not fully expressive without a header or an explanatory caption (see [MRM+96]).

Another obvious application scenario for the proposed diagram design system is as a front-end to a database information system. Since EAVE works on relational data it is rather obvious that it may be coupled with conventional relational databases without major changes. A problem occurring in such a setting would be, however, that EAVE is not designed for very large data sets, because visualisations should only convey a moderate amount of data in one presentation. To bridge the gap between the mass data, stored in a database, and the need to view them we consider it useful to build an intermediary tool, that makes use of data mining and knowledge discovery techniques to compute views of moderate size. These views, small databases themselves, could serve as the input to the EAVE system, and the classification techniques proposed in this thesis could then operate on them, rather than on the actual database itself.

A third application scenario conceivable for EAVE would be to use it as a system that supports graphics experts such as designers or cartographers in their work. As we have argued in the introduction, a considerable amount of time (in the order of hours) passes by until an expert may come up with a first hand-made design if the data set is sufficiently complex. EAVE could, for instance, be redesigned to generate the k best designs offered to the expert so that he could select the best solution from which to start off and do further aesthetic refinements. In this way such a system could also help make a conventional desktop publication process more cost effective.

8.4   Interesting Unsolved Problems

In this section, we will sketch research problems we consider worth working on in the future. The first is concerned with the data classification process. Instead of looking only for functional dependencies in the case of n-ary relation classification we may also investigate ordinal dependencies, a stronger form of functional dependencies. Ordinal dependencies link the concept of functional dependencies and that of linear order relations imposed on the domains to define order-preserving mappings. From such mappings relating, e.g., a temporal domain to the number of paintings created (as in Figure 4.4) we could , for instance, derive meta facts such as "with the centuries passing by the number of paintings increased" if this was the case.

Another problem concerned with data classification is the detection of structural data regularities as those considered by [Mar91]. In this case, a systematic classification is, however, impossible, since many problems concerning the instance-based detection of such graph regularities are np-complete or even np-hard (see [GJ79]). Nevertheless, as [Mar91] has shown, specific well-defined topologies may be detected with moderate computational costs. A detection of such structural patterns may be particularly useful in applications where it is known that specific types of such regularities occur sufficiently often in the data.

A major problem which we have only touched in section 6.3.9 is concerned with object network encoding. Research effort needs to be put on the development of resource allocation algorithms proceeding network dependency lattices.

Also, a more effective combination of a task model with the given data-driven approach is desired. We do, however, not believe that tasks directly influence the visualisation. We rather consider tasks to influence on the selection of the data to be visualised. In this way they could help defining the views in the database application scenario discussed before. Instead of only relying on formal methods for data reduction, they could bring in the semantics.

Apart from task models also the definition of user-defined visualisations is an interesting research topic. One possibility to support user-defined visualisations within the famework we proposed could be to offer style sheets in which the importance of graphical relations may be defined by experts (graphic designers, cartographers) in order allow for an application-customised look and feel of the visualisations.

Another interesting problem is concerned with the design of an evaluation of the produced design according to graphical complexity criteria. In this case a couple of designs could be generated and then evaluated to find the most effective with respect to a complexity value. Still another interesting question is concerned with the use of different modalities to express the same set of facts. Concretely, when is it sensible to generate graphical output, when to generate textutal output, and when to generate both? As already mentioned in chapter 2 [MRM+96], have conducted research into this direction, but we should also mention [And95] who has proposed a plan-based approach to multimodal presentations.

The last open problem we want to address here is concerned with the use of the EAVE system in an interactive scenario. Interaction is a problem, because the flexibility of design decisions may lead to inconsistent displays of data in an interactive session. To illustrate that consider the following scenario: a query extracts in a first step a binary relation instance from a database. The instance is then analysed and assigned a given relation type so that an adequate visualisation is the result. In the following step a refinement of the query takes place and the data are analysed again which leads to the assignment of the resources defined at a subtype. In this case it is likely that the visualisation of the same relation instance may lead to different results which is a consistency problem. Another scenario could be that two data relations were already displayed separately in some earlier interaction steps and now they have to be displayed at the same time. Since a resource allocation conflict occurs it must be decided which relation is assigned the most effective graphical resources. In this case it may happen that one of the two graphical relations cannot be assigned the same graphical resource as before. In other applications were visualisations are only generated from time to time this might not be a problem at all. This indicates that a solution of this problem could be to let the application control the consistency, e.g., by introducing a consistency value that effects on the selection of graphical resources.

Bibliography

[ABD+89]   M. Atkinson, F. Bancilhon, D. DeWitt, K. Dittrich, D. Maier, and
           S. Zsdonik. The object-oriented database system manifesto. In
           *Proceedings of the First International Conference on Deductive and
           Object-Oriented Databases*, pages 40–57. Elsevier, December 1989.

[ABL91]   C.S. Ai, P. Blower, and R.H. Ledwidth. Extracting reaction infor-
           mation from chemical databases. In G. Piatetsky-Shapiro and W.J.
           Frawley, editors, *Knowledge Discovery in Databases*, pages 367–
           382. AAAI Press, 1991.

[And95]   E. Andre. *Ein planbasierter Ansatz zur Generierung multimedialer
           Präsentationen*. PhD thesis, Universität des Saarlandes, 1995.

[AR96]   Melina Alexa and Lothar Rostek. Computer-assisted corpus based
           text analysis with tatoe. In *Proceedings of ALLC-ACH '96*, Bergen,
           Norway, June 1996.

[Bee89]   C. Beeri. A formal approach to object-oriented databases. In
           *Proceedings of the First International Conference on Deductive
           and Object-Oriented Databases*, pages 370–395. Elsevier, December
           1989.

[Ber83]   J. Bertin. *Semiology of Graphics*. University of Wisconsin Press,
           1983.

[Bur91]   P. Burmeister. Mermalimplikationen bei unvollständigem wissen. In
           W. Lex, editor, *Arbeitstagung Begriffsanalyse und k"nstliche Intelli-
           genz - Informatik Berichte*, 1991.

[Cas91]   S. Casner. A task-analytic approach to the automated design of
           graphic presentations. *ACM Transactions on Graphics*, 10(2):111–
           151, 1991.

[CCH91]   Yandong Cai, Nick Cercone, and Jiawei Han. Attribute-oriented induction in relational databases. In G. Piatetsky-Shapiro and W.J. Frawley, editors, *Knowledge Discovery in Databases*, pages 213–228. AAAI Press, 1991.

[CM84]   W.S. Cleveland and R. McGill. Graphical perception: Theory, experimentation and application to the development of graphical methods. *Journal of the American Statistical Association*, 79(387):531–554, 1984.

[Cod88]   E.F. Codd. *The Relational Model and Beyond*. Database Programming and Design, 1988.

[Con87]   J. Conklin. Hypertext: An introduction and survey. *IEEE Computer Magazine*, 20(9):117–122, 1987.

[CW91]   K.C.C. Chan and A.K.C. Wong. A statistical technique for extracting classificatory knowledge from databases. In G. Piatetsky-Shapiro and W.J. Frawley, editors, *Knowledge Discovery in Databases*, pages 107–124. AAAI Press, 1991.

[Ead84]   P. Eades. A heuristic for graph drawing. *Congressus Numerantium*, 42, 1984.

[eta95]   Kathryn Hamilton etal. Arbeiten mit microsoft office für windows. Technical report, Microsoft, 1995.

[FDFH90]   J.D. Foley, A.v. Dam, S.K. Feiner, and J.F. Hughes. *Computer Graphics: Principles and Practice*. Addison-Wesley Publishing Company, 1990.

[Gan87]   B. Ganter. Algorithmen zur formalen begriffsanalyse. In B. Ganter, R. Wille, and K.E. Wolff, editors, *Beiträge zur Begriffsanalyse*, pages 241–254. B.I. Wissenschaftsverlag, 1987.

[GJ79]   M.R. Garey and D.S. Johnson. *Computers and Intractability: A Guide to the Theory of NP-Completeness*. W.H. Freeman and Co. San Francisco, 1979.

[Gna81]   S. Gnanagmari. *Information Presentation Through default Display*. PhD thesis, University of Pennsilvania, 1981.

[GRKM84]   J. Goldstein, S.F. Roth, J. Kolojejchick, and J. Mattis. A famework for knowledge-based interactive data exploration. *Journal of Visual Languages and Computing*, 1984.

[GW96]   B. Ganter and R. Wille. *Formale Begriffsananlyse – Mathematische Grundlagen*. Springer Verlag Heidelberg, 1996.

[Haa96]   A. Haake. *Versionenunterstützung für strukturierte Hyperdokumente im Elektronischen Publizieren*. PhD thesis, Technische Hochschule Darmstadt, 1996.

[Hem95]   M. Hemmje. Lyberworld – a 3d graphical user interface for fulltext retrieval. In *Proceedings of CHI U95, Video Summaries*, May 1995.

[Heu92]   A. Heuer. *Objekt-orientierte Datenbanken: Konzepte, Modelle, Systeme*. Addison Wesley, 1992.

[KAN93]   W. Klas, K. Aberer, and E.J. Neuhold. Object-oriented modelling for hypermedia systems using the vodak modelling language (vml). In *Object-Oriented Management Systems*, NATO ASI-Series. Springer Verlag, 1993.

[KHMS96]   T. M. Kamps, C. Hüser, W. Möhr, and I. Schmidt. Knowledge based information access for hypermedia reference works: Exploring the spread of bauhaus ideas movement. In M. Agosti and A.F. Smeaton, editors, *Information Retrieval and Hypertext*, pages 225–256. Kluwer Boston/London/Dordrecht, 1996.

[KKR95]   Thomas M. Kamps, Jörg Kleinz, and John L. Read. Constraint-based spring-model algorithm for graph layout. In Franz J. Brandenburg, editor, *Graph Drawing, Symposium on Graph Drawing '95*, Lecture Notes in Computer Science, pages 349–360. Springer-Verlag Berlin Heidelberg, Passau, Germany, October 1995.

[KR95]   Thomas M. Kamps and Klaus Reichenberger. A dialogue approach to graphical information access. In W. Schuler, J. Hannemann, and N. Streitz, editors, *Designing User Interfaces for Hypermedia*, Research Reports Esprit, pages 141–155. Springer-Verlag Berlin Heidelberg, Darmstadt, Germany, 1995.

[Mac86]   Jock D. Mackinlay. *Automatic Design of Graphical Presentations*. PhD thesis, Computer Science Department of Stanford University, 1986.

[Mar91]   J. Marks. *Automating the Design of Network Diagrams*. PhD thesis, Harvard University, 1991.

[MBC93]   N. Max, B. Becker, and R. Crawfis. Flow volumes for interactive vector field visualization. In G.M. Nielsen and D. Bergeron, editors,

IEEE Proceedings of Visualization '93, pages 19–24, San Jose, California, October 1993. IEEE Computer Society Press.

[Mic96]   Microsof. Encarta '97 enzyklopädie – ein umfassendes nachschlagewerk. Technical report, Microsoft-Unterschleißheim, 1996.

[MR93]   Wiebke Möhr and Lothar Rostek. Tedi: an object-oriented teminology editor. In *Proceedings of TKE '93: Third International Congress on Terminology and Knowldege Engineering*, Cologne, Germany, August 1993.

[MRC91]   J.D. Mackinlay, G.G. Robertson, and S.K. Card. The perspective wall: Detail and context smoothly integrated. In *Proceedings of the ACM SIGCHI U91 Conference on Human Factors in Computing Systems*, pages 173–180, New Orleans,LA, May 1991.

[MRK95]   Kathleen McKeown, Jacques Robin, and Karen Kukich. Generating concise natural language summaries. *Information Management and Processing*, 31(5):703–733, 1995.

[MRM⁺96]   V.O. Mittal, S.F. Roth, J.D. Moore, J. Mattis, and G. Carenini. Generating explanatory captions for information graphics. In *ICCAI Proceedings of the International Joint Conference on Artificial Intelligence*, volume 2, Montreal, Canada, August 1996.

[NA93]   Nemcics and Antal. *Farbenlehre und Farbendynamik – Theorie der farbigen Umwelt*. Muster-Schmidt Verlag, Göttingen/Zürich, 1993.

[Par92]   ParcPlace. Object works smalltalk userUs guide release 4.1. Technical report, Parc Place Systems Inc. Sunnyvale, California, 1992.

[RKG95]   Klaus Reichenberger, Thomas Kamps, and Gene Golovchinsky. Towards a generative theory of diagram design. In N. Gershon and S. Eick, editors, *IEEE Proceedings on Information Visualization*, pages 11–18, Atlanta, Georgia, October 1995. IEEE Computer Society Press.

[RM90]   S.F. Roth and J. Mattis. Data characterization for graphics presentation. In *CHI '90 Proceedingd*, April 1990.

[RM94]   Lothar Rostek and Wiebke Möhr. An editor's workbench for an art history reference work. In *Proceedings of the ACM European Conference on Hypermedia Technology*, pages 233–238, Edinburgh, UK, September 1994. ACM, New York, NY.

[RMF94]   Lothar Rostek, Wiebke Möhr, and Dietrich Fischer.   Weaving a
          web: the structure and creation of an object network representing
          an electronic reference work. In C. Hüser, Wiebke Möhr, and Vin-
          cent Quint, editors, *Proceedings of the Fifth International Confer-
          ence on Electronic Publishing, Document Manipulation and Typog-
          raphy*, volume 6, pages 495–505, Darmstadt, Germany, April 1994.
          Wiley Chichester, New York, Brisbane, Toronto, Singapore.

[RRKB96] K. Reichenberger, J.C. Rondhuis, J. Kleinz, and J.A. Bateman. Effec-
          tive presentation of information through page layout: a linguistically
          based approach. Technical Report 921, German National Research
          Center for Information Technology GmbH, 1996.

[Sal89]   G. Salton. *Automatic Text Processing: the Transform ation, Analy-
          sis, and Retrieval of Information by the Computer*. Addison Wesley,
          Mass., 1989.

[Sha95]   J. Shaw. Conciseness through aggregation in text generation. Tech-
          nical report, Columbia University, Department of Computer Science,
          1995.

[SHT89]   N. Streitz, J. Hannemann, and M. Thüring. From ideas and arguments
          to hyperdocuments: Travelling through activity spaces. In *Hypertext
          '89: Special Issue of SIGCHI Bulletin*, pages 343–364, Pittsburgh,
          USA, November 1989.

[Smi78]   A.R. Smith. Color gamut transform pairs. In *SIGGRAPH ACM Pro-
          ceedings 1978*, pages 12–19, 1978.

[SSS91]   M. Siegel, E. Sciore, and S. Salveter. Rule discovery for query opti-
          misation. In G. Piatetsky-Shapiro and W.J. Frawley, editors, *Knowl-
          edge Discovery in Databases*, pages 411–430. AAAI Press, 1991.

[TB94]   E. Teich and J.A. Bateman. Towards the application of text gener-
          ation in an integrated publication system. In *Proceedings of the 7th
          International Workshop on Natural Language Generation*, Kenneb-
          unkport, USA, June 1994.

[TC91]   H. Turtle and W.B. Croft. Riao '91: Efficient probabilistic inference
          for text retrieval. In *Proceedings of RIAO '91*, pages 644–661, 1991.

[Tuf83]   E.R. Tufte. *The Visual Display of Quantitative Information*. Graphics
          Press, 1983.

[USM95]   S.K. Ueng, K. Sikorsky, and K.-L. Ma. Fast algorithms for visualiz-
            ing fluid motion in steady flow on unstructured grids. In G.M. Nielsen
            and D. Silver, editors, *IEEE Proceedings of Visualization '95*, pages
            313–319, Atlanta, Georgia, October 1995. IEEE Computer Society
            Press.

[Wil82]   R. Wille. Restructuring lattice theory: An approach based on hierar-
            chies of concepts. In I. Rival, editor, *Ordered Sets*, pages 445–470.
            Reidel, Dordrecht/Boston, 1982.

[Wil95]   M. Will. Visualisierung von baumordnungsstrukturen als inklusions-
            diagramme.   Master's thesis, Technische Hochschule Darmstadt,
            1995.

[WN91]   A. Weber and E.J. Neuhold.   Distributed publishing of electronic
            newspapers and mailorder catalogues.   Technical Report 574, Ar-
            beitspapiere der GMD, 1991.

[YLRM95]   R. Yagel, S.C. Lu, A.B. Rebello, and R.A. Miller. Volume-based rea-
            soning and visualization of diecastability. In G.M. Nielsen and D. Sil-
            ver, editors, *IEEE Proceedings of Visualization '95*, pages 359–362,
            Atlanta, Georgia, October 1995. IEEE Computer Society Press.

[ZB91]   J.M. Zytkow and J. Baker.   Interactive mining of regularities in
            databases. In G. Piatetsky-Shapiro and W.J. Frawley, editors, *Knowl-
            edge Discovery in Databases*, pages 31–53. AAAI Press, 1991.

[Zic91]   M. Zickwolff. *Rule Exploration: First Order Logic in Formal Con-
            cept Analysis*. PhD thesis, Technische Hochschule Darmstadt, 1991.

Appendix A

Definition of Relational Properties

Let $R \subseteq D \times D$ define a binary relation on the finite domain D. Then, we define the following list of relational properties:

Definition A.1 (relation properties) *Let $D = X \cup Y$ be a finite set. Then, a relation instance R is called*

- *symmetric, iff $\forall x, y \in D$: $R(x,y) \Longrightarrow R(y, x)$.*

- *antisymmetric, iff $\forall x, y \in D$: $R(x,y) \wedge R(y,x) \Longrightarrow x = y$.*

- *reflexive, iff $\forall x \in D$: $R(x,x)$.*

- *irreflexive, iff $\forall x \in D$: $\neg R(x, x)$.*

- *transitive, iff $\forall x, y, z \in D$: $R(x,y) \wedge R(y,z) \Longrightarrow R(x,z)$.*
  The smallest subset $P \subseteq R$ such that R is a subset of P's transitive closure $R \subseteq Trans(P)$ is called the intransitive kernel T_K of R (also, $T_K(R)$).

- *linear, iff $\forall x, y \in D$: $R(x,y) \vee R(y,x)$.*

- *a path $((x_1, x_2), \ldots, (x_{n-1}, x_n))$ from x_1 to x_n for $D = \{x_1, \ldots, x_n\}$ iff the x_i are distinct with the possible exception that $x_1 = x_n$ in which case we call it a cycle. We call n-1 the length of the path, and in case of $n \geq 2$ we speak of a non-trivial path. If there is a path from x_i to x_j we say that x_j is reachable from x_i.*
  R is called a semipath, iff R is a sequence of tuples of the form (x_i, x_{i+1}) or (x_{i+1}, x_i) in which the x_i are distinct for all $x_i \in D$.

R is called strongly connected (strong), iff x_i and x_j are mutually reachable for all $x_i, x_j \in D$. It is called unilaterally connected (unilateral), iff x_i is reachable from x_j or x_j is reachable from x_i for all $x_i, x_j \in D$. It is called weakly connected (weak), iff x_i and x_j are joined by a semipath for all $x_i, x_j \in D$.

- *acyclic, iff $\neg \exists S \subseteq R$ such that S is cycle.*

- *an antisymmetric tree, iff R is antisymmetric, weakly connected, and $|R| = |D| - 1$.*

- *a symmetric tree, iff R is symmetric, strongly connected, and $|R| = 2|D| - 1$.*

- *bipartite, iff R is antisymmetric, acyclic, and $\exists V, W \subset D$ for which $V \cup W = D \wedge V \cap W = \emptyset$ such that $\forall (x, y) \in R$ with $x, y \in D$: $x \in V \wedge y \notin W \vee y \in V \wedge x \notin W$.*

- *oriented (set-valued mapping), iff R is bipartite and $\forall x, y, z \in D$: $R(x,y) \implies \neg R(y,z)$.*

- *unique, iff R is oriented and $\forall x, y, z \in D$: $R(x,y) \wedge R(x,z) \implies y = z$.*

- *surjective, iff R is unique and $V \cup W = D$.*

- *injective, iff R is unique and $\forall x, y, z \in D$: $R(x,z) \wedge R(y,z) \implies x = y$.*

- *bijective, iff S is surjective and injective.*

- *strictly ordered, iff $R (=$"$<$"$)$ is antisymmetric, irreflexive and transitive. If for $B \subseteq D \exists c \in D$ such that $\forall b \in B : c \leq b$, c is called a lower bound of B. If $C \subseteq D$ denotes the set of lower bounds of B in D and $\exists \tilde{c}$ such that $\forall c \in C : \tilde{c} \geq c$ we call $\tilde{c} \in C$ the greatest lower bound of B and denote it by $\inf (B)$. Dually, we define the concepts upper bound and least upper bound $(\sup (B))$.*

- *lattice order, iff R is strictly ordered and $\forall x, y \in D \exists \sup (x, y) \wedge \inf (x, y)$.*

- *complete lattice order, iff R is ordered and $\forall B \subseteq D \exists \sup (B) \wedge \exists \inf (B)$.*

- *a tree order, iff R is a strict order and $T_K (R)$ is an antisymmetric tree.*

- *a discrete linear order, iff R is a strict, linear order and there exists a bijective mapping $f : D \mapsto N$.*

- *a real-valued linear order, iff R is a strict, linear order and there exists a bijective mapping $f : D \mapsto R$.*

- *an equivalence relation, iff R is symmetric, reflexive, and transitive.*

Appendix B

Relation Type Concepts

In this chapter we present the relation type concepts that constitute the relation type lattice. Each concept of the type lattice is formally composed of a pair of sets comprising an extension (a set of objects and and intension, a set of attributes). Each such concept satisfies equation 5.2 in chapter 5.1. The list of all concepts of the type lattice is given below.

1) **concept extension:** $\emptyset$
concept intension: {SymmetricRelationType, SymmetricTreeType, EquivalenceRelationType, AntisymmetricRelationType, AntisymmetricTreeType, StrictOrderRelationType, LatticeOrderRelationType, TreeOrderRelationType, DiscreteLinearOrderType, RealValuedLinearOrderType, AcyclicRelationType, BipartiteRelationType, OrientedRelationType, UniqueMappingRelationType, SurjectiveFunctionRelationType, InjectiveFunctionRelationType, BijectiveFunctionRelationType}

2) **concept extension:** {g18}
concept intension: {AntisymmetricRelationType, AntisymmetricTreeType, StrictOrderRelationType, LatticeOrderRelationType, TreeOrderRelationType, DiscreteLinearOrderType, AcyclicRelationType, BipartiteRelationType, OrientedRelationType, UniqueMappingRelationType, SurjectiveFunctionRelationType, InjectiveFunctionRelationType, BijectiveFunctionRelationType}

3) **concept extension:** {g17, g18}
concept intension: {AntisymmetricRelationType, AntisymmetricTreeType, StrictOrderRelationType, TreeOrderRelationType, AcyclicRelationType, BipartiteRelationType, OrientedRelationType, UniqueMappingRelationType}

4) **concept extension:** {g16, g17, g18}
concept intension: {AntisymmetricRelationType, AntisymmetricTreeType, Stric-

tOrderRelationType, AcyclicRelationType, BipartiteRelationType}

5) **concept extension:** {g15, g18}
concept intension: {AntisymmetricRelationType, AcyclicRelationType, BipartiteRelationType, OrientedRelationType, UniqueMappingRelationType, SurjectiveFunctionRelationType, InjectiveFunctionRelationType, BijectiveFunctionRelationType}

6) **concept extension:** {g14}
concept intension: {AntisymmetricRelationType, StrictOrderRelationType, LatticeOrderRelationType, TreeOrderRelationType, RealValuedLinearOrderType, AcyclicRelationType}

7) **concept extension:** {g13}
concept intension: {SymmetricRelationType, EquivalenceRelationType}

8) **concept extension:** {g12, g15, g18}
concept intension: {AntisymmetricRelationType, AcyclicRelationType, BipartiteRelationType, OrientedRelationType, UniqueMappingRelationType, InjectiveFunctionRelationType}

9)
concept extension: {g11, g15, g18}
concept intension: {AntisymmetricRelationType, AcyclicRelationType, BipartiteRelationType, OrientedRelationType, UniqueMappingRelationType, SurjectiveFunctionRelationType}

10) **concept extension:** {g10, g18}
concept intension: {AntisymmetricRelationType, StrictOrderRelationType, LatticeOrderRelationType, TreeOrderRelationType, DiscreteLinearOrderType, AcyclicRelationType}

11) **concept extension:** {g10, g14, g18}
concept intension: {AntisymmetricRelationType, StrictOrderRelationType, LatticeOrderRelationType, TreeOrderRelationType, AcyclicRelationType}

12) **concept extension:** {g9, g11, g12, g15, g17, g18}
concept intension: {AntisymmetricRelationType, AcyclicRelationType, BipartiteRelationType, OrientedRelationType, UniqueMappingRelationType}

13) **concept extension:** {g8, g9, g11, g12, g15, g17, g18}
concept intension: {AntisymmetricRelationType, AcyclicRelationType, Bipar-

titeRelationType, OrientedRelationType}

14) **concept extension:** {g6, g10, g14, g17, g18}
concept intension: {AntisymmetricRelationType, StrictOrderRelationType, TreeOrderRelationType, AcyclicRelationType}

15) **concept extension:** {g5, g10, g14, g18}
concept intension: {AntisymmetricRelationType, StrictOrderRelationType, LatticeOrderRelationType, AcyclicRelationType}

16) **concept extension:** {g4, g5, g6, g10, g14, g16, g17, g18}
concept intension: {AntisymmetricRelationType, StrictOrderRelationType, AcyclicRelationType}

17) **concept extension:** {g2, g16, g17, g18}
concept intension: {AntisymmetricRelationType, AntisymmetricTreeType, AcyclicRelationType, BipartiteRelationType}

18) **concept extension:** {g2, g7, g8, g9, g11, g12, g15, g16, g17, g18}
concept intension: {AntisymmetricRelationType, AcyclicRelationType, BipartiteRelationType}

19) **concept extension:** {g2, g4, g5, g6, g7, g8, g9, g10, g11, g12, g14, g15, g16, g17, g18}
concept intension: {AntisymmetricRelationType, AcyclicRelationType}

20) **concept extension:** {g2, g4, g5, g6, g7, g8, g9, g10, g11, g12, g14, g15, g16, g17, g18, g19}
concept intension: {AntisymmetricRelationType}

21) **concept extension:** {g1}
concept intension: {SymmetricRelationType, SymmetricTreeType, AcyclicRelationType}

22) **concept extension:** {g1, g13}
concept intension: {SymmetricRelationType}

23) **concept extension:** {g1, g2, g3, g4, g5, g6, g7, g8, g9, g10, g11, g12, g14, g15, g16, g17, g18}
concept intension: {AcyclicRelationType}

24) **concept extension:** {g1, g2, g3, g4, g5, g6, g7, g8, g9, g10, g11, g12, g13,

g14, g15, g16, g17, g18, g19}
concept intension: ∅

Appendix C

Quantitative-Perceptual Limitation Constants

In this chapter we present the complete list of limitation constants that are used in the EAVE system to verify the quantitative-perceptual effectiveness criteria developed in chapter 6.

graphical resource	grouping number	frequency	capacity
font	1	1	2
caps	1	1000	2
typeFace	1	1	4
indentedList	1000	1000	1000
frameGrouping	3	3	10
nestedRectangles	8	3	10
hue	1	1	5
hueClass	1	1	5
texture	1	1	5
saturation	1	1	1000
brightness	1	1	1000
orderedHue	1	1	1000
orderedBrightness	1	1	1000
position	1	1000	1000
borderLineStyle	1	1	3
borderLineHue	1	1	2
borderLineHueClass	1	1	2
borderLineSaturation	1	1	1000
borderLineBrightNess	1	1	1000
width	1	1000	1000
height	1	1000	1000
radius	1	1000	1000
length	1	1000	1000
lineStyle	1	5	3
borderLineWidth	1	1000	1000
fixedXPosition	1	1	1000
fixedYPosition	1	1	1000
fixedZPosition	1	1	1000
fixedHue	1	1	1000
fixedBrightness	1	1	1000
rightExtent	1	1000	1000
leftExtent	1	1000	1000
topExtent	1	1000	1000
bottomExtent	1	1000	1000
attachments	2	2	5
spatialGrouping	3	1	1000
belowBottomBoundary	1000	1	1000
aboveTopBoundary	1000	1	1000
rightOfRightBoundary	1000	1	1000
leftOfLeftBoundary	1000	1	1000
equiDistance	1000	1	1000
line*	1000	1	1000

all types of line relations have the same quantitative-perceptual properties

Figure C.1: *Limitation constants.*

Appendix D

Coloured Illustrations

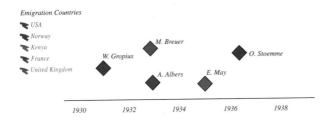

Figure D.1: *Diagram D) represents artists emigrating to different countries.*

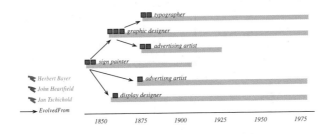

Figure D.2: *Diagram F) describes how and when different professions in advertising emerged.*

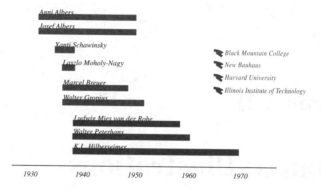

Figure D.3: *Diagram I) represents an alternative design for the data underlying diagram E).*

Figure D.4: *Visualisation using classified colours.*

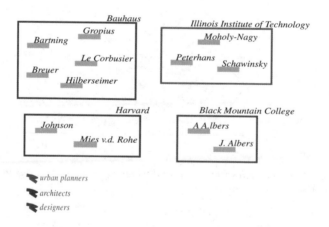

Figure D.5: *Visualisation using nested rectangles and colours.*

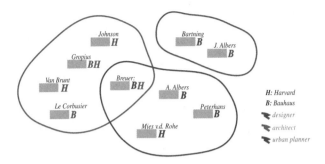

Figure D.6: *Visual representation of set-valued-functionally dependent facts.*

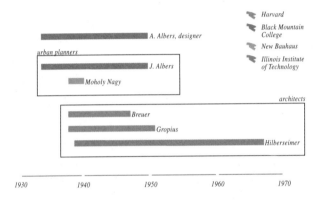

Figure D.7: *Visualisation of PerformedProfession facts.*

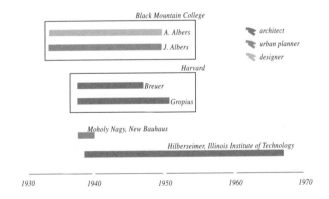

Figure D.8: *Alternative visualisation of PerformedProfession facts.*

Springer
and the
environment

At Springer we firmly believe that an
international science publisher has a
special obligation to the environment,
and our corporate policies consistently
reflect this conviction.
We also expect our business partners –
paper mills, printers, packaging
manufacturers, etc. – to commit
themselves to using materials and
production processes that do not harm
the environment. The paper in this
book is made from low- or no-chlorine
pulp and is acid free, in conformance
with international standards for paper
permanency.

Druck: Strauss Offsetdruck, Mörlenbach
Verarbeitung: Schäffer, Grünstadt